Marjorie Reeves, MA (Oxon), PhD (London), D. Litt (Oxon), F.R.Hist.S., F.B.A. was educated at the High School for Girls, Trowbridge and St Hugh's College, Oxford. She was Vice Principal of St Anne's College, Oxford between 1951 and 1967 and a member of the Central Advisory Council, Ministry of Education from 1947–61. In 1975 she spent a semester at Columbia University, New York, and in the summer of 1977 was Distinguished Professor in Medieval Studies at the University of California, Berkeley. Dr Reeves divides her time between Oxford and Wiltshire, where her interests are music, gardening and bird-watching.

D0489547

Marjorie Reeves

Sheep Bell & Ploughshare

the story of two village families

A PALADIN BOOK

GRANADA
London Toronto Sydney New York

Published by Granada Publishing Limited in 1980

ISBN 0 586 08349 9

First published in Great Britain by
Moonraker Press 1978
Copyright © Marjorie Reeves 1978

Granada Publishing Limited
Frogmore, St Albans, Herts AL2 2NF
and
3 Upper James Street, London W1R 4BP
866 United Nations Plaza, New York, NY 10017, USA
117 York Street, Sydney, NSW 2000, Australia
100 Skyway Avenue, Rexdale, Ontario, M9W 3A6, Canada
PO Box 84165, Greenside, 2034 Johannesburg, South Africa
61 Beach Road, Auckland, New Zealand

Set, printed and bound in Great Britain by
Cox & Wyman Ltd., Reading
Set in Intertype Times

Granada ®
Granada Publishing ®

Contents

Figures in the text in parentheses, thus (1)
indicate references to the illustrations.

Part of the Whitaker family tree—I

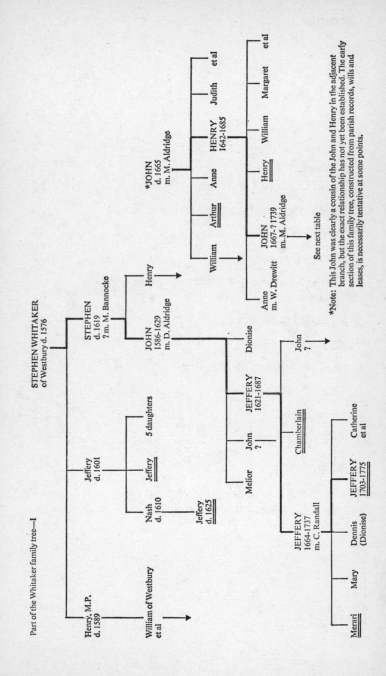

STEPHEN WHITAKER
of Westbury d. 1576

Note: This John was clearly a cousin of the John and Henry in the adjacent branch, but the exact relationship has not yet been established. The early section of this family tree, constructed from parish records, wills and leases, is necessarily tentative at some points.

Part of the Whitaker family tree—II

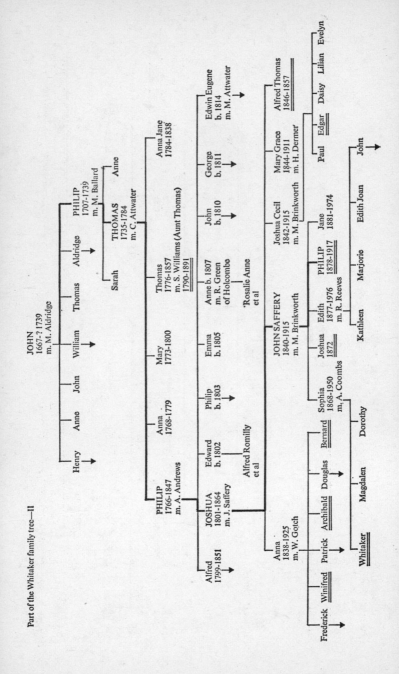

The Reeves family in Bratton

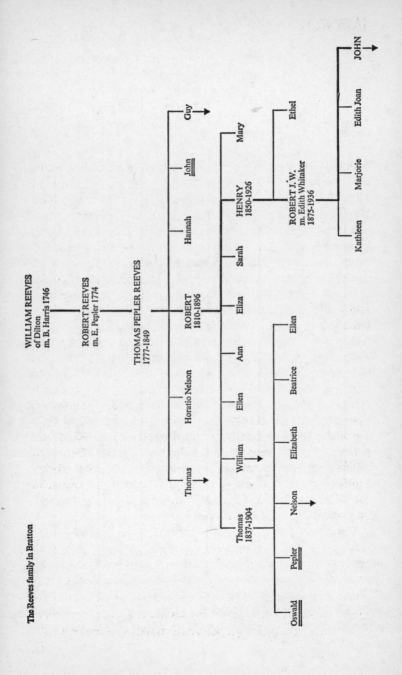

WILLIAM REEVES
of Dilton
m. B. Harris 1746

ROBERT REEVES
m. E. Pepler 1774

THOMAS PEPLER REEVES
1777-1849

ROBERT
1810-1896

Thomas | Horatio Nelson | Hannah | John | Guy →

Eliza | Ann | Ellen | William → | Sarah | HENRY 1850-1926 | Mary | Ethel

Thomas 1837-1904

Oswald | Pepler | Nelson → | Elizabeth | Beatrice | Ellen

ROBERT J. W.
m. Edith Whitaker
1875-1936

Kathleen | Marjorie | Edith Joan | JOHN →

Foreword

Much of the material on which this book is based came into my possession on the death of Jane Saffery Whitaker in 1974. It had been accumulated over the generations by the Whitakers of Bratton and finally gathered together in the last family home they inhabited in the village, whence it was transferred by Miss Whitaker to the house into which she retired in 1946. This material included a wide variety of documents, such as deeds and wills, diaries, farm records, petty-cash accounts and receipted bills, original writings and letters, which ranged from the seventeenth to the early twentieth century. In addition, there were many family possessions to illuminate domestic life, and books, magazines, music, etc., to throw light on their tastes, not to mention ephemeral survivals which often gave the most curious and vivid view of all. Of a completely different type were the records of R. & J. Reeves & Son Ltd of Bratton Ironworks, documenting the history of a family business, rather than the life-style of a family. A third source of material was provided by the records of the Bratton Baptist Church to which both Whitakers and Reeveses were attached. Today much of the documentary material is already deposited in the Wiltshire Record Office at Trowbridge, and the rest will be eventually.

For other information upon which I have drawn, I must thank Mrs Jean Morrison who supplied me, *inter alia*, with material from the Longleat archives, and much else besides from her wide and detailed knowledge of the locality; the Vicar of St James Church, Bratton, for permission to use the Parish Registers; Mr Michael Lansdown for permission to search the early files of the *Wiltshire Times*; Mr Kenneth

11

Ponting, for permission to quote his words. I must also thank Mrs Deirdre Wheatley for much specialized advice and for permission to quote from her tape of Miss Whitaker's reminiscences, and my sister, Miss K. M. Reeves, for a great deal of advice and assistance.

MARJORIE REEVES
January, 1977.

NOTE

After this book had gone to press more information on George Whitaker came to light. His further education was at Charterhouse and Queens' College, Cambridge (1829–33) where he gained a first-class tripos in classics and mathematics in 1833. He was a Fellow at Queens' (1833–40), was ordained an Anglican priest (1838), became vicar of Oakington (1840–51) and was appointed the first provost of Trinity College, Toronto, in 1851. He occupied this post from 1852 to 1880. He then returned to England to become vicar of Newton Tony, Wiltshire, where he died in 1882. His portrait hangs in Trinity College Hall. See M. Reeves, 'George Whitaker (1811 – 1882)', *Wiltshire Archaeological Magazine*, 72/73 (1980), pp. 135–9.

M.R.

1 From Cloth to Land

Houses can be human nests which families make for themselves out of their possessions – nests composed of flotsam and jetsam as well as more solid material, which both shape, and are shaped by, succeeding generations. Where a house is continuously occupied by one family over a considerable period, and when that family happens to be a hoarding one, the materials of which their nest is built become astonishingly rich in variety, even when they pursue quite ordinary lives. When the generations of the living have gone, their 'shape' still lingers, the profile of a family sketched in their material remains, or – to change the metaphor – a family memory-house. When the house is finally dismantled, its contents are ruthlessly sorted into categories: 'rubbish' and 'to keep'; documentary, personal, furniture, silver, books, and a pathetic category of ephemera, or oddments. Everything worth saving may be efficiently distributed to appropriate quarters in museums, record offices, libraries and the like, but an organic whole has been destroyed; a family image has been torn in shreds. Before the fragments are wholly scattered by the application of neat analytical methods, an attempt is made here to recover something of the profile of two families that lived in Bratton for nearly 400 years in one case, and 200 in the other.

Bratton (1) sits on a ledge below the northern escarpment of Salisbury Plain. Behind it, to the south, the line of the downs rises another 300–400 ft, sweeping up westward to the earth-work known as Bratton Castle, with the White Horse beneath it, and to another high point eastward, now called Picket Hill. Northward, it slopes down through apple-orchards and a tangle of little lanes to the lower-lying pastures. From the chalk two small streams issue and join in the Stradbrook which flows roughly northwards, eventually to join the Avon. Through the middle of the village, running east/west, is the road between Devizes and Westbury. This has always been the main line of communication, and from the middle of the eighteenth century it was a turnpike road. The older farms and cottages were scattered, some along this road, some by the Stradbrook, some among the lanes and on the Lower Road to the north; probably there was a cluster around the church under the downs. Indeed, in the medieval period Bratton appeared as three hamlets: Milburne by the stream, Stoke by the church and Bratton by the Court House on the Lower Road. Early in the nineteenth century Bratton Iron Works came into being beside the main road and this may have helped to draw the village together, with a focus on the Works, the Duke Inn and the shops.

The Whitakers appear in this part of Wiltshire in the sixteenth century as already quite a widespread family, with branches in Westbury, Bratton, Tinhead and further afield. The Bratton branch at one time or another inhabited several farm homesteads in the village, but as early as 1682 they were already in possession of the house which became the final repository of the family material. It was then, apparently, called Smarts. This house, partly rebuilt after a fire in 1789, still stands on the Lower Road looking up through the apple-orchards towards the downs. In the nineteenth century it was renamed the Yew Trees, and – though anachronistic – I shall generally use this name. The yews are in the garden on the north side, originally an avenue of six fine ancient trees which imparted a venerable quality to the garden. There is no record of their planting and much speculation on their age. The house itself has a high Georgian front of mellow brick, with older parts behind it. With attic rooms and generous old cupboards, it was a comfortable, accommodating home, a place for welcoming relations and accumulating stuff. The last Whitakers to live there hoarded every memento with care. What is astonishing is that when the Yew Trees was finally sold in 1946 most of the Whitaker material was decanted into a converted cottage-cum-dairy on the home farm. There it retained something of its living character so long as Jane Saffery Whitaker sat in the midst of it. Now it is mostly dead stuff packed away in boxes.

The backcloth to Bratton is the downs. Today, with fewer sheep and more cattle-grazing, the downs are increasingly masked in boscage of various kinds, but throughout most of the previous 400 years that backcloth must have been one of smooth slopes and little hills of fine turf, powdered with thyme and other small hill-flowers. This was the product of traditional sheep-grazing. For the mouth of a sheep is a finer lawn-mower than the tearing teeth of cattle and the traditional method by which the shepherd slowly moved his flock across the downland – so regularly that you could tell the time by his position – meant that the slopes were systematically cropped and young bush-shoots mown off. But running up like fingers into the downs are the coombes, rounded dry bottoms, then as now quite good for arable farming, and the evidence suggests that in the period which concerns us there was much arable cultivation on the top of the downs and in the coombes. The constant mention of 'closes' indicates the growth of enclosures, some medieval, many more in the seventeenth century, but Bratton common fields, the West Field towards Westbury and the East on the Edington side, remained in being until the final Enclosure Act of 1808. Down to the north lay the moister pastures, good for dairy farming as well as arable. So Bratton on the edge of the downs was, by its position, a community given to mixed farming.

It shared this position with a row of villages under the edge of the downs, settled on the water-line where the springs emerge at the foot of the chalk: Edington, Tinhead, Coulston, Erlestoke, Cheverell. Like them its economics were determined by the fact that it lay between the Plain and the Wiltshire Vale. The shelf on which these villages stand drops away finally down to Trowbridge, Hilperton, Bradford-on-Avon. Here cloth manufacture was booming in the fifteenth and sixteenth centuries, and in the valleys of the Avon, the Frome and their tributaries the mills hummed.

17

Our row of villages felt a double pull. Kenneth Ponting, writing on next-door Edington, has said:

Edington ... lies where the hill country of the Plain meets the Wiltshire Vale, a division that dominates the country not only topographically speaking but also economically. The hill was, and to a limited extent remains, sheep; the Vale was cloth, of which a few vestiges can yet be found. One would therefore expect to find in the history of Edington parish traces of the two great trades that have dominated the economic history of Wiltshire [i.e. wool and cloth].

This is true for Bratton also. Along with arable and dairy farming, sheep have played a continuing role in the village. Now they generally live comfortably in prepared pastures, but within living memory the sheep-bells still tinkled above the village as a flock moved at sheep's pace through a sleepy summer afternoon. Cloth was, and is no more. In the sixteenth century Bratton men built mills on the Stradbrook. They tried to catch the tide in the market for undyed broadcloth and at one time there were at least four mills on the little stream. But, in the seventeenth century, boom was followed by slump. Lacking capital, perhaps, or foresight, to move into the new line of the coloured-cloth trade, the mills in Bratton languished, yet remained for a later revival. In the meantime the basic farming economy continued and by the seventeenth century the more substantial Bratton families can be seen establishing themselves in land. The Whitakers were among these.

By tradition the pedigree of the Bratton Whitakers starts with Stephen Whitaker, who was reputed to have come from Holme in Lancashire in the reign of Elizabeth and settled in Westbury. But the only authority for this is a statement by Sir Richard Colt Hoare in his *Modern Wiltshire* for which he gives no source, and the only basis appears to be a similarity in coats of arms. In 1560 arms were granted to Stephen Whitaker, described as: Sable, a Fess between three Mascles Argent; Crest: Horse statant Or. These were based on those of the more distinguished family of Whitakers in Holme. But at the Visitation in 1565 Stephen Whitaker of Westbury 'disclaimed the name of gentleman'. Perhaps a grander origin had been sought when a humble family began to prosper, but the honour was found to be not worth the financial burden. The coat of arms was, however, later cherished by the Bratton Whitakers who used a modified version as a book-plate in the eighteenth century.

Stephen Whitaker and his immediate family did indeed prosper.[1] In the 1560s he was a clothier of considerable property, buying land in Westbury, Westbury Stourton, Bratton and Steeple Ashton, but also owning a mill at Penleigh – and incurring a fine for faulty white cloth. His eldest son, Henry, at one point M.P. for Westbury, moved to Plymouth where he married Judith Hawkins, while retaining his Westbury connections. In his will, proved in 1589, he is described as 'gentleman' and leaves property to his sons in Westbury. His brother Jeffery, described as 'clothman of Tinhead', established what appears to have been a flourishing cloth business in the Edington and Bratton area. In a survey of 1573:

William of Westbury, grandson of Stephen, is recorded as owning: one fair mansion house . . . with a large fulling mill and loft over it and all things fitting for the dressing of cloth, the water being better for scouring than most other mills, having a clear course from the springhead. Also a garden and yard to the said capital mansion and three acres of arable land . . . Bitham house and mill, Bigwood tenement, fifteen acres of arable and seven acres of meadowland . . . and three acres between Westbury town and the hill.

At this period Stephen and his family could almost be compared with the great clothiers of the area – the Stumpes, Hortons and Longs.

But there were obscure Whitakers already active in the district before Stephen rose to prominence. The earliest we know is a John Whitaker who, in 1466, seems to have been the biggest clothier in Westbury, paying tax on 120 cloths as compared with the next highest, 80. The first Whitakers we

---

[1] The material on pp. 19–21 is drawn mainly from *Victoria County History of Wiltshire*, VIII, pp. 168–9, 172–4, 243, 245–6 and *Wiltshire Notes and Queries*, IV, pp. 107, 111.

know in Edington and Bratton are John, a clothier who probably built the 'New Mill' in Edington parish in 1519, and Richard, another clothier, who was a juryman in Bratton in 1522 and collector of a lay subsidy there in 1538. Both prospered: John held a Westbury estate from 1522 to 1551 and in 1545 held the lease of a fulling-mill in Westbury Leigh; Richard Whitaker had about 160 acres and a sheep-house in Westbury in 1545. In Bratton there was also a Widow Whitaker who, according to a perambulation of 1575, held Bratton Mill (the Lower Mill). In 1585 a grist mill in Bratton was sold to two brothers, Christopher and William Whitaker, whose father may have been the Richard just mentioned. In 1586 Christopher paid a lay subsidy.

Meanwhile Jeffery, Stephen Whitaker's second son, was building his own little cloth empire, centred on mills in Edington and Bratton. He acquired the lease of Leigh fulling-mill, bought Mompesson lands in Edington and Tinhead and had a watermill in Bratton some time before 1599. In 1600 he owned a fulling-mill at Langham, North Bradley. In his will, proved in 1601, he left his eldest son, Nash, and his second son, Jeffery, lands and mills in Tinhead, Edington, Ashton, Langham and Westbury, and animal stock, including a flock of sheep. His legacies totalled £3,000, in which he remembered, besides his sons and daughters, his nephews, his servants, and the poor of Edington, Westbury, Bratton, Warminster and Devizes, 'forty shillings apiece'. He also left a house and household stuff, including glass and hangings. The house, according to Kenneth Ponting, is the fine Becketts House still standing in Tinhead. To Jeffery he left specifically his best cloth mark: 'commonly called the yellow cross'. This was the high water-mark of the Whitaker clothiers in Edington and Bratton.

Their decline may have been partly due to family bad luck. Nash died very soon, in 1610, leaving his 'Bratton Mill' and best cloth mark to his son Jeffery. This Jeffery died without issue in 1625. In 1613 he had been described as a clothier; at his death, as a gentleman – but this may not indicate increased prosperity. He left land in Edington and Steeple Ashton to his uncle Jeffery, but no more is heard of the cloth mills. The elder Jeffery, too, seems to have died without direct heirs. Apart from family misfortune, the crisis had now set in in the undyed broadcloth trade which – according to Mr Ponting – was virtually destroyed by the mid-seventeenth century. By 1625 the direct line of Jeffery Whitaker of Tinhead was almost extinct and little more is heard of the Whitakers as clothiers in Edington and Bratton. One is mentioned in 1674 but the fact that a Thomas Whitaker, fuller, occurs in 1638 and a William Whitaker, clothworker, in 1693 suggests that the Whitakers who remained in the trade mostly sank to the level of workers.

But there was no lack of Whitakers in Bratton in the seventeenth century, obscure at first and traceable only from parish registers and other official records. In 1585 a Stephen Whitaker married Margery Bannocke in Bratton Church. This Stephen was probably the youngest son of the great Westbury Stephen and the founder of the branch of Whitakers which most concerns us. His son, John, was baptized in Bratton in 1586 and married there to Dionise Aldridge in 1618. Nine years later in 1627 another John Whitaker married Margaret Aldridge. Thus already two leading Bratton families were intertwined in an alliance characteristic of this society. About this time the initials JWD were carved on a beam in the Court House at Bratton and it has been suggested that John and Dionise settled there. Two Whitakers, John and William, made payments in the lay subsidy of 1625 while again they were both recorded in the Wiltshire Freeholders' Book of 1637–8.

By 1666 we reach the firm ground of the oldest document preserved at the Yew Trees which specifically names the Whitakers. It is a copy of the Court Roll of the Manor of Bratton concerning land in Southaye, Thorncombe Bottom, 'Portwai furlong', Sandes and Brodelayne held by Arthur and Henry Whitaker, customary tenants by copyhold of 1649. These were the sons of John and Margaret Whitaker, married in 1627. It was from the younger brother Henry that the line of 'Yew Trees Whitakers' finally descended. The next document in the family archives is an agreement between Anne Whitaker, Henry's widow, and John Drewitt, yeoman in Bratton, concerning his marriage with Anne's daughter, Anne. Here we meet another of the family alliances which cemented Bratton society together.

There are many Whitaker baptisms and burials in the Parish Registers for this period and it is clear that the family was proliferating in Bratton. We can trace the ramifications in wills and land leases. Much, though not all, of the village was in the Manor of Bratton, belonging to the Longleat estate. In the 1680s this was being reorganized and a survey of Bratton was made in 1682. Leaving aside other land-acquiring Whitakers and pursuing our own branch alone, we find a lease of 1670 which shows Jeffery Whitaker, a son of John and Dionise, together with Jeffery and Chamberlain, his sons, in possession of a tenement which, through the 1682 Survey and a later note in it of 1735, can be identified as Smarts, that is, the Yew Trees. In 1683 Henry Whitaker was entering into possession of land under Picket Hill at Deanly and Patkin Hill. He was probably the Henry Whitaker who signed the 1682 Survey and added a grumbling note about the changes in the pattern of farming caused by the Longleat reorganization.

A few early wills put some flesh on the bones.[2] The Henry just mentioned was able to distribute lands and money throughout his ample family, though his last two daughters came off poorly: to John, the leasehold called Axfords; to Henry, the leasehold of Horsecates; to William, Francklens, and Thomas, Redlands; to Philip, 40 acres of arable in Bratton (common) Field; to his daughters Anne and Margaret, £200 each; to Judith and 'Dinius' (Dionise), £100 each. In the inventory of his goods are included 'a peace of virgenholes (virginals), a viall and base viall', worth altogether £4. A taste for music seems to have begun already. He left 905 sheep and the total value of his estate was £2,344.15.0. In the next generation his son Henry, in a will made in 1691, remembered his sister, Anne Drewitt and her children, and all the rest of his brothers and sisters. In 1697 Chamberlain Whitaker – an odd name in this family – left bequests to

2 For these wills, see *Wiltshire Notes and Queries*, IV, p. 202.

brothers, cousins and friends in lieu of direct heirs. He is described simply as 'husbandman', yet he was able to leave money to the poor of the Baptist congregation meeting at Leigh, and out of a total value of £87.13s. his books were valued at 15s.

Thus we have a little evidence of some culture and much of family solidarity. One feature of this family tree is a recurrence of distinctive Christian names amidst the endless Johns, Williams and Henrys: Dionise or Dennis, Melior and Judith turn up in different branches, while the Yew Trees branch revives the earlier name of Jeffery in three successive generations. This feature supports the view that the Whitakers in this area were all ultimately of one family. Another characteristic which we have already noted is the close intertwining of a certain group of families, in marriages, in bequests, in the management of affairs and exchange of land. Whitakers, Aldridges, Ballards, Drewitts, Blatches, less frequently Frowdes and Seagrams – these dominate Bratton in a kind of family oligarchy, operating together almost in a stately ritualistic dance. A few other names appear and some smallholders stand respectfully on the edge of affairs, but these are the families who manage. In 1660 John Ballard married Catherine Whitaker and the Ballard connection remained a constant factor, even though not always agreeable. In 1710 Humphrey Whitaker took a lease of the Ballard homestead and for the next century it passed back and forth between the two families. The will of Mary Ballard, wife of William Ballard, which was proved in 1714 illustrates the family network well. She herself was an Aldridge, her sister had married into the Blatch family, while she leaves 'my black satin gown that I had against the time I was married' to her husband's daughter, now the wife of John Whitaker. The Whitaker/Aldridge connection, begun before 1615, was continued three generations later when three of Henry Whitaker's children married Aldridges. The names Aldridge Whitaker, Aldridge Ballard and Ballard Blatch underline this interwoven pattern, and the cross-threads of cousinry must have been hard to disentangle. To give one more later example: in 1780 a tenement called Aldridge's was leased to

Thomas Whitaker on the life of Philip Ballard Blatch and a new lease to Thomas, son of Philip, in 1788 names him as trustee for William Aldridge Ballard, Ann Ballard and the children of John Blatch.

2 Schoolhouse and Meeting-house

By 1700 the Jeffery Whitakers were comfortably settled in the house which stood on the site of the Yew Trees. The second of the three Jefferys, called 'the elder', reigned with his wife Catherine, whom he had brought from Trowbridge, thus breaking the inter-marrying Bratton pattern. The back wing of their home, with ample kitchens below and the 'long room' above, was probably much as we see it today. The front part, as we shall see, was dramatically burnt down in 1789 and rebuilt. Inevitably, farming their land was a major preoccupation. We pick out the pattern of their holdings from the legal documents and records which survive. Like those of other local farmers, the Whitaker holdings were scattered through the three main areas of Bratton farming: the downlands, the medley of pastures and orchards in which the homesteads themselves were located, and the lower, damper fields indicated by names like Withymead and Marsh. Some parts were still in the common fields, but there were many enclosures, such as Redlands, Butts and Coldharbour. Running up into the downs was a surprising extent of arable land, in fields with names which we often still meet – Patkin or Patcombe, Thorncombe, Longcombe. The lease granted to Jeffery the Elder by Lord Bath in 1735 gives a full account of the land which went with Smarts or 'Jeffery Whitaker's Home Living' (i.e. the Yew Trees). Besides the tenement itself, with 'Backside Garden and Orchard', and two little grounds called the Close and Redlands, he held meadow and pasture in Stoke Mead and Stoke Parrock, and arable land in the Butts, on Patcombe hillside, in Longcombe, at Heaven Cleave and Hipley (?), on Yerburies hill, on Lower Stoke hill, on West Stoke hill, in

Deanleigh, at Brandiers, at Cats well, Combe bottom, Kingsthorn, Coleman and one or two more – all in parcels of land ranging from half an acre to seven. He also had the right to 10 Beast Leaze, 1 Horse Leaze, 64 Sheep Leaze on Cow Down and 64 in Stokecombe Field.[1] This sort of evidence is the topographer's paradise and readers are invited to do their own perambulation.

Jeffery farmed these lands in the midst of a clan of similar landholders who must often have discussed crops and flocks in pubs and parlours. In the mid-eighteenth century Whitakers were also living at or holding Winckes' (now the Court House), Trulands, Frickers' (now Court Farm), Tinkers' Tenement (now Ivy Cottage), Ballards', Bucks' (now East Marsh Farm), Whites' (now Reeves Farm) and Hodges' (now Emms' Farm). From these names it would seem that they had ousted many former families. They were active and busy men, these Whitakers, much involved in local affairs. They appear as paymasters and jurymen, they collect taxes, take inventories of dead men's goods, act as estate agents for the Thynnes of Longleat, serve as trustees of wills and guardians of children. Sometimes they are described as yeomen, sometimes as gentlemen, but they belong to that key group in English local life who upheld the fabric of society.

If they had been only farmers we might have got no further than this in trying to recall them to life. Luckily for us the Whitakers were more. A document now in the Wiltshire Record Office tells us that in 1701 the house of William Whitaker, 'now in the occupation of Robert Bathe situated in Bratton' is 'set apart and from henceforth intended to be used as a meeting-house for the exercise of religious worship by Protestant dissenters'. This was witnessed by Jeffery Whitaker the Elder and his cousin, William Whitaker. Almost certainly this licence was for a Baptist conventicle. We do not know what made these Whitakers turn away from the Established Church, but there had been a committed Baptist group in Erlestoke, three miles towards Devizes, from the early 1660s, and Frowdes, who

[1] Leaze = common pasture land and hence pasturing rights.

were Whitaker connections, were much associated with this cause. We also do not know where this house was or what happened to the conventicle meeting there. Presumably it collapsed, for the next stage in the story sees Jeffery and his wife, Catherine, walking through the fields on a Sunday to worship with the Baptists in Westbury. Preachers and congregations walked far in those days and coming in the opposite direction was John Watts, minister of the Erlestoke group. The story is told in the Minute Book of the Erlestoke/Bratton Church:

... our brother Watts ... he living in Westbury, came to us [i.e. Erlestoke] Lord's Days and so did return home. Many times he met Mr. Jeffery Whitaker of Bratton and his wife in the field as they were going from the meeting at Westbury home. On a time his wife, Mrs. Catherine Whitaker, asked him if he would preach once at their house, to which he readily complied and so he did at the time appointed, many being at the meeting he freely appointed to be with them that day month and so continued some time beginning the meeting at six o'clock in the evening, then he was desired to be with them once a fortnight which he was with some success. Then they prevailed to have a meeting every week beginning at three o'clock in the afternoon ... and so he went on with comfort, the Lord disposing and inclining some of worth to attend the meeting at Bratton.

This story of the Sunday walk and meeting in the fields can evoke an idyllic picture, but we should remember that it could mean hard, muddy walking in all weathers. Perhaps Mrs Catherine's request spoke of tired feet. Traditionally, the Bratton group gathered in the large, flag-stoned kitchen at the Yew Trees and there we can picture it meeting until in 1734 the group 'were inclined to build a Meeting-House for the more commodious worshipping of God'.

Jeffery Whitaker the Elder allows us to see very little more of him, but unexpectedly we catch one glimpse in the parish register. The births of his six children are all recorded in a beautiful and distinctive hand, with the precise hour and minute of birth. These entries are so unlike the rest that Jeffery, one concludes, must have entered them himself. The fact that these and some children of other families are registered as *born*, not *baptized*, shows that these families were already committed to a Baptist theology. Again, Jeffery's death is also entered in a distinctive gothic hand, suggesting that the younger Jeffery was following his father.

Nothing has survived about these children's education, but two bits of flotsam – 'refugee books', as it were – turn up at the Yew Trees to show us what was taught and learnt in Baptist families. One is an exercise-book which belonged to a cousin and is inscribed: 'John Drewett his Multiplication Table February The: 27: 1701'. It is the very acme of an arithmetic book. Each page is wonderfully and elaborately set out, with flowing lines and scrolls and little decorations. From Tables it proceeds to Multiplication, Reduction, Division in the manner of the Golden Rule, Long Measure, Avoirdupois and so on, all so beautifully lettered as to suggest that this was a fair copy – except for a large red blot which runs through several pages. Under what stress, one wonders, did the toiling John make it? One of the touches which bring these old papers so vividly close are the later scribbles on blank pages, and here we find draft letters, bills of exchange, notes on surveying the Queen's Highway and some accounts for Bratton Farm, 1711/12.

The other is a printed book which may well have been used in the upbringing of Whitaker children, although this particular copy is inscribed 'Anna Gay, her Spelling book'. She was a more distant cousin. The light-hearted little rhyme on the fly-leaf

Whose pretty Book is this?
My little dearest Miss
Will you give me a kiss?

stands in sharp contrast to the horrifically Protestant title-page (2) which is anything but pretty':

The Protestant Tutor, Instructing Youth and Others, In the Compleat Method of Spelling, Reading and Writing True English: Also Discovering to them the Notorious Errors, Damnable Doctrines and Cruel Massacres of the Bloody Papists; which England may expect from a Popish Successor, with Instructions for Grounding them in the Protestant Religion. To which is added The Preamble to the Patent for Creating the Electoral

Prince of Hannover a Peer of the Realm, as Duke of Cambridge.

This edition was published in 1713, with a frontispiece of Queen Anne. It mirrors the hopes and fears of radical Protestant families at the moment when the Hanoverian succession was in the balance. The Preface, to all Protestant Parents and Schoolmasters, refers to recent times 'in which the enemies of the Protestant Religion and of the Liberties and Properties of Freeborn Englishmen' were countenanced to such a degree that 'they had infested the Principles of our Youth with the Libertine Spirit of Atheism and Debouchery, so that ... England was next Door to Ruin, Popery and Slavery, ready to deluge us in a Flood of execrable Miseries and Calamities'. Even now the Jesuitical Sowers of Discord still lurk in holes and corners, hence the reprinting of this little book to save 'our Youth' from swallowing the 'Hellish Notions of their Idolatrous Religion'. If the little Whitakers were brought up on this, they would get their spelling mingled with most powerful anti-Papist propaganda. They would learn a catechism in which Popery was refuted from the Bible, as thus:

Q. What confirmation hath the Popish way?
A. Devilish, 1 Thes. 2.3.
Q. Have Peter pence their Original from Peter?
A. No. Acts 3. 6.
Q. May the Pope absolve us from our Oath of Allegiance?
A. No. Eccles. 8.2.

They would learn history with an astonishing slant and be called upon in a New Litany for children to pray:

That it may please thee, let there be
Pour'd down from Heav'n Felicity
On all the Hanover Family, We beseech thee etc.
Princess Sophia still protect,
And with thy Counsel her direct;
And all Pretenders Lord! reject, We beseech thee etc.
Keep bloody Papists from this Nation,
And let us all in ev'ry station
Be mindful of their Extirpation, We beseech thee etc.
That never more may England Blaze,

As once in cruel Mary's Days;
And that we all may give thee Praise, We beseech thee etc.

The peaks of Papal iniquity are high-lighted in vivid little woodcuts that must have powerfully infected childish imaginations with the Protestant myth. It is a relief when the book descends again to weights and measures, bills and receipts. We seem a long way from Popish plots with this:

The Hosier's Bill, June i, 1702.

	l	s	d
Six pairs of Silk Stockings for your Wife at 15s per pair	4	10	0
3 Pair for yourself Worsted Stockings at 3s per pair	0	9	0
2 Pair for your daughter Molly, Silk	1	0	0
A Knit Silk Wastecoat for your Wife	10	0	0
A Knit Worsted one for yourself	0	15	0
	16	14	0

The elder Jeffery's first-born, Merari, rather surprisingly joined the Horse Guards, so when Jeffery died in 1737 it was to his bachelor son, Jeffery the younger, that he left all the beds and bedding on the upper two storeys of the Yew Trees, while his widow, Catherine, had the house. There were 14 beds, and thus we come on the first clue that there was a school in the house. In 1740 the younger Jeffery wrote in his diary: 'This day 22 years ago I began teaching school'. So, in 1718, at the age of 15, he started in – surely at the Yew Trees in the school which his father must have been conducting. To his own education he only makes one allusion, when he mentions the death of his old school-master, Philip Ellis of Shrewton.

We can now see the mid-eighteenth-century Whitaker household through Jeffery the younger's diaries, of which three survive, two in little homemade notebooks and the third in a small exercise book with the head of a 'Turck from Constantinople' on one side and a 'Iannitser' (Janissary) on the other. They run from 8 March 1739 to 7 July 1741, with one missing (28/10/39 to 2/4/40). Since they begin and end abruptly, there must have been others. They start just when Jeffery's father's affairs have been wound up after his death: a new lease of the Yew Trees has been negotiated and Jeffery continues to live there with his mother, Catherine Whitaker, and his sister, also Catherine. Also in the house are a 'Cousin Whitaker', probably Elizabeth, widow of Henry Whitaker, Ben Bourne, a troublesome school assistant and Tom, a servant who could be 'very wicked and stubborn and once provoked me to beat him'. In addition there are the boys, and about six permanent farm labourers attached to the establishment.

Jeffery is a precise, pedantic man who gives for each entry, not only a date, but the day of the week in an astronomical symbol thus: Sunday ☉, Monday ☽, Tuesday ♂, Wednesday ☿, Thursday ♃, Friday ♀, Saturday ♄. He makes corrections and cross-references and notes times very precisely, as 'An Eclipse of the Sun observ'd the end at 29' after 5 p.m.' (24/7/39). At this time he is reading on Sundays Foxe's *Book of Martyrs* which he cites by its proper title as he meticulously records how many pages he has read, until: '28 June, 1741: '. . . finished reading Fox's *Acts and Monuments* have read the three vols. in fol. printed 1641, began reading the Third vol. Sep. 28, 1740'. Like his father, he is interested in parish records and in separate notebooks makes a careful copy of part of the parish register which he checks in 1748. As for his personal appearance, we can only discover that he wore a wig, had a light grey suit and got his great coat washed. He was nervous about his health and often sent to Warminster for physic. Sometimes 'it worked', sometimes it didn't. When he had boils, he could not sit down. When he had a bad attack of colic in 1739, he recorded that the doctor 'was very much shocked with my Disorder, finding a very sensible alteration in all the Animal Oeconomy'. This is the man who records for our reading all the petty doings of his household in a small, beautiful hand with many flourishes. The entries are brief, laconic, sometimes ludicrously dead-pan:

17 March, 1739. Rode to Warminster before Dinner. three Rioters to be hanged.
24 September, 1739. having a bad Cold did not go up into the School all Day. Spaniards proclaim War.
28 September, 1739. The Dog Lion hang'd. Dick Halliday

fought with R. Cook and J. Ballard one after Another at pipers. Uncle sold a bed bedstead and Bolster Cord and mat for 32s A carved Tester.

4 September, 1739. Aunt Whitaker Died this morning at $\frac{1}{4}$ after 5. Agreed with Mr. Knapp for freestone Coping for the Wall before the School and house against the Street.

11 June, 1740. Took physick ... I was ill Mobbing at Froom about Corn.

The business of a respectable farming household goes on industriously all the time. The labourers thatch and dig and plant, 'put the flower garden in order', and mend gates and drains. The state of the weather is anxiously noted as William Henwood cuts the acre of clover at Coleman or the fine weather brings 'a very quick harvest'. At home his mother and sister organize the big washes which he notes every few weeks and supervise the meaty dinners recorded by Jeffery – to which we will return later. Jeffery himself spends much time riding round the countryside on business connected with family property, school fees and local government. Within the radius of Westbury, Warminster, Frome, Trowbridge, Bradford, Melksham and Devizes there is much coming and going of both men and women on horseback. They cover considerable ground in a day and 'lie with' friends or relations when they cannot return. Once Jeffery 'mounted at Salisbury $\frac{1}{4}$ before 6 and (was) home $\frac{1}{4}$ after Ten in the morning. Rode to Marsh Fair'. Another time he did a long round with his sister, probably collecting school fees: Durrington, Amesbury, Salisbury, Fordingbridge, Tisbury and home via Crockerton, spending three nights on the way. There was much sociability involved in these rides and once Jeffery records: 'lay at Mr Collins's memdm. not to drink so much another time'. But sometimes his journeys are simply for shopping: 'rode to Bradford $\frac{3}{4}$ after 4 for paint it got out of the bladder and painted my Cloathes'.

But what about those boys packed away in the 14 beds at the top of the house? There is maddeningly little about them and one suspects that Jeffery preferred riding round the country to 'attending the school', as he grudgingly records from time to time. Even the numbers are hard to get at: there seem to have been usually between 15 and 23 boarders; in June 1740 there were certainly 18 boarders and 14 day boys. The school occupied the two upper floors of the house and the schoolroom was probably the long room to which there was access by an outside flight of steps up to a balcony. There was an Easter holiday and a break in May from which the boys drifted back rather casually before the end of June. Most of them went home for Christmas. If we had only Jeffery's diaries we should discover precious little about the curriculum, except that 'the Boys learn'd to bow' (6/5/40), but by a marvellous stroke of luck one of Jeffery's own handwritten advertisements has survived, rescued by a local antiquarian, Edward Wilton, 100 years later and sent to Joshua Whitaker in a letter. With beautiful flourishes it announces:

At Bratton in the County of Wilts are taught Writing in all hands Practical and Ornamental. Arithmetick Vulgar and Decimal. Geometry Superficial and Solid. Trigonometry Plain and Spherical. With the Application thereof to Surveying of Land, Gauging, Navigation etc. Also Merchants Accts.
July 30, 1750.   Jeffery Whitaker

Thus the school was a miniature 'dissenting academy', turning away from the classical studies of the Establishment and catering for the rising classes of farmers, tradesmen and merchants, so many of whom were Nonconformists.

As for equipment, Jeffery buys books from a London bookseller, Ward, and sends Tom to Warminster and to Gadsby's of Devizes to fetch boxes of them. But what exactly was he doing when he 'began to write Titles on the edge of printed books'? Ben was sometimes employed making 2d, 3d, or 4d exercise books and he also wrote out arithmetic and geometry books on, for instance, 'operations in the Double Rule of three', 'Tare and Trett Sums with opperations',[2] 'Sperical Geometry' and Rules in the use of the Square Root'. By another stroke of good luck, a fragment of one of these books has survived in which the beauty of the curve is given full play on the elegant title page,

[2] *Tare* = deduction from gross weight for packing etc. Tret(t) = deduction allowed for wastage in transferring goods from one container to another.

'Practical Geometry', and another title in the shape of a swan with 'Mensuration' on the neck and 'Solids' on the body (3). Making ink was a major operation. Four gallons which Jeffery started to make on 22 July 1740 were not finished until 1 August, and again the gallon he began to make on 31 March 1741, took until 17 April. 'This is writ with it', he remarks, and a very good advertisement it is – would that he had left us the recipe. Other equipment is only mentioned casually: a watchmaker comes 'to set going the Horologe'; a back board is bought for one of the boys 'to make him hold up his head'; from a 'Traveller that Gilds with powder' Jeffery buys the receipt for doing this and ten 'Quicksilver Lookinglasses' – for what purpose, we wonder?

We hear more about extra-curricular activities. The boys go nutting, pick crab-apples and in October 'Lammas the orchard'.[3] What excitement there must have been when on 4 May 1739, 'a man came with a Man Tiger to show to the Boys'. The Beckington boys are allowed to go home in August for the Rode Revel and on November 5th there is a holiday and 'Bonfire as usual'. If we can trust an 1823 reminiscence of Jeffery Whitaker, he was an enthusiast for King Alfred and used once a year to assemble the boys on the White Horse to commemorate Alfred's victory over the Danes by scouring the horse. This conjures up a pleasant picture of a swarm of little boys gambolling all over the Horse, while exhorted to noble deeds by their earnest schoolmaster. Was it Alfredian sentiment also which prompted Jeffery to have his bookplate made from the Whitaker coat of arms with the white horse *statant* above? Was he also an amateur archaeologist? A rumour, recorded by Colt Hoare in *Ancient Wilts*, reports, that 'Mr Whitaker, the late schoolmaster, investigated Bratton Castle, finding Roman coins, querns and nearly a cart-load of large pebbles'.

Naughty Ben Bourne was a constant source of irritation, chiefly because of his propensity for going to fairs and revels and staying out late:

[3] This use of 'lammas' as a verb is unusual, not recorded in the N.E.D. *Lammas* (1 August) is the festival of the harvest first-fruits.

30 May, 1739. Ben having taken a haunt of late to stay out till 10 o'clock most nights, but last night i Having set up till 11 he did not come all night but this morning about ½ an hour after 9 he went to Bed till 12 without saying anything and left the School to me. I have endeavoured all I can to reclaim him by fair means.

15 Sept., 1740. Gave Ben leave to go to Marsh fair . . .

16　'　' Ben did not come as he promis'd.

8 Oct., 1740. Ben not minding the Boys to my liking in the Evening. I blam'd him but he in a Mog refus'd to go up with us to prayers.

10 Nov., 1740. Ben did not come till after Dinner, he is careless of coming at all, don't like confinement.

Jeffery's disapproval of his frivolous assistant was probably all the greater because he disliked jollifications himself. 'A parcel of fools new dressing the Maypole in the lower street', he writes angrily on 1 May 1739. Bratton Revel must have tried him sorely, for it seems to have lasted two days:

23 July, 1739. Bratton Revel. Ben out from leaving work time till 2 a Clock Tom out till ½ after 10.

24 July, 1739. Ben . . . did not come home all night. I sat up till after 10.

25 July, 1739. Ben home about 5 in the morning went to bed I attended the school . . . a great ado at Revel this year but I thank God I saw none of it.

How we wish he had – and told us what he saw. Fairs and sheep-shearings were more respectable because they combined business with pleasure. At Edington, Warminster and Marsh Fairs, for instance, the Whitakers bought cheeses. Funerals, of course, were great occasions. When Aunt Whitaker died there were six pall-bearers, white gloves and scarves were furnished to the men and gloves to the women. Again, describing a Crockerton funeral, he records: 'I was one of the pall Bearers Gloves Hatbands and Sashes white silk few people but handsomely manag'd.' Mourning rings or lockets, with pictures of funerary urns or hair in them, were distributed to members of the family and various Yew Trees specimens bear witness to the strength of family clan feeling. In Jeffery's record there is a striking absence of celebration at Christmas and New Year. On 22 December 1740 he 'gave the poor a penny a piece'. The 25th he spent reading Foxe, adding in his diary: 'by abstemious living and confinement I think I am thinner than I have been this 7 years but I bless God I am better or at least as well in health as I have been this many years'. New Year's Day he spent 'in the Closet' sorting his father's papers. There is a tinge of melancholy in this schoolmaster but we must remember that Nonconformists had reacted sharply against the 'pagan superstitions' of pre-Reformation England.

All this sounds very ungregarious, and yet there was a continual round of sociability among families of the 'middling sort' in Bratton and the district, while Jeffery takes good care to record with satisfaction his contacts with the Phipps family who were 'county'. He says nothing ill of these acquaintances – with one exception. The Ballard family was too close for comfort. John Ballard was his particular *bête noir*. Once, when Ballard had been worsted in some business, Jeffery writes with glee: 'Mr John Ballard looks mighty budge', and when Ballard was an assessor of Land Tax, Jeffery was obviously worried: 'J.B. partial about assessing me and himself'. When, in a small-pox epidemic, the two brothers, Jonathan and John Ballard, both died within a few days, Jeffery was moved to a unique outburst which is worth quoting:

17 Nov., 1740. At 3 this morning died Mr. Jonathan Ballard of the Small pox a facetious Companion Given to Drinking and idle Company . . .
20 Nov., 1740. Mr. John Ballard Died this morning about 8 a Clock of the Small pox. He was stubborn and perverse in his temper Tyrannical in his family. Arbitrary in the neighbourhood and when he had drink'd Quarrelsome in Company positive and self-will'd in his assertions ambitious and despising others and given to law. his life more desired by his dependants and those that losses by him than others. I wish I could say as much on the bright side of his Character. I hope the Lord gave him a true sight and sense of his folly before his Death.

This shows us what Jeffery could do when roused.

As those who kept the machinery of local government going, these people often joined conviviality with business, or even occasionally got the first while evading the second.

Jeffery was very pleased when he attended a Court, to find that there was none, but 'the Dinner good Victuals large in Quantity and well Drest good Beer and good Attendance'. We see him walking to Westbury Parish Meeting in the company of several young men and a whole bevy of girls: 'came home after midnight'. He dines at the Search Hoop in Warminster when he called on the Hundred Jury. Evidently he could be obstinate, for when summoned to Sessions at Westbury Leigh for renewing Alesellers' Licences, he refused 'to write a certificate for J. Callaway or any other'. Did he feel there was too much drinking in Bratton? On another occasion, when he 'rode to Sessions with Sister behind me', he would not set his hand to a presentment about a road. The chores of local government which fell to his lot in Bratton were tiresome. On 28 April 1739 he starts to collect the Land Tax; on 2 May he anticipates difficulty in getting it in; on 12 May, however, he thankfully carries it to Westbury. In August of the same year he is dealing with assessments for Window Tax and the next year he is somehow mixed up with a problem of churchwardens: '7 April, 1740. Mastr. Horlock and Mastr. Lucas to see me at Tuckers'. Church Wardens not bringing in their Accts. Chose others'. Obviously you could get unpleasant jobs landed on you if you did not attend meetings. Once Jeffery was fairly caught out by not going to the Westbury parish meeting, where T. Phipps nominated him as overseer. Then he *was* in a stew, rushing round to various people to get him off, until family influence did the trick: 'Co. Blatch got me off from being overseer'. We can picture him thumbing through the copy of *Parish Law, or a Guide to Justices of the Peace, Ministers, Church-wardens, Overseers of the Poor, Constables, Surveyors of the Highways, Vestry Clerks, and all others concerned with Parish Business*, published in 1734, which sat on a bookshelf at the Yew Trees.

Very little disturbed the even tenor of the Yew Trees household. Jeffery sometimes notes oddities: the Aurora Borealis appears 'very Red and Surprizing'; a great storm smites them with 'hail Stones bigger than Boys marvels, pointed ends near an Inch long and water running down

Tinkers' Lane almost enough to drive a mill'; a snake is seen coming out of the barn-wall, and the appearance of 'naish an Hermophrodite' is recorded without comment. But the high-light at this period of Jeffery's life must have been his trip to London to see his brother in May, 1740. On the 19th he 'sent to take a place in the Caravan[4] being Resolv'd to go to London next week'. On Sunday, 25th, after hearing Mr Watts preach, he rode to Devizes. Perhaps one of the two miniature trunks of this period which were found at the Yew Trees was strapped behind him. He set out in the 'caravan' at midnight, carefully noting in his diary the change of date. They breakfasted at Marlborough, dined at Thatcham and lay at Reading. On the 27th Jeffery was in Maidenhead for breakfast, at Colebrook for dinner and got to 'Hide Park Corner' about 6 p.m., where his brother met him. His pastimes in London were certainly not frivolous. He looked over books at Mr Ward's and pursued his feud with John Ballard into the Court of King's Bench and Common Pleas. On Sunday, of course, he heard a well-known preacher, Dr Gifford. But he did see the 'Duke and the princesses' at St James's and also 'the Curiosities of the Royal Society'. He started home again on 5 June, reaching Devizes at 5.30 in the evening of the 6th. He had lost a mourning ring in transit but was, perhaps, relieved to have suffered no further damage: 'Rode home. I thank God I came home in good health'.

But he returned to a far less healthy situation in Bratton. In April he had already recorded, 'rumour'd that John Croom has the small pox' and a few days later: 'John Croom died last night of the small pox'. During the whole summer smallpox rumbles like a not-so-distant thunder, breaking in full storm over Bratton in November and December, 1740. We catch Jeffery's apprehension when he writes in June: 'Dream'd I was going to bed to young Croom. If God in his providence should think fit that I should have the small pox I hope I should Rely alone on him for support' . . . and then, characteristically: 'Rode to

[4] *Caravan:* stage waggon conveying passengers and goods. There was a regular service between Devizes and London.

Westbury to Dr Bayley for Physick.' In November nerves were shaken by the deaths of the two prominent Ballard brothers, and a Day of Prayer and Fasting was called at the Baptist Meeting House. On 12 November the Whitakers were alarmed to hear that 'Hollowayes boy at the next house has had the Small pox more than a week unknown to the Neighbours'. Letters were sent round to the parents of the schoolboys to fetch them home, if they thought proper; but many seemed to care as little as Mr May of Worton who 'don't design to fetch his Son home'. Jeffery, however, did care and from Sunday, 16 November, onwards 'abode at home with the Boys and Servants that hath not had the Small pox'. He read them funeral sermons instead: no wonder he was 'low-spirited'; they were, too, no doubt. All the Ballards were stricken, but somehow the Yew Trees escaped, except for a late victim in Cousin Whitaker. All through November and December Jeffery's melancholy record goes on, while his mind turns often to Physick:

28 November. last night I took one pill and this morning 3 more of Extract of Rudii[5] to prepare for the Smallpox but it worked but very little.
28 December. Sent William Henwood to Warminster to Mr. Pearsehall for advice of preparation for the small pox.

On 19 December he notes a sinister detail: 'I smelt burnt Woollen or Hair in our garden. Supposed to be burnt at one of the Small pox houses'. There is a sombre record of deaths at Christmastime and it is not till the end of January that the epidemic is seen to be waning. Finally, on 1 March, Jeffery records: 'I with the Boys went to meeting, not having been there since November 9th last on Account of the Small pox'. Did Jeffery, one wonders, draw a moral from the contrast between the near immuunity of the Yew Trees and the tragic fate of the Ballard households?

Personal emotions sometimes erupt even in the best-conducted families. Mrs Catherine Whitaker was probably a

---

[5] *Extract of Rudii:* probably some preparation from marigolds (used as a stimulant and an aperient), since *ruddes* was a country name for marigold.

redoubtable old lady and Sister Catherine pig-headed. In the summer of 1740 suddenly an affair is seen to be flaring up when on 4 July, Jeffery remarks: 'Sister resolv'd for a husband'. Next day Catherine announced her intention to marry and there was a 'great disturbance' between herself and her mother. When the sweetheart arrived, Mrs Whitaker forbade him the house and Jeffery had to take him to Mr Watts the minister's house, where they had 'abundance of talk'. Poor, mild Jeffery, caught between the two warring women! Although friends tried to mediate, the old lady remained adamant. The suitor was John Collins, a tradesman of Devizes, whom she obviously thought beneath the Whitakers in station. He could, however, force the pace. On 15 July Jeffery writes: 'this powerful Sweetheart would have an Answer possitive to be married this morning. Sister being drove to such a pinch, like a fond fool consented to be married tomorrow. William Henwood began mowing the Orchard'. So on 16 July 'at half-an-hour after 7 Sister went from home in order to be married, as it was against our Consent, Mother forbid the man's coming here so they lay at Blatches' '. This near elopement must have set the village a-buzz, but in Jeffery's laconic telling it all settles down surprisingly quickly. Sister rides with Tom to Warminster and Frome to buy wedding clothes and there are many friends to ride some way with her when, on 6 August, she sets out 'behind her husband'. Tom took her box to Devizes next day. The old lady climbed down pretty quickly, for, by the following year, Collins was sufficiently accepted to stay at the Yew Trees where he presented his mother-in-law with a trout and Jeffery with a crook stick. Jeffery remained a bachelor – but not from choice. Suddenly – while still in the dark days of smallpox – the pace of the diary begins to quicken and Jeffery starts the story of his own timid little love-affair: '10 December, 1740: Dream'd a pleasant Dream that I was married to Mrs. M. —m, with all the pleasant Circumstances thereof.' But the courting of Mrs Mary Adlam of Bull Mill, Crockerton, did not really get going till next April. The story is best told in his own words:

9 April, 1741. Advise with Mrs. Collins about a Certain momentous affair.

18 April. At 25 min. after 6 mounted my Horse Rode to Bull Mill made an offer of myself and Substance to Mrs. Molly Adlam and also told her Mother my intention and had a favourable Answer and 2 or 3 hours of Mrs. Mary's Company for which I bless God for his mercy being persuaded if I obtain her it will be in mercy.

2 May. At 6 in the morning mounted my horse Rode to Froom spent the Day till ½ an hour after 7 at Mr. James Collins's most of it with and in the Company of Mrs. Mary Adlam which was greatly to my satisfaction and pleasure.

10 May. Rode to Crockerton Heard Mr. Wilkins from Mark 14.38. Din'd at Bull Mill spent the afternoon with Mrs. Adlam very agreeable. (More agreeable visits follow, until . . .)

18 May. Myself, Bro. and Sister Collins Rode to Crockerton and with Mrs. Adlam, Mr. James Collins of Froom and his Wife, Mr. John Moody and his Wife and Mr. King Rode to Norington by Dinner time . . .

19 May. at Norington apprehensive of being Sleighted by Mrs. Adlam and jealous of F. Fricker but however danc'd with her in the Evening.

20 May. All of the aforementioned with F. Fricker . . . Rode to Sutton Mandeville and Din'd with Mr. H. Fricker. Mrs. Adlam Rode behind F. Fricker she sleighted me much more to my great grief and disappointment had thoughts of Riding away but by my best Friends persuaded to the Contrary.

21 May. We Breakfasted and Din'd at Mr. John Lawes's . . . being so vext and Disappointed found myself not well and Mrs. and myself were Aukward Company and neither could be free with the Company of each other.

23 May. Being resolv'd to know Mrs.' mind more perfectly, she discharg'd me quite and will hear no more on that head. her mother vext about it . . . her Brother saith he should have been glad if she had accepted me. no objection was made against my person Character or Circumstance but as I think Mrs. being naturally brisk and airy and I being used to Reading and Study am thoughtful and grave in Countenance which she cannot like and perhaps willing to try another. Oh! most unfortunate Journey this Week to lose my chiefest delight in this World!

24 May. at Home all day being greatly vext at my late disappointment can hardly bear up under it God of his infinite mercy either turn her heart or Support me under all trouble this being the greatest I ever met with.

15 June. . . . am very thoughtful about things since may 23 last. I hope my health nor senses will be impair'd.

That little chronicle epitomizes, I think, the society and the conventions within which Jeffery moved, as well as giving us a flash of self-revelation. After this the diary sinks back to its usual hum-drum level.

Pious sentiments fall naturally from Jeffery's pen and, although fervour does not seem to be part of his nature, we are always aware of the Meeting-House as his background. It was new in 1734 – a great achievement for a small committed group – built amidst the Bratton orchards 'on a piece of ground commonly known as Brown's Berry', and there it still stands, a mellowed red-brick building with high-pitched, stone-tiled roof and stone facings, a perfect example of eighteenth-century Nonconformist architecture. On the south-west side there is still an area called Berry or Bury. The licence for the new meeting-house was witnessed by an impressive group of Baptist worthies: Wm Axford, John Aldridge Ballard, John Blatch, Henry Whitaker, Edward Frowd (Edington), Jeffery Whitaker the Elder and Philip Whitaker. These formed the first trustees. The familiar family names roll out, and it is clear that this Church was, humanly speaking, founded on and sustained by this close group of families. Gradually the leadership shifted from the parent church of Erlestoke to its offspring at Bratton, perhaps because of a succession of vigorous men, until in the 1750s the Erlestoke Church vanished, leaving Bratton as the focus of Nonconformist piety in the district.

The affairs of an eighteenth-century Baptist Church were conducted with a dignity and pious solemnity that expressed itself in sonorous, flowing sentences and a special vocabulary derived from the Bible. What survives of the early records at Bratton came to light in the Yew Trees, from which we deduce that the two Jefferys wrote many of them, while we owe their survival to the hoarding instincts of the Whitakers. Not all scribes, however, had the penmanship or literary skill of the Whitakers. Among the Yew Trees hoards was this epistle of 1732, so characteristic, in its aberrant spelling and overtones of St Paul, of the young Baptist democracies:

42

From the Church of Christ in Sarum to our Brethren of the Church meeting in Stock (Erlestoke) Baptised upon profession of faith and holding the principals of the doctrine of Christ mentioned hebr. 6.2. we wright greeting wishing all grace mearcy and peace from god the Father and our Lord Jesus Christ etc.

For as much as it is through the providence of god the Lot of our brother Henry Best to be cast near and to reside amongst you and he being desieris to join communion with you and we not haveing nothing to accuse him of, or lay to his charge we resine him up to your christian care hoping that you will accept him in christ and wach over him in the Lord and Live togither to the credit of reiligen and Glory of god and we subscribe ourselves your brethren in Christ Jesus.

Then follow all the members' signatures.

The highlight of Baptist life was the annual or bi-annual Association Meeting which moved round among member churches. At that time Bratton belonged to the Western Association which covered a wide area in the West of England. It was surely a tribute to the vitality of this small Church that the very next year after the building of the meeting house 'Ministers and Messengers, streamed into Bratton in May, 1735, for the Association Meeting. What did the village think about this astonishing influx and where did they accommodate them all? We do not know and, indeed, would not know anything at all about this unusual village event were it not for the Whitaker hoarding habit. Each church sent a letter 'To the Ministers and Messengers of the Several Churches of Christ meeting in Association at Bratton near Westbury on the 28th May, 1735'. Probably it was Jeffery the elder – himself a 'messenger' – who salvaged some of the original letters, those from Grittleton and Malmesbury, Yeovil, Crewkerne, Plymouth and Pen y garn (Pontypool). Each gives an account of the present spiritual state of their church. Grittleton 'has cause to bless God, that we have peace amongst ourselves and have not as we know of not so much as one discontented Member belonging to us. Neither have we any snarling nor frowning looks, either between member and member, or between minister and people'. Pen y garn hopes 'that the Lord is about to do great things in this place and to gather in Many Stray Sheep'. Plymouth is in a low state: 'it is a very mournful time which we live in for Corruptions Both in Doctrine and practice do mightily abound which things we Judge call for days of Deep Humiliation before the Lord'. The Church at 'Crook-horn' also mourns 'the present low and desolate state of Zion'. These are fragments of the canvas which must have been painted in Bratton on that day in May. To change the metaphor, we catch here something of the authentic flavour of eighteenth-century Nonconformity. How did they discuss the scene, we wonder, what resolutions did they pass before they all got on their horses and rode away? No other record survives.

Once we can hear the authentic voice of the Bratton Baptist Church itself, and the chances are strong that what we have here is a draft of Bratton's letter to the Association Meeting in Bristol in 1738, written by Jeffery the younger. Because of its characteristic style and theological awareness, I shall quote several sentences:

The Church of Christ Meeting at Earl Stoke and Bratton Baptised on a personal profession of faith Maintaining the Doctrines of the Trinity of persons in the Unity of the Godhead or divine Nature, personal Election, particular Redemption, efficatious grace in our Vocation together with the Saints, perseverance till they are brought to Glory ... To our Honoured and beloved brethren Meeting in association in Broad Mead, Bristol ... As to our Church State, we have cause to morne but not to dispaire, we have had none added for a long time; death hath defaced our Glory but not (blessed be God) broken our peace; our Numbers of hearers do not deminish; though it is somewhat like the Moon; two Meetings every Lord's Day; one at Stocke, the other at Bratton; Church meetings once a month; some times meetings of prayers; evening lecture Lord's Day many times but the waters of the Sancturary is but littel stirred, tho' we hope not altogether still ...

Like other Baptist causes in the mid-eighteenth century, Bratton Church does seem to have sunk into the doldrums. After the death of John Watts in 1747 it had no regular minister for 30 years, a situation which encouraged divisions. Even before this Mr Ballard was being awkward, for Jeffery Whitaker tells a curious story: '18 July, 1740. Mr J. Ballard being Affronted with Nimrod for leting old Gwin into the Meeting House with whom he was at Law that he lock'd up the House and would not suffer the Meeting there as appointed so the meeting was at our house'. But on the whole the 'family cement' kept the Church together and ensured that its affairs were conducted in orderly fashion. One salvaged scrap of paper gives a list of new trustees for the Meeting House in 1756, with all the flourishes of Whitaker handwriting. The names include Merari Whitaker, John Blatch the younger, Thomas Whitaker and William Ballard. It is interesting to find Merari, the Horse Guardsman, coming back into the Bratton picture. He had already, in 1741, got a foothold there by acquiring a lease of Tinkers' Tenement, just opposite the Yew Trees, which his brother Jeffery sublet for him for some years. Perhaps he came back to Bratton to live before his death in 1761. Jeffery, curiously, does not figure in this list of trustees, but at some point we know that he was made a deacon of the church, the only one we can name in the eighteenth century.

It goes without saying that Sunday was a day of services and sermons. Jeffery regularly took the boys to the afternoon service at the chapel to hear Mr Watts, and he usually noted down the text. But his relations with the Established Church were quite amicable. He and the boys sometimes went to Bratton or Westbury parish church and we have already met him mixed up in a problem of churchwardens in 1740. Indeed, other Whitakers were faithful supporters of the parish church at Bratton, supplying from 1750 a succession of churchwardens and leaving their tombstones in the church-yard. On the whole, the two religious communities in Bratton lived side by side with little animosity, both stable and dutiful in their own commitments. In the Baptist congregation piety centred on the preaching services and the Lord's Supper. The sermon nourished their minds (and tongues) on Biblical treasure and the monthly communion gave them the elements of their faith in the simple form they desired. Another precious scrap of paper gives an account of the 'Collections taken monthly at the Lord's Supper', balanced by an account of what 'Mr John Blatch gave to the Poor from the Collections at the Lord's Supper and for Wine'. The account runs from 1769 to 1772 under Blatch's treasurership. In January, 1773, Jeffery Whitaker takes over, writes out the account, and signs for the balance of £1.6.6.

But in 1775 Jeffery Whitaker died at the age of 72, and the members of the Church penned a disconsolate letter to the trustees of two funds for the relief of poor churches. They mourned the irreparable loss sustained by the death of our 'truly pious and worthy friend and deacon'. In his will he left a capital sum of £350 to the Baptist Meeting-House, the interest to be used for the support of a regular minister, for an annual sermon to save young people from the evils of Warminster Fair, to help the poor of Bratton and to provide instruction for poor Bratton children in reading and writing. I think this was characteristic: he wanted true learning to reign from the pulpit; he wanted to get a dig at those wicked fairs; he wanted to do something for education. For, in spite of his grumpiness about 'attending school' in Ben's absence, I think he believed in it. Perhaps the school was his real monument. It must have trained several generations of Bratton boys (and others) in elegant writing and neat accounting. We can guess that a bunch of young Whitakers went there and perhaps this schoolmasterly tradition helped to form the literary tastes we shall meet in them later. But in his diaries Jeffery guards his own personality closely. Except for that revealing bit of self-analysis evoked by his love affair, he seldom allows it to peep out. We see him as a precise, methodical person, mostly absorbed in a conventional routine, either totally lacking in humour, or given to the dead-pan sort which defies detection from this distance. He does not show much humanity, even under the pall of small pox, but when in love reveals himself as a shy and sensitive man. He ended a bachelor, and with him died out the Jeffery Whitakers. His brother, too, had no children, so here this branch of the family ends.

The school was carried on, first by Jeffery's later assistant,

Thomas Morgan, and then by the Rev. John Cooper, the Baptist minister, and Mr Thomas Williams of Trowbridge. In 1787 an advertisement in the *Salisbury and Winchester Journal* shows it still running on the same lines:

BRATTON SCHOOL

At this School Young Gentlemen are genteely boarded and carefully instructed in the learned Languages, and in every other branch of Literature necessary to form the scholar and man of business, by the Rev J. COOPER and Mr. WILLIAMS.

The above school was conducted by the late worthy Mr. Jeffery Whitaker for more than half a century with the greatest reputation and is highly esteemed for its healthful and pleasant situation. Its distance from Devizes is 10 miles, from Frome 10, Warminster 6, Trowbridge 5, and Westbury 2½   (5/2/1787)

Two years later, however, a poor crazy scholar burnt down part of the Yew Trees and made a second attempt to destroy the school in temporary quarters before committing suicide. The drama caused a considerable sensation in the local press. The school carried on in obscurity, though in what building is not clear. We trace it by advertisements until 1820. Then it vanishes. For the time being the Yew Trees passed out of Whitaker hands and we shift our story to Whitaker cousins live at Bratton Farm (now Manor Farm).

3 Parents, Children – and an Aunt

When Thomas Whitaker became a chapel trustee in 1756 he was only 21 years old – more than 30 years younger than his cousin Jeffery, and two generations removed. It looks as if he dived into life energetically, for he brought home an interesting bride, Caroline Attwater, from Bodenham, near Salisbury; with her bred five children, bought or leased much land, managed chapel affairs – and was buried at the age of 49 with a laudatory funeral sermon which was carefully copied out by the preacher and respectfully presented to his widow. Among the property transactions in which Thomas's or Caroline's names appear, two acquisitions are particularly interesting. In 1772 Thomas obtained from John Houlton of Seagry the lease of Grants Farm on the Plain, a beech-enclosed cluster of farm dwellings and buildings with an extensive acreage of arable land and sheep pasture around it. Right down to 1913 it remained one of the best-loved Whitaker holdings. The other was Dunge Farm, mid-way between Bratton and West Ashton.

At the chapel Thomas had to step into Jeffery's shoes in 1775 just at a critical moment: the roof was near to falling in. Once again, it is a piece of paper in the Whitaker hoard which tells us that a new roof was 'absolutely necessary'. The estimated cost was £30 and already, so we learn, 20 people had pledged themselves to subscriptions ranging from five guineas to 2s 6d and totalling £32.13s. The list is headed by Thomas Whitaker and Jeffery (just before his death) and ranges through the familiar roll-call of Frowdes, Drewitts, Ballards and Blatches to names of families that have an honourable place among Bratton labourers – Bristow, Sweetland, Burgess, Baggs and so on. This is Nonconformist democracy at work. Alas – the roof actually cost £62.6.9d, and the hat had to go round a second and even a third time to meet the bill. How careful they were in accounting for every penny. A second little sheet of paper records some details: the roof took $56\frac{1}{2}$ ft of oak timber (£4.6.0d) and then later 224 ft of the same (£16.16.0d); tiles cost £2.5.0d, while the men hauling timber got 1s 8d-worth of beer. Other details of expenditure have not survived, but they made £7.12.6d by selling old roof iron, etc., and ended with a deficit of 6d. Thomas, it seems likely, kept this account. In such ways the methodical Whitakers made their contribution to the Baptist Church.

Perhaps Thomas's bride made a stir in the village when he brought her home. The Attwaters of Bodenham sprang on the maternal side from the Gays who provided Bath with a mayor and the name of Gay Street, and Nonconformity with an eminent seventeenth-century preacher, Richard Gay, who corresponded with John Bunyan and languished for a time in Ilchester gaol. It was probably the Nonconformist commitment that first linked Whitakers and Attwaters and no accident that some of Richard Gay's sermons as well as Anna Gay's lesson-book, *The Protestant Tutor*, turned up at Bratton. The interesting thing about Caroline is that through her coming to Bratton we are able to uncover a little-known literary circle which centred on Bodenham and Broughton just over the Hampshire border. It becomes for a moment part of our story because of its influence on the Whitakers. Its 'flavour' is unusual: a blend of strict Baptist piety and typical eighteenth-century classical pastoralia. Its presiding goddess was Anne Steele, who never left the environment of Broughton where her grandfather and father were pastors of the Baptist Church. Having poetical gifts, she naturally wrote hymns, published in two volumes in 1760, and equally naturally she has been chiefly studied by hymnologists. But her pen-name, Theodosia, strikes an odd note for a pious Baptist and a volume of *Miscellaneous Pieces*, published after her death in 1778, reveals another side to her literary personality. It is, however, the collection of poems, letters and diaries which have come to light at the

Yew Trees that really lifts the curtain and shows us a circle of literary ladies and gentlemen gathered around her who write with all the mannered sentiment and convention of the period through which at times the religious soul-searchings of a Nonconformist conscience strike with a distinctive but not discordant note. How did this unexpected treasure arrive in a Whitaker household? Caroline, no doubt, was responsible for some, but it was her extremely communicative sister Jane – Aunt Attwater to the young Whitakers – who probably collected most of it.

Through Jane's literary outpourings we discover the graceful group which poses around 'Theodosia': 'Sylvia' is a Miss Steele, probably Anne's niece; 'Myrtilla' can be shown to be Jane Attwater herself and 'Dorinda', her sister Caroline; 'Florio' is, I think, Anne Steele's brother or nephew and 'Philander' perhaps Jane's brother. We also meet 'Amira', 'Aminta', 'Maria' (some of whose poems we have) and others unidentifiable. 'Myrtilla' often comes to stay with her sister in Bratton, writing thence the eloquent epistles to her 'ever-valued Sylvia' and other friends which express the style of the group so perfectly. Her voluble pen often runs away with her in ungrammatical and unpunctuated sentences, but here is a view of the Bratton landscape, seen in May, 1771, through her romantic spectacles:

Dorinda and your Myrtilla have taken a very agreeable Evening's ramble up by the Church Where viewing the gardens the slooping hills the Lovely fields Cloth'd with richest verdure the blossom'd Orchards yield a sweet perfume and help to compleat the rural prospect All beautious and serene – The Lofty Elms hung pendant o'er the purling rills which gently murmuring sooth each care to rest and calls (sic) the Mind to pleasing Melancholy Meditation Near our sight on the top of the impending hill were the Receptacles of our fellow Mortals there stood the Church in ancient form Rear'd by the hands of those who perhaps once inhabited this very spot There now they lies (sic) in heapless ruin all there are deposited the master and the slave Mouldered alike in Dust and soon shall this frail Body which now surveys these Mansions of the Dead sink into Death's Cold Arms...

So Bratton inspired its own elegy in a churchyard.

Some of the poems these friends wrote to each other turn up in manuscript among the Whitaker papers, although – alas – nothing of Dorinda's has come to light. One of Jane Attwater's notebooks contains this by Sylvia on the joys of country life:

To me more fair my dear lov'd native scene
The Corn-clad Hill the stream the daisied green
The scattered tillage and the lowly Tow'r
To all the Charms inventive art can show'r . .
O bear me to some deep embow'ring Gloom
Awfully silent as the peaceful Tomb
There wrapt in pensive pleasing thought I'll stray
And muse the silent stealing hours away . . .

It is nice to think of these ladies, who undoubtedly lived busy lives, fancying they would enjoy the pleasures of solitude.

On the Whitaker bookshelves, besides copies of Theodosia's poems given to 'Dorinda' and 'Myrtilla', were several books, printed in Bristol and now rare, which emanated from this group. The most interesting is a long poem entitled *Danebury or the Power of Friendship, A Tale, with Two Odes. By a Young Lady*. There were two copies at the Yew Trees, one containing an inscription in which Sylvia, as authoress, presents it to Myrtilla with the ardent wish that their friendship may equal that of the girls in the tale. The tale is an Anglo-Saxon legend of a battle at the 'ancient camp' of Danebury (near Stockbridge) in which the Danes were defeated and a girl named Elvira saved from death by her friend Emma. Another note pinned into this copy gives a glimpse of Theodosia and her friends going on an expedition to Danebury, where a 'Miss H. More' is moved to extempore poetry – and this turns out to be no less than Hannah More. So Anglo-Saxon attitudes could be struck by a group of ladies on Danebury as well as by a schoolmaster and his boys on the White Horse.

It would be amusing to know what Thomas and Caroline's children thought about their voluble Aunt Jane and her literary friends. Philip, born in 1766, was only 13 years younger than this aunt. The next in the family, Anna (1768), died at the age of 11, but the other three, Mary (1773), Thomas (1776) and Anna Jane (1784), all grew up. We meet these children in their lesson books. Philip has left us no exercise books, but in 1772 his 'Aunt jenny Attwater' gave him a new miscellany, just published, of the curiosities beloved of that age: *Choice Emblems Natural, Historical, Fabulous, Moral and Divine for the improvement and pastime of Youth, ornamented with near fifty handsome Allegorical Engravings ... The whole calculated to convey the golden Lessons of Instruction under a new and more delightful Dress.* Beneath a touching frontispiece of two earnest children being instructed in a garden by the Muse, the author's educational philosophy is expounded thus:

Thus prudent care must rear the Youthful mind,
By Love supported and with Toil refin'd,
'Tis thus alone the Human Plant can rise,
Unprun'd it droops, and Unsupported dies.

The 'emblems' are abstractions, each expounded in relation to its own symbolic picture. Thus Silence is represented by an ancient philosopher with pyramid and obelisk as backcloth; Purity by the Sensitive Plant; Guilt by the Bat; Instability by Fortune with her wheel; Precipitation by Plato's rash charioteer; Perseverance by Jason and the Golden Fleece; Industry by the Woodpecker – and so on. Granted that moral teaching was the *sine qua non* of children's books, this must have been attractive stuff, but Aunt Jenny was surely forcing the pace a bit to give it to a boy of about six. The only other child's book which we can identify as Philip's is *Christmas Tales for the Amusement and Instruction of Young Ladies and Gentlemen in Winter Evenings* by Solomon Sobersides who instructed all booksellers 'to make a Present of it to Good Girls and Boys, they paying sixpence only to defray the Expence of Binding'. Amusement and instruction go together: this is characteristic of the eighteenth-century books we are looking at.

Because Anna died young, there was a gap of seven years between Philip and his sister Mary. So he was probably always the elder brother, and must have grown quickly into manhood with the death of his father. We meet Mary as a child through her own peculiar style of 'signature'. In 1787 she was given one of J. Newbery's delightful little books for children: *A Compendious History of the World From the Creation to the Dissolution of the Roman Republic compiled for the use of Young Gentlemen and Ladies* ... If one looks closely at the quaint frontispiece of the Creation, one realizes that it has somewhat irreverent additions – some comic extra animals with spirited tails and a little man in a high hat sitting on the elephant, presumably God. When we look into another of Mary's books we find her style is unmistakable. In front of *A Collection of Pretty Poems for the Amusement of Children Three Foot High*, by Tommy Tagg, she has made a spirited sketch of what looks like Papa chasing daughter on horseback. She has also paid attention to the pictures accompanying the poems. Perhaps the way she disfigured True Beauty expresses her irritation at this verse:

What is the blooming Tincture of a skin
To Peace of Mind or Harmony within?
What the bright sparkling of the finest Eye
To the soft soothing of a calm Reply?

Another book which she decorated was *Early Piety or Memoirs of Children Eminently Serious* in which Master Billy and Miss Betsy Goodchild are introduced to a variety of moral stories, ranging from Mount Vesuvius to the Penitent Prodigal.

Amongst the pile of exercise-books, again, Mary Whitaker's arithmetic book is easily recognizable – even without the inscription 'Mary Whitaker. her Book Feb. 17, 1784' – because it starts with a lively little pen-and-ink drawing of a lady in an immense crinoline and head-dress. Perhaps this was to keep her spirits up, for the first half of the book is a formidable model with huge, intimidating long-division sums. In the second half the work is more convincingly childish, but still beautifully lettered in parts. There were samplers, too, to be accomplished. At nine she was being taught a lesson 'Against Idleness' by toiling through four verses of 'How doth the little busy Bee

Improve each shining hour' – with some difficulty over cross-stitching the word 'skilfully'. Then she moved on to a long poem, 'Sensibility', surrounded by a fine flower border and probably worked in 1784. It declares:

Since Trifles make the sum of human things
And half our misery from our foibles springs . . .
A solitary blessing few can find
Our joys with those we love are intertwined
And he whose helpful tenderness removes
Th' obtruding thorn which wounds the brest he loves
Smooths not another's rugged path alone
But scatters roses to adorn his own.

We can imagine Caroline selecting this rather unusual piece from her own literary repertoire, but did she, one wonders, explain it to her daughter? Mary seems an individual child, perhaps disliking conventional piety. Even her recipe books which we shall look at later have an individual touch. She did not marry and died quite young, in 1800.

Thomas – as well as his elder brother Philip – probably went to the Yew Trees school. Perhaps they were both instructed through *The Polite Academy or School of Behaviour for Gentlemen and Ladies* on how to behave to superiors, equals and inferiors, in Church, at Meals, on keeping Company, on how to salute, make a bow, take your leave and so on. If Thomas faithfully followed the instructions for a ceremonial bow and leave-taking, it would have taken him about five minutes to get out of the room. In 1784 Thomas was given *Youth's Pleasing Historian and Entertaining Companion through English History . . . after the manner of Dr. Goldsmith,* but this time the title is deceptive, for the frontispiece of Britannia instructing Youth in the Beauties of English History is much more entertaining than the rest. In the front of his copy of John Clarke's *Compendious History of Rome* Thomas bravely wrote: 'Thomas Whitaker me jure tenet', so he must have been learning Latin. And, no doubt, English grammar. For the children possessed *The English Accidence designed for the Use and Adapted to the Capacity of Young lads . . .* in which masters are urged 'to enjoin their Scholars to get it by Heart

... as a Task at Breaking up or other vacations'. At the age of nine Thomas was given *The First Principles of Religion and the Existence of the Deity explained in ... dialogues adapted to the Capacity of the Infant Mind.* That sounds tough going, but actually the author tries to carry out Locke's pronouncement 'that philosophical reasonings at best amaze and confound, but do not instruct children'. So we get such charming dialogue as the following:

Maria. Did one God make all the cows and horses and fishes and trees and flowers and everything?
Mamma. Yes, my dear, God made everything.
Maria. Was not God tired then?
Mamma. No, God is never tired.
Maria. That is very strange! Papa told me he was tired of making horses for me last night, when he had only cut out four, and card is not so heavy to hold as a live horse would be; and there are a great many horses in the world. I think God must have been tired before he made all living things.
Mamma. No, indeed, my dear, God is never tired. Your papa is tired because he is only a man, and men are soon tired; but God is not a man.
Maria. If God is not a man, is God a woman? or what is God?

The question of questions! If only we knew how the Whitaker parents would answer it!

On 14 October 1789 Master Thomas Whitaker, aged 13, was writing in beautiful copper-plate all down the first page of his exercise-book: 'Attend to rule and order when you write'. The book had a nice picture of a horse and rider on the cover and Thomas proceeded steadily through it, copying on one side of the page rhyming directions for good writing, such as 'Be sure to place your pen and self aright' and 'The downward strokes make full, the upward fine', while on the other side penning various aphorisms, as 'Quiet minds enjoy life' and 'Nature is always various'. Each page is dated at the foot until, on 29 March 1790, he is triumphantly covering the last page with 'Zeal, care and patience soon will conquer all'. He may also have owned more of these exercise-books with attractive pictures on the front of Duck-shooting, a Guardsman firing at full gallop, and Vauxhall Gardens. In September, 1790, Thomas was making out immaculate 'Bills of Parcels' to such fascinating characters as 'The Reverend Mr. Euclid Peachy' and 'Madame Strawberry, bought of Manywords, Milliner'. The bills themselves are of great social interest, but who invented the fancy names? One arithmetic problem which these children worked shows what people did with their silver:

A gentleman sent 455 oz 1 dwt 16 grs of old Plate to his silversmith with Order to make it into the following articles viz Punch Bowls each 27 oz 4 dwts, tankards each 11 oz 14 dwts, teapots each 10 oz 10 dwts, lamps each 20 oz 17 dwts 21 grs, plates 127 oz 11 dwts per dozen, spoons of 36 oz 17 dwts 20 grs per dozen. How many of each must he make supposing for each dozen of plates and spoons he is to make one of each of the other?

More of Anna Jane's possessions survive than of the other children. She had a terrific *Universal Spelling Book* which amazes us with what it offered:

Tables of words in one, two, three and four syllables . . . adapted to the Capacity of Children from Three Years . . . and yet so full of sense that such as can already read may receive very material Instruction: Comprehending . . . passages both on moral and divine subjects, as also Fables and pleasant Stories . . . A very easy and rational Guide to English Grammar . . . A Collection of near 5000 of the most useful Words . . . explained for the . . . Information of such Persons as would know the meaning of what they read and write, being a useful Instructor for the School, Shop, or Compting House. Many useful Things necessary to help the young Beginner . . . Chronological Tables of the Succession of the Kings of England and many of the most memorable Occurrences in sacred and profane History; with some short Remarks on the seven stages of Life, which . . . may be of great service to prevent Youth from falling a sacrifice to the common Temptations of Life and their own unbridled passions.

No doubt she was really thankful when she wrote a little verse at the end, beginning 'Lord, make me thankful unto thee'. She moved on to Entick's *New Spelling Dictionary* which was even more severe, with no pictures.

But eighteenth-century writers knew how to gild the pill in charming little moral tales with lively wood-cut pictures.

Anna Jane had a very quaint collection with a title which must be quoted in full: *The Picture Exhibition, containing the Original Drawings of Eighteen Disciples, to which is added Moral and Historical Explanations ... under the Inspection of Master Paul Rubens, Professor of Polite Arts.* The contents are most curious, as, for instance, 'The Washing of the Lions at the Tower', a story with the moral that April-fooling is a bad thing. More conventional was another of her books, *The Village School, or a Collection of Entertaining Histories for the Instruction and Amusement of all Good Children.* This is peopled with bad boys (Master Crafty, Jack Sneak, etc.) and good girls (Jenny Meek, Sally Neatwood and so on) who portray the life of the village school in vivid picture and story. In 1791, when she was seven, her brother Philip gave her *Tea-Table Dialogues between a Governess and Misses Sensible, Thoughtful, Bloom, Hopeful, Sterling, Lively and Tempest.* The recipe is still the same: artless little stories, transparent morals and first-class little black-and-white pictures.

It was surely her mother who gave her Theodosia's *Verses for Children*, in which the duty of obeying parents is uncompromisingly, though charmingly, presented:

My dear little boys, I send you no toys,
For those are for babies, you know,
But since to good sense, you show some pretence,
Attend to the Counsel below.
What papa says is right, observe with delight,
Mama too with pleasure obey;
If you strive to be good, and behave as you should,
Their praise will be sweeter than play.

Anna Jane received as a present in 1795 *Letters on the Improvement of the Mind* addressed to a young lady, and probably two other books for girls were hers also: *The Whole Duty of Women*. By a Lady, and *The Young Lady's Pocket Library and Parental Monitor*. This latter contained no less than three separate works of parental advice to daughters (with, in one case, a charming picture of the three daughters sitting in a row taking it), and Moore's 'Fables for the Female Sex'. Anna Jane probably enjoyed them but these books should not be read in the light of the Sex Discrimination Act.

We meet Anna Jane's handiwork in various forms. First, there are four of her exercise-books and the cover of another. Her copper-plate in the copy-book shows excellent muscular control, but she can't manage the spacing: 'Imitate the virtuo/us' defeats her all down the page. We can't inspect her sums properly, for another little Whitaker, about 1842, seized hold of this exercise-book and used it for a scrap-book. In 1796 she was carefully copying out an anthology of religious verse which got into the hands of irreverent scribblers (one was her brother Thomas) who decorated it with faces, signatures, etc. Similarly, her 'Poetical Book' of 1799, in which she has laboriously inscribed a long poem, 'The Hermit', has been decorated on the back page by an amusing sketch of three ladies. Perhaps she invited these attentions because she was a solemn girl.

We have one of her samplers, of the Lord's Prayer, with a delicate strawberry border, which she finished on 28 May, 179? (undecipherable). But if tradition is right, her greatest achievement in embroidery was an oval map of Europe worked on grey silk with a border of twining flowers. If she did this in the later 1790s she was using an out-of-date map, almost certainly one which we still have. It shows Poland before it was finally partitioned in 1795, while Little Russia, Little Tartary, the German Ocean, United Provinces and other features all mark the eighteenth-century scene. At the top, embroidered in a fine, flowing line is 'The Frozen Sea' and at the foot 'Barbary' in Africa (4).

Anna Jane comes over as a dutiful girl. Hers is probably the little notebook with marbled cover in which, from 1798 onwards, the preachers' texts are faithfully recorded Sunday by Sunday. A little later we shall find her teaching in the Sunday School. She did not marry, but became 'Miss Whitaker', with her own silver teapot. We still have the undertaker's account for her funeral in 1838.

We can actually furnish these children's nursery a little more completely. On the walls they probably had Riley's *Biographical and Chronological Tablet of English History*, a wall-chart picturing all the monarchs from William I to George II with a succinct judgement on each. Here is the pronouncement on George II: 'Was choleric – but neither vindictive nor malignant: he was brave, determined and intriguing.' The children who gazed at this picture-gallery must have felt that English History was a very stable affair in which black and white were clear and things came out right in the end. Perhaps they also had some of the big wall-pictures of English History which cost 3s, 'pasted on boards for hanging up in Nurseries'. At any rate a pocket version comes to light of *Prints of English History designed as Ornaments for those Apartments in which Children receive the first rudiments of their education*, complete with Mrs Trimmer's commentary. History in this version is full of surprises – starting with the Druids. We have already looked at their bookshelves; surely their cupboards held the many little fancy boxes in which girls, at least, used to hoard their treasures, so that now we can pry into their secrets by lifting the lids. Here is a little eighteenth-century 'trunk' in thin painted wood. On the lid sit a quaint couple in rural surroundings, at the ends are portrayed The King of Prussia and The Princess Dowager of Wales, inside are riddles on scraps of paper. Here is one:

Once I was a merry thought
In a little hen
Now I am a little slave
Made to wipe a pen.

(Does anyone make pen-wipers today?) Next we look into a child's workbox which holds a little hoard: a small oriental doll, a tape-measure in a cowrie shell, fragments of a tiny necklace carved from cherry-stones in a small wooden box which advertises Improved Portable Pens, and a scrap of poetry dated 1804 which begins: 'Sister this trifle with you take/And wear it for ye giver's sake'. Another miniature trunk, covered with embossed leather and lined with eighteenth-century newsprint, contains pieces of patchwork, a needlebook and some gold braid. Little 'housewives', pin-cushions and homemade boxes come to light; a small, heart-shaped needlebook is embroidered in cross-stitch on one side 'For my Mother' and on the other 'Mary 1085'. Was this Mary Whitaker, and did she mean 1785? Not many actual toys emerge, but we come on a gaunt wooden doll which bears mute witness to much fondling, and a pathetic waif of a tiny eighteenth-century doll which was found lying in comical incongruity beside a well-fed, prosperous doll from the early twentieth century, with pink-and-white china face, 'real' blue eyes and flaxen hair (5). Carefully stored in a little Wedgwood dish is a miniature set of ivory glasses, decanters and other vessels for playing at dinner-parties and with this, perhaps, goes a small set of bone knives, spoons and two-pronged forks, carved by hand and complete in their tiny wooden box.

Perhaps the model carriage (6) and the games and puzzles belonged more to the boys. There are thin wooden spillikins and a set of miniature dominos, hand-carved in bone with the neatest little bone box, which go up to double seven. Some games are openly educational. Pill-boxes of thin wood hold the letters of the alphabet on tiny squares of cardboard, one such box still bearing its label: 'Pectoral Lozenges Prepared from the Genuine Balsam of Tolu by J. Shepherd, 176 Fleet Street, London.' In a French box with a picture of Perpignan are sets of instructive card games. Bowles's Geographical Cards give 'A View of the Principal Cities of the Known World; Designed as a recreation for Young Gentlemen and Ladies and the Use of Boarding Schools'. They were designed by John Ryland, a Baptist and missionary enthusiast. It is not surprising that one detects a pronounced Protestant slant: Catholic cities are labelled 'Romish', while the statement 'The Established Religion is Protestant' naturally covers Dublin. A set of the monarchs of England provides some curious 'facts', such as 'William I subverted the English Constitution 1074', 'Arts and Sciences taught again at Cambridge 1110', 'Cards invented for the French king 1391'. A little leather trunk contains slips of paper with nouns and adjectives to be matched up, while a set of 'emblem cards' each with picture and verse is obviously for moral teaching, as thus:

The Anchor safely holds the Ship
When boist'rous winds assail,
Let Reason then the anchor be,
When Passion blows the Gale.

The soft *Guitar's* enchanting notes
Delight the player's ear
And study brings such sweet reward
To those who persevere.

Just like the *Kite* the giddy Youth
Soars upon pleasure's wing,
Forgetting that some skillful guide
Should regulate the string.

Even jig-saw puzzles could be didactic. The Whitakers had
'The Pilgrim's Progress Dissected or a Complete View of
Christian's Travels from the City of Destruction to the Holy
Land, Designed as a Rational Amusement for Youth of
both Sexes'. In spite of rationality, its vivid little scenes are
absorbing to put together. In a similar style is a 'Dissected
Map of the World for Young Learners in Geography' which
gives the eighteenth-century world in two hemispheres. A
milking-scene has no obvious moral but a pair of puzzles,
Courtship and Matrimony and Matrimony and Happiness,
teach very clear lessons. The first is a trick puzzle, as the
illustration may reveal (7). All these are primitive as jig-
saws, with no interlocking pieces except round the edges, but
none the less they must have been fun to do. Indeed, the
general impression left by all their books and possessions is
that these Whitaker children at the end of the eighteenth
century had parents who chose carefully for them and
wished to give them delight as well as instruction. Of course
discipline in education was severe and moral teaching never
far round the corner, but the emphasis on 'entertainment' is
striking and – saving grace – these children at least were
allowed to doodle as they pleased.

Philip had to grow up very quickly. When his father died in
1784 he had, at the age of 18, to assume the headship of the
family. No doubt his mother supervised the education of the
younger children, but he had plenty on his plate. He quickly

became a man of affairs and public works. New leases had to be negotiated for his father's holdings on the Longleat estate; Grants Farm on the hill meant another big acreage to manage; in 1788 he was already acting as trustee for Ballard and Blatch relations. Perhaps among the local government chores that fell to him was responsibility for highway surveying, for the Account Book for Bratton Tything Highways, 1768–1836, turned up at the Yew Trees. In 1789, at 23, he became a trustee of the Caleb Baily Trust, a newly reorganized charity which had originated about 1750 for the support of preachers in the Baptist, Congregational and Presbyterian denominations. How he came to be associated, when so young, with a regional charity outside Bratton is a mystery, but his appointment began a connection of Whitakers and their relations with this charity that only ended in 1975.

We catch a different glimpse of him from an ancient brown-paper parcel with his name on it. Inside are family papers, indentures, wills, land conveyances and notes on family history, all carefully gathered together. The oldest document is a narrow slip of a land conveyance, dated 27 December 1346, with the seal still intact. It conveyed land in Bratton and Milbourne to a Roger le Hoppe and had obviously been preserved in connection with some land which later came into Whitaker hands. The rest are later deeds specifically relating to the Whitakers. There are various versions of the Whitaker family tree going back to the mid-seventeenth-century Henry Whitaker, and a version of the Whitaker coat of arms with notes on it. Philip had also pursued his Gay/Attwater ancestry and made a family tree of this. He was even interested in the family tombs of the Houltons from whom his father had acquired Grants Farm. This shows us a man with a sense of history.

At the chapel he stepped into a situation where much activity was afoot but where leadership had been thin since the deaths of Jeffery and Thomas Whitaker. In 1786 the Church embarked boldly on a programme of enlarging and improving the meeting-house. The Church Minute Book records:

The enlargement ... was about 12 feet backwards, Lord Bath and Mr. J. Nevill gave the land and the congregation defrayed the expenses of the building, amounting to £177.4.3d. The vestry was built in the spring of 1784. Mr. Ballard gave the land...

Once again the original accounts have survived among Whitaker papers. Twenty-one people subscribed £180.17.0d in sums ranging from £60 to one guinea. The amounts of subscriptions have gone up noticeably, as well as costs, but the subscribing families remain much the same. For embellishment '4 Pair Brass Sconces and Carriage at £1.13.6d' was added to the bill. Among the payments for labour to the tiler, plaisterer, carpenter, joiner, glazier and plumber, is one 'Reeves the Blacksmith, paid 19/5d', whom we shall meet again. Philip probably kept the account for this operation and, from the amount of correspondence which remained in his hands, it would seem that he was church secretary, although he is not recorded as a deacon until 1800.

Jeffery Whitaker's will had stimulated the Church to look once more for a regular minister and in 1777 they had cordially invited Mr Cooper, a former Trowbridge clothier. This necessitated regular financial support for his salary and so, once again on an odd surviving piece of paper, we come across a list headed 'We whose names are hereunder written do voluntarily propose to subscribe the sum of money annexed to each of our names towards supporting the Revd. Mr John Cooper, if he shall be inclined to settle amongst us as our Minister'. Thomas Whitaker was still then alive and he heads the list, followed by 15 of the faithful names. For a considerable time the Church flourished under Mr Cooper: 30 were added to the membership and the congregation grew. Then anxieties about the Minister's theology began to arise. Theology was of deep importance, and aroused passionate emotions. Philip Whitaker's soul was racked with anxiety, but in the end he felt bound to raise his doubts with Mr Cooper. We still have what are almost certainly drafts of

63

his letters defending his theological position and some replies from Cooper. They are very revealing in their soul-searching concern to find the true God and the dignity of their Christian courtesy towards each other. At one point Cooper, who had cited Isaac Watts in defence of his position, feels he must write to retract this argument which, on further study, he believes to be erroneous. Finally, he left in 1797.

Here we see how farmers and men of business could be deeply concerned with theology. They could not leave it to the clergy. The articles of faith of the Bratton Baptist Church, drawn up by all the church members c. 1737, are an eloquent testimony to this. But then, the sermons they listened to Sunday by Sunday were full of theological meat as well as Biblical teaching, and afterwards they would carefully record in diaries and notebooks the text and sometimes the subject. We have the remains of such a text book which begins:

Mr. Cooper A.M.
Psalm 63: 3. Because thy loving kindness is better than life.
Ditto P.M.
Acts 8: 39. And he went on his way rejoicing.
Ditto in the evening.
Heb. 4: 9. There remaineth therefore a rest for the people of God.

Appropriate, perhaps, at the end of a long Sunday, with three services and a sermon at each. But there was little rest for poor Mr Cooper who kept up this record without a break until the notebook disintegrates. Occasionally a *cri de coeur* accompanies the faithful text-recording. Thus in 1776 Jane Attwater wrote: '. . . heard Mr Walter preach from Ecclesiastes . . . I must omit setting this discourse down, as I have now forgot the method of it – my every faculty now bears a near resemblance to every external object which is benum'd and froze with the chilling blasts of winter.'

This constant attention to sermons must have stimulated the capacity for self-expression in these congregations. Their language was nourished on Biblical simile and the rolling periods of the sermon. Then they found they had something to communicate and their words flowed. Nonconformity loosened tongues and touched off pens. This happened to Philip Whitaker, although, in his case, the self-communication started rather formally. At the beginning of 1786, when he was twenty, he equipped himself with a large vellum-bound book, with chased brass clasps and beautiful vellum pages. The second page is inscribed in copper-plate hand:

Texts preached from at Bratton and Memorandums of some remarkable Occurrences beginning with the Year 1786.

Opposite we read:

The following lines were written to me by my Aunt j. Attwater and desir'd to be inscribed at the beginning of this Book:
Sacred to Memory and Religion pure,
Let these Mementoes, and these lines endure:
With pious awe, the Truths of Scripture hear,
Trace o'er in Thought and pour your Wants in Prayer . . .

And so on for 32 lines. So Aunt Attwater was encouraging the young Philip in self-expression. She did not immediately have much success. Philip's first entry reads:

Sunday Jany 1st. Mr. Cooper A.M. from Prov. 27: 1. Ditto P.M. from Psalm 24: 4 the last was the subject of a Funeral Discourse for Joan Demay and Thos. Walter two aged Members who were bury'd this Day at the meeting.

The diary continues with a meticulous recording of preachers and texts but a disappointing absence of 'notable occurrences', except the following: 'This day my brother Thomas was inoculated with Miss Blatch and Mrs Morgan's Children may Divine Goodness protect them and bring them safe through it'. In June he attended Baptist Association Meetings at Bristol, but only recorded more sermons. This seems to be the limit of his literary ambition and even this soon wanes, for in February 1787 the diary peters out, and with about 7/8ths of those beautiful pages abandoned pure and clean. But before we leave this disappointingly immaculate book, it has another secret to tell us, carrying us for a moment into Philip's later family life. Slipped at intervals between those vellum pages are comic little cut-outs, done by or for a child: a wooden-looking dog making no real effort to catch a lively hare; a boastful cock confronting a man on a galloping horse; a house and garden; a sailing-ship. What is even more amusing is that they have been cut out of a Baptist Missionary Appeal to which we shall return later. Who was the child who seized on this book for a grand repository for treasures? Was it one of Philip's offspring?

Philip was discouraged and perhaps his aunt gave him up. She herself found the words flowing at breakneck speed off her pen and was already accumulating a pile of breathless notebooks. It is a strange chance that two such piles of notes finally landed at the Yew Trees – mixed up together, dis-ordered, with no authors and sometimes no dates. It took a considerable amount of rabbiting among internal clues to establish the fact that there were two separate authors pour-ing out their inner thoughts on paper at roughly the same time. It was very satisfying to discover beyond a doubt that these two were Philip and his Aunt Jenny. Did they know about each other's writing? I think not, for Jane wrote a good deal of hers away from Bratton. But Philip may well have been stimulated to start again by his literary aunt.

So, about ten years after he had abandoned vellum, Philip starts again, this time in humble little homemade notebooks now falling to pieces. He begins in a mood of spiritual gloom and introspection:

On *Sunday Evening 29 May, 1796*, I began this little Book in an unstable wandering Frame of Mind after attending the Word and the solemn Ordinance of the Lord's Supper in a very dark Frame, reviewing with painful reflections the Backsliding of the past Month ... I'm little better than a mere Formalist, Lord assist me in self-examination and if to this hour I'm a Stranger to myself and thee, give me now a right Knowledge of myself and thee ...

Sunday Morn. June 5th. It is all smiles in Creation. Spring has clothed the whole vegetable world in so full Dress, and this delightful morning loudly proclaims the Wisdom, Power and Goodness of the great God: thus it is without. Lord, help me to take an impartial View of the little World within. I know thou canst make that to flourish and though it may have been a long Winter's Season with me, may I not despair of the Return of Spring...

Sunday Evening, June 19. .... the Cares and Anxieties of Life occupy my mind too much. I want to know what it is to be diligent in Business but at the same time fervent in Spirit...

Monday Morn. August 1st. If I kept a faithful Diary of all my Experiences, the time since I wrote last in this book would be filled with an Account of Strange Perplexity, Wanderings, Unbelief and I know not what. Yet I'll not yet leave a Throne of Grace... The Vision is for an appointed time, whither Lord shall I go but unto thee?

So his spiritual wanderings go on until, on 1 January 1797, a new note appears. Unfortunately a vital bit has disintegrated and we pick up the sentence at an exciting point:

,.. the obtaining such a worthy Object who is I believe one of thy own dear Children; the Matter yet hangs in Suspense and it is a Season with me when Prayer is peculiarly necessary.

Then he goes into long heartsearchings as to whether he has sinned in 'seeking that in the Creature which is only to be found in thee' and asks that he may receive 'a Partner in life as a Covenant Blessing'. If there is a latent thorn on either side, he prays, that would hinder the advancement of vital Godliness 'and thy Glory in us and by us', 'let Mercy blast my too fond hopes'. And then a revealing touch: 'deliver me from being so much embarrassed'. So Philip in love is torn between fear and delight.

It is some time before we discover who she is and it remains a mystery as to how he met her, unless it was through his Bodenham relations who had Salisbury contacts. For she was a Miss Anne Andrews, of a London family, but then working in Salisbury. She had become sufficiently intimate in the family of John Saffery, Baptist Minister in Salisbury, to be called a 'daughter' by him. So Philip consulted Saffery about his courtship and on 12 January the latter wrote to Philip full of concern about propriety and suggesting that the two could meet in Saffery's parlour – which they evidently did. We trace the progress of the courtship in Philip's writing:

Sunday Evening Jany 22, 1797. .... I do now I hope earnestly and sinserely pray for the temporal and spiritual Happiness of that Object who has engrossed as much (perhaps more) of my Affection as Creature ought, bless her, guide her, bless us, guide us, dispose of us . . .

Sunday Evening, June 17, 1798. .... There is another subject I ought to have recorded, the leadings of Providence in my Acquaintance with that dear and valuable Anne Andrews. Oh thou heart searching God. thou knowest whether my Affection for her is pure and founded on a right basis. As far as I can Judge of my Own Heart and the Duty of Christians in these Matters, I hope it is, I love her because she is a Child of God, but I love her with the kind of Affection which I feel of no other Creature. Thou has been merciful to me in the Progress of the Affair and I believe . . . Affection is mutual . . . I am to go to Sarum on Tuesday to be united for Life to her, if thou permit . . . may we ever count it our highest Honour to be enabled to act for God, keep me from all irregular Affections and Desires, and may the Marriage State be made by the constant Influence of the Spirit upon us a holy one indeed. .... help us to begin with good rules not to suffer any Engagements to thrust our Religious Duties and as to an Increase of worldly goods, give us such share as thou see best . . .

So he was married, and on the following Sunday records 'I hope I more than ever view my dear Wife as an unremitted Gift of God to me . . . she has a heavenly soul and is very likely, I hope, to be the Means of quuickening my dull soul in divine Things'.

After this the diary settles down into near contentment. He records 'Months of Health, Peace and Joy of an earthly kind'. A year later the first baby is on the way – not well-timed from a farmer's viewpoint – and he writes:

Mercy is still following me. Oh that I knew my soul prospered in my earthly prosperity . . . The dear Partner of my Joys and Cares is near approaching the Hour of Child Birth. Lord preserve her and spare the little one if thy Glory can be answered by it . . . And through the ensuing busy season of the year in which Patience must be exercised, keep me from dishonouring thee.

The diary breaks off soon after this. Courtship and marriage had done much for Philip and perhaps he had no further need of introspective musings. Certainly he would have had less time, for he and Anne brought up a large family of lively children whom we shall meet later. He had become the prosperous *paterfamilias*. But before we leave his courting days we must look at a tiny relic of his wedding day, which must have belonged to one of his sisters: it is a small painted vanity case, with an inner lining covered with silver braid. Inside is a little comb, a tiny cylinder and ivory writing tablets with the inscription (almost rubbed out), on one side 'My dear Brother was married the 19th of June, 1798', and on the other, 'To a worthy lady ... Miss Ann Andrews'.

Jane Attwater's love affair was far more drawn out than her nephew's. Indeed, it seemed at first that her later notebooks must have belonged to another person. She began these personal revelations in 1769, when she was 16, and – with some gaps – they run right down to 1825. They are vivid and appealing, tempting one to quote much, but here we will concern ourselves only with her relations to Mr B., since this is how we discover why she and her diaries finally took up their abode in Bratton. She travelled around a good deal, visiting relations and friends. We have already seen her staying at Bratton with her sister, Mrs Thomas Whitaker, and it is while she is staying with another sister in Bradford in 1776 that she plunges us straight into her great problem:

My mind is now greatly perplexed and the affair goes on and I am yet undetermined. My mind is totally averse to a union of that kind with anyone. My heart shuders and recoils at the thought of entering into such a connection ... Many reasons there are for and against. I would wish to set them in a balance and to see which preponderates ... but I cannot do it. I am totally averse to what is said to be the general conduct of our sex – to give transient encouragement to him whom they never mean to accept, so that I can by no means let Mr. B-s visits be continued ... my Friends are all for it ... (they tell) me how much my honored Mother will be grieved should I give him a positive denial ...

He pays great respect to her mother and Jane is impressed by this but just a little suspicious about his motives and though she fears to 'distress my dear, my ever much loved and fond mother in refusing him, yet how can I do otherwise when I know I must not keep him in suspense'. So she weighs the issue back and forth trying to screw herself up to the point:

I must not trifle – tis a matter of too great importance . . . O for divine Guidance . . . If it may tend to promote thy Glory and . . . the means of doing Good then I hope I would wish to say Incline my heart to accept Him if none of these valuable Ends are to be answered by such a Union, deliver me from the least thought of entering into it – I dread the Interview – I must be decisive.

Then on 9 February we read:

Tis past. I have now confirmed my former denials by giving him a positive one . . . I could do no other way, for my heart dictated what I said. I cannot act so disingenious to keep anyone in suspense let it be ever so much against my future peace! . . . I fear the effects of what I last said as Mr. B-'s professions this time were more solemn than ever. I sincerely wish him every Blessing and that he may (? meet) every in-quietude of Life with calmness and becoming Fortitude.

Mr B. did not take his life or go into a decline. He remains hovering in the background of the diary, while Jane is absorbed in problems exercising her soul, such as whether to join the Baptists by the rite of Believers' Baptism. She had witnessed the ceremony at Bratton and been much impressed but wavered for some time: 'I am like the door on its hinges going from one privilege to another'. When her beloved mother died in 1784 the theme of her diaries for a long time was inordinate grief: 'My dear parent is gone from me and with her my usefulness and my pleasure is fled . . . what do I live for, to be a silent, inactive Spectator – useless, unheeded and unnecessary to my Friends . . .' Perhaps it was this vacuum in her life which enabled Mr B. to slip back into view again. Thirteen years had passed since the scene in Bradford, but he was still waiting. On 24 May 1789, Jane wrote in her 'friendly diary':

My mind is much perplexed about temporal affairs, having long had the earnest Solicitations of I believe a good young man which I can by no means discard. I have tried every method in

70

vain. He seems determined ... professing an assurance that it is the will of providence we should be united ...

She goes on treating him 'with rudeness and contempt' for some time, but providence finally intervenes in the person of a much-loved preacher and the tone begins to change:

11 October, 1789 ... Mr. J. B. accompanied us home ... my mind is much oppressed and agitated. I know not how to act or what to do ... my Happiness and if I may credit Mr. B's word his seem to be much at stake. I know not how to go forward or backward ... Mr. Burgess a good old Gentleman, with tears of affection in his eyes becomes his advocate ...

She owns that she is moved by the entreaties of 'this aged man' and decides that 'things must take their course'. This 'course' was a very pious one: Mr B. came home after church and read aloud a sermon, after which they 'improved the time in prayer, etc.' Jane still declared that she would give no encouragement to his addresses unless she believed him to be a 'partaker of the grace of God'. On 27 June she was worried because Mr J.G.B. left her feeling 'very poorly'. In August she wavered, and in some penetrating reflections explored the psychological cost to an independent and withdrawn personality of being thrust into the forefront of active affairs and allowing one person to 'possess my whole heart'. She admits that she does not like Mr J.G.B. to come on a Sabbath Day because 'it naturely tends to take up too much of my attention'.

At last, in October 1790 she accepts him. In her diary she confesses that if a disappointment were to ensue now, when she has built up so much affection for the man whom she believes God to have appointed for her, she would need great strength from above to bear it. She writes:

My mind is now at peace and all tranquil within. I seriously believe myself to be in the path of duty, my Inclination happily united to make me happy ... The more I know of him the more similarity I find in thought as well as in word ... My soul does magnify the Lord.

And so: 'Nov. 18, 1790. This day I went to Church with Mr. Blatch ...' The description of her wedding feelings is too long to quote. Now at last we know who Mr B. was: Joseph Goodenough Blatch, living then at Amesbury but belonging to the Blatch family of Bratton who were so closely connected with the Whitakers. It was, after all, an intimate circle of friends in which these Baptist families moved.

There is an outburst of joy in the diary when Anna Jane Theodosia was born in 1793. The next book, dated 1795, begins: 'This Book is design'd for a mutual depository for particular providences that occur & thoughts on them for J.G.B. & J.B.' So the marriage of true minds had taken place and Jane's fears of being 'possessed' by another had proved groundless. The conjugal diaries, however, are less individual, except for the time of deep sorrow when their beloved child died at the age of 16. Before 1800 the Blatches came back to Bratton to live, for at that date Joseph Blatch became a deacon of the Baptist Church, together with Philip Whitaker. So Philip and his Aunt Attwater lived their later years in close contact. The days of the romantic, poetical frame of mind, of spiritual outpourings in secret diaries, were over. The two Attwater sisters, Caroline and Jane, were now ladies of consequence in Bratton society, while by 1800 Philip and his wife were busy with an increasing family. Yet, as we shall see, the literary flavour persists in the Whitaker clan. It is striking that two marriages – one introducing the Attwater connection and the other, through Anne Andrews, bringing her poetess sister, Maria Grace, into the Whitaker circle – should have made such an imprint on the outlook of a very ordinary and localized farming family.

4 Family Possessions

Eighteenth-century people bought to keep. The Whitakers were prospering in a modest way at this time and so whatever furniture there was of an earlier age disappeared. This was the Age of Mahogany and the houses filled up with grand solid pieces. Cabinet-makers worked from pattern-books and rarely signed their pieces, so we cannot tell where the Whitakers bought their furniture nor date it exactly. There is an ample wing armchair with lovely downward-sweeping lines and cabriole legs decorated with the shell pattern of the early eighteenth century: imagination fills it with the *paterfamilias*, perhaps Jeffery Whitaker the Elder. In 1754 Thomas Chippendale published the first edition of his *Gentlemen and Cabinet-makers' Director*. This set the fashion for provincial cabinet-makers, so when the Whitakers refurnished their dining-room it was with 'Country Chippendale', a set of chairs complete with the carver at the head of the table. This was plainer than the grand stuff, but pleasing in its sober design and good workmanship. Later fashions were also reflected: when Hepplewhite issued his *Cabinet-Maker's and Upholsterer's Guide* in 1788, and Sheraton his *Cabinet-Maker and Upholsterer's Drawing Book* between 1791 and 1794, the Whitakers bought Hepplewhite and Sheraton styles. The solid stools on which the children sat were just local.

The growth of letter-writing encouraged its own furniture in the form of writing bureaus and tables, while the accumulation of treasures stimulated a desire for display. So they bought two fine Sheraton secretaires equipped with drawers and writing-desk below, and glass-fronted shelves above. Occasional tables proliferated – pembrokes, pedestals, consols, pie-crusts – according to the designs of the great furniture kings. This was also the day of grandfather clocks. No doubt originally belonging to different establishments, two finally came to rest at the Yew Trees. One is a 1770 clock by Edward Marsh of Sarum, with a sober case but beautiful face, decorated with filigree brass-work, and a musical chime. The other is a grander affair of about 1750, made by Caleb Evans of Bristol. It is decorated with a moon and stars and a hunting-scene and it records days of the month and phases of the moon as well as the time. These clocks saw many generations of Whitakers through their lives. Had the experience of time, one wonders, a different quality when it was regulated by the little preliminary whirr, and then the slow, musical chime of the grandfather, rather than by the sharp, worrying little pips of the radio?

Beds are, perhaps, more expendable than most furniture, so within living memory only two or three traditional four-posters remained to be enjoyed by the last grandchildren, though some lovely fluted posts lingered forlornly to the end. In his diary however, Jeffery Whitaker mentions a carved tester to a bed which was sold for 32s. in 1739. But feather beds survive many accidents and are a problem to destroy. Misguided members of the present generation have battled with their volatile contents in an effort to re-cycle them. For storing clothes and linen, chests of the medieval type and dower chests were still used, but the higher chests of drawers now becoming popular quickly invaded Whitaker bedrooms. Essential adjuncts to the principal bedrooms at least were a mahogany night-stool and a copper warming-pan. There was a social hierarchy in the former and the Whitakers' respectable mahogany articles probably came somewhere in the middle of it.

It is in the small things which a family gathers around itself that a way of life is most revealingly discovered. Old candlesticks of all grades from silver, Sheffield plate and brass down to base metal, remind us vividly of the lighting problem. With them go candle-snuffers, an iron candle-box and candle-trimmers, that is, scissors fitted with a little box to catch the bits. Old knives are hard to come by. They were, no doubt, demoted in favour of stainless steel and have disappeared in kitchen or garden. But spoons and forks take us back to the eighteenth-century dining table, especially silver spoons, slender in design and good in the mouth. A long-handled silver ladle, with shell-patterned bowl, suggests a large soup tureen or meat dish with gravy well. Perhaps it is the very ladle that 100 years later, Joshua gave his son, John, on a birthday occasion. One or two of the monumental dishes on which the head of the house carved sirloins of beef still survive, as well as tureens and plates in willow-pattern china and stoneware, now cracked and brown with much baking. Pewter plates and a primitive pewter hot-plate (with an inter-space into which you poured hot water) are probably survivals from an earlier age. A pewter flagon and mugs remind us that homemade cider and ale were everyday drinks, calling for much pressing and brewing, not to mention 'wringing' of perkin. But a silver brandy-warmer and an elegant punch ladle conjure up a flicker of conviviality in this sober household. The George II silver tankard is probably the one mentioned by Jeffery Whitaker in his will. Wine would be bought locally – once Jeffery Whitaker records walking to Tinhead to buy wine – but customers provided their own bottles which bore their stamp on the side, imprinted on a disc of thick glass. These often survived the demise of the bottle and so we still have one of them bearing the inscription:

K

In°   Mary

Whitaker

1714

Thus it belonged to John and Mary (née Aldridge), who were cousins of the Jeffery Whitakers, and grandparents of the Thomas in the last chapter. But what does the *K* stand for? Tea-drinking was coming in. The Whitakers left two of those mahogany caddies, with zinc linings and keys, in which households then stored the precious stuff. Yet, on 2

July 1739, Jeffery recorded: 'Tea lost', and on 4 July: 'Mr Ballard searched for Tea. found some on Francis Merritt's wife'. The Whitaker ladies drank tea from white and gold tea-bowls with no handles – lovely fluted china which was so far out of fashion in Victorian days that some bowls are stained brown by hot red-currant jelly. A silver teapot was, no doubt, the centre piece of the tea-drinking equipage, but none survives from the eighteenth century.

The china which the Whitakers collected for display shows us what the modestly affluent could buy, as distinct from the grand collectors. It was quite varied: Worcester and Wedgwood pieces, Delft bowls, ironstone plates, china figures and a tea-set with the monogram of *M* on it, probably spare pieces from a set made to order. It is interesting that this very provincial family, away in a corner of Wiltshire, caught the craze for *chinoiserie*. So far as I can discover, they had no relations who went to the Orient, but much of their treasured china consisted of eighteenth-century Chinese porcelain – bowls, plates and cups in a variety of designs which give a spot of exotic colour to their china shelves that one might not have expected.

Perhaps until the present era the kitchen has been the most traditional part of the house. We do not always comprehend what a revolution has taken place here in our lifetime, nor its social significance. In the eighteenth-century kitchen at the Yew Trees, with its stone-flagged floor, huge dresser and ample fireplace, domestic work was carried on by the methods and with the utensils which had been used for centuries and would be, in some cases, for another 100 years at least. Traditional models often did their work very well: the well-bucket, for instance, wider at the waist than top or bottom, was designed to sink and fill. Equally antique in design were the roasting-jack, the iron tripod for boiling over the fire and the brass trivet, while earthenware crocks and pitchers also take us back to the Middle Ages. A little brown crock with a handle is well designed to keep gruel or porridge hot by the fire. A heavy brass ladle, with a beautifully shaped, perforated bowl and long iron handle, conjures up large stew-pots with juicy lumps to be fished out. Copper stew-pans, kettles and coal-scuttles gleamed in days when servants and mistresses worked together and labour was the most expendable commodity. Their preparation of food started much further back than our prepackaged meals. Spices were ground by hand in a pestle and mortar: perhaps the oldest one at the Yew Trees was the heavy little alabaster one, with the traditional 'ears' by which to grip it, which was unearthed in the garden. A more sophisticated brass one was used right down to the end of the nineteenth century. The wooden spice-box, elaborately lettered for pepper, mace, cloves and cinnamon, has compartments which screw on top of each other. In days before cheap glassware, the lemon-squeezer consisted of two heavy wooden bats hinged together. Sugar came in long bars which had to be cut up with sugar-cutters, rather like iron tongs (8). Choppers and chopping boards remind us that everything was cut up by hand.

We are lucky that Jeffery Whitaker was both methodical and interested in food, so that we really get some idea of the dinners cooked with these utensils from his daily note of the menu. They ate a good deal of meat and rang the changes on all the well-known joints. In addition, we meet: 'the thick end of Neats Rand', 'pidgeon pie', 'mutton pye', 'pigs feet and hocks', 'Ears, blade bones etc.'. Boiled mutton or beef with broth was a stand-by, as also Bacon and Cale. They sometimes had 'pudding' or apple dumplings with their meat, and once pancakes. Once he records 'Rump of Beef and Cale, garden stuff being very Scarce' and again 'Pigs Chaps, hocks etc., pudding'. The Whitakers often had visitors for dinner and frequently served two or three joints at once.

'Our people washing' is also a recurring comment in Jeffery's diary, but, from its infrequency, this appears to have been a big affair, probably monthly, done in the separate wash-house where there was a large 'copper' for heating the water and boiling linen.

In 1780 an Attwater lady passed over her cookery book to 'Mrs Whitaker Senior'. It is called *The Universal Cook: or Young Woman's Best Guide in the Whole Art of Cookery*, by Mrs Ann Partridge, and has a wonderful frontispiece in which a much be-capped and curled lady presents it to the demure serving maid, with the caption: 'The cheapest present for a Servant Maid'. It advocates good, plain cooking. A recipe which catches the eye is for making a White Portable Soup (yes – *portable*, not potable.) You do innumerable things to a leg of veal and two dozen chicken feet until you have jelly in china cups as thick as glue. You turn these out on to a piece of new flannel 'to draw out all the moisture' and in a little while 'they will be so hard that you may carry them in your pocket without the least inconvenience'. Now why should you want to? Was it for taking nourishment to poor sick people?

Mary Whitaker (Philip's sister) used Mrs Glasse's *Art of Cookery made Plain and Easy*, the pre-Mrs Beaton. How universal was her art the table of contents shows:

I. How to Roast and Boil to Perfection every Thing necessary to be sent up to table.
II. Of made Dishes.
III. How expensive a French cook's sauce is.
IV. To make a number of pretty little dishes for a Supper or Side-dish and little Corner dishes for a great Table.
V. To dress Fish.
VI. Of Soups and Broths.
VII. Of Puddings.
VIII. Of Pies.
IX. For a Lent dinner; a Number of good Dishes which may be made use of at any other time.
X. Directions to prepare proper food for the Sick.
XI. For Captains of Ships; how to make all useful Dishes for a Voyage; and setting out a Table on board.
XII. Of Hogs Puddings, Sausages etc.
XIII. To pot and make Hams etc.
XIV. Of Pickling.
XV. Of making Cakes etc.
XVI. Of Cheesecakes, Creams, Jellies, Whipt Syllabubs etc.
XVII. Of made Wines, French Bread, Muffins etc.
XVIII. Jarring Cherries and Preserves etc.
XIX. To make Anchovies, Vermicelli, Catchup, Vinegar, and to keep Artichokes, French Beans etc.
XX. Of Distilling.
XXI. How to market; the season of the Year for Butcher's Meat, Poultry, Fish, Herbs, Roots and Fruit.

XXII A certain Cure for the Bite of a Mad Dog, by Dr Mead.
XXIII. A Receipt to keep clear from bugs.

Not content with this, a section on Perfumery is added: the Whitaker ladies surely could not go wrong.

If the Bills of Fare set out for each month in the year exhibit cooking on the grand scale, Mrs Glasse was not above giving instruction in the cooking of those Pigs' Feet and Ears and other odd bits of animals and birds which were so useful on a farm. Here is her recipe for cooking Cocks-Combs:

Let them be well cleaned, then put them into a pot, with some melted bacon, and boil them a little; about half an hour after add a little baysalt, some pepper, a little vinegar, a lemon sliced, and an onion stuck with cloves. When the bacon begins to stick to the pot, take them up, put them into the pan you would keep them in, lay a clean cloth over them, and pour melted butter clarified over them, to keep them close from the air. These make a pretty plate at a supper.

It is fatal to linger, but a few titbits cannot be resisted:

To dress Larks Pear Fashion. You must truss the larks close, and cut off the legs, season them with salt, pepper, cloves and mace: make a force-meat thus: take a veal sweet-bread, as much beef-suet, a few morels and mushrooms, chop all fine together, some crumbs of bread, and a few sweet-herbs, a little lemon-peel cut small, mix all together with a yoke of an egg, wrap up the larks in force-meat, and shape them like a pear, stick one leg on top like the stalk of a pear, rub them over with the yolk of an egg and crumbs of bread, bake them in a gentle oven, serve them without sauce; or they make a good garnish to a very fine dinner.

(All that work for a garnish!)

A Salmagundy. Take two pickled herrings and bone them, a handful of parsley, four eggs boiled hard, the white of one roasted chicken ... chop all fine separately, that is, the yokes of the eggs by themselves and the white the same; scrape some lean boiled ham very fine, hung beef or Dutch beef scraped. Turn a small China bason or deep saucer into your dish; make some butter into the shape of a pineapple, or any other shape you please, and set it on top of the bason; lay round your bason a ring of shred parsley, then whites of eggs, then ham, then chicken, then beef, then yolks of eggs, then herrings, till you have covered the bason and used all your ingredients. Garnish the dish with whole capers, and pickles of any sort you choose, chop fine; or you may leave out the butter . . . and put a flower at the top or a sprig of myrtle.

Her 'standing crust for a great pie' is quite a curiosity. You boiled 6 lb of butter in a gallon of water and skimmed it off into a peck of flour. You then worked it well up into a paste and pulled it to pieces till it was cold. You could then make it up into whatever form you wished, such as the walls of a goose pie.

Without the aid of modern science everything was so laborious. Ice-cream was made in tubs of salt and ice; pickling lemons took a month's attention. Mary Whitaker's own handwritten Recipe Book of 1792 is a vivid reminder of how they laboured. It is arranged alphabetically, starting under *A* with 'to preserve Apricots' and 'to make antimony'. Under *B* a recipe for making Shoe-blacking shows us how far back they started in their chores:

Take a quart of strong beer, $\frac{1}{4}$ lb of Ivory black, $\frac{1}{4}$ brown sugar and a bit of glew, boil it till it is all dissolved stirring nearly all the time, then put in bottles for use.

Good food for leather, no doubt. The recipe 'to make Catchup that will last 20 years' has a note: 'this mama have made and have proved very good'. We see Caroline and her daughter at work in the kitchen and then Mary writing out the recipe in her own style:

Take a gallon of stale strong beer, 1 lb of anchovies . . . 1 lb of shalots peel'd $\frac{1}{2}$ oz of mace $\frac{1}{2}$ oz of cloves $\frac{1}{4}$ oz of whole pepper 3 or 4 large races of ginger 2 quarts of the large mushrooms rub'd to pieces cover all this close and let it simmer till it is half wasted then strain it through a flannel bag let it stand till it is quite cold then bottle it a little of with melted butter makes a fine fish sauce.

Most of the items are very workaday, but 'Oister Sauce' to serve with fresh cod or boiled turkey looks a little exotic beside 'Potato Pudding' or 'Plumb Pudding'. The recipe for Eve's Pudding is in verse:

If you want a good pudding pray mind what is taught
Of eggs take twopennyworth when twelve for a groat

Then take of the fruit of which eve was first cousen'd
Well-pared and well-chop'd at least half a dozen
Six oz of bread let Moll eat the crust
The crumb you must crumble as small as the dust
Six oz of currants from the stones you must part
Lest you break out your teeth and spoil all the sport
Four oz of sugar won't make it too sweet
Some nutmeg and Lemmon will make it compleat
Four hours you must boil it without any flutter
And then if you please you may add melted butter

And now Mary gets out her recipe book again, for the maids must keep all the pots and pans gleaming and she has a whole page on scouring – iron, brass, copper, pewter, Queen's metal and silver. There is no Vim or Ajax to fall back on. To do the pewter they start with fine hay and a peck of rudder'd ashes which they boil for some time. Now listen!

Dip in the Pewter one thing at a time leting it stay but a little time then have ready a coars Cloth with hay under it and well rub it with yellow sand and some of the lye from the boiler then have ready a tub of clean water and a woolen Cloth and when it is well wash'd in that rub it with white sand and a liquid made of Perl ashes and strong beer (to ½ lb of Perl ashes put 2 quarts of beer and boil it for some time) then well wash it in another tub of clean water and put in the shade or some distance from the fire.

How often did they do this, one wonders, and did the process give the kind of patina to pewter which we cannot get today? And why does beer turn up so often and so unexpectedly as an ingredient? Another question we cannot answer is how much of the kitchen work was done by the maids and whether the mistress confined herself to the more elegant tasks. It seems likely.

Mary also had a companion book of Medicinal Recipes which starts with a drastic remedy for the Ague which 'cured Mr Tylee of Bath of an ague which lasted him 3 years'. Home doctoring started with herb gathering: tansy was good for gout, hempseed for jaundice and archangel for shingles. The poor child with 'Hooping Cough' got rubbed with 'garlick'. Perhaps Mary picked Colts Foot Roots and Leaves to boil and sweeten with sugar or treacle and administer to someone 'in a Decline'. Teeth should be rubbed with charcoal and the bite of an adder or viper with sweet oil and salt. And here is a real herb recipe 'for the Evil':

Take Elicompane roots handful water-bittony handful water-parsnip 4 roots picked dock handful wild broom boil it in a galon of spring water ½ hour let it stand 24 hours then strain it of(f) drink of it once a day.

The range of remedies in this little book shows that the women were still the traditional doctors, although Jeffery Whitaker – fussy as he was about his health – often sent for doctor's or chemist's medicines.

The industry of women in this period seems phenomenal. For when they had cooked, scoured, washed and concocted potions, they sat down to yards of the finest sewing. Drawers stuffed with their work have now yielded up their treasures. It is significant that, while top clothes have mostly disappeared, underwear has survived. The materials are fine and durable – linen, cotton, muslin – and the stitchery is such that, when the garments did wear out, the embroidered pieces were often saved to be used again. Voluminous night-gowns and even larger night-shirts for men have survived well, buttoning down the front with linen buttons that would stand up to a wringing in the huge mangle. Also voluminous are women's underskirts of muslin or fine cotton, with rows of minute tucks or flounces, or heavily quilted. Apart from beaded slippers and smoking-caps, little else remains of men's apparel, but the ladies evidently treasured their own handiwork.

They concentrated their decorative efforts on the head, neck, sleeves and hem-line. Caps of all sorts survive: muslin mob-caps which frilled the face and tied under the chin, lace caps, cotton caps like close-fitting bonnets decorated with lace or embroidery, and little close skull caps, some with elaborately stitched patterns that simulate quilting. Neck-wear, with its varieties of fichu, kerchief, collar or band, offered much scope. You could embroider on muslin or net, or make your neck-wear of finely tucked linen, or choose cotton with a lace edging. Some perfectly plain kerchiefs of linen and muslin are exquisitely stitched. For the frills on sleeves 'white work' embroidery was in vogue, with delicate pierced flower patterns and minute button-holing. Finely pleated elbow sleeves were made separately with draw strings to keep them up. Cuffs, pleated, embroidered, or edged with lace, were also made separately: Jane Attwater once sent Caroline a finely-stitched pair in a letter. Flounces, with rolled or scalloped edges, decorated the yards of the hem-line. Everywhere we see tiny stitches and ponder on the hours of gathering, tucking and embroidering that they represent. Because these were country ladies, they also made sunbonnets in lilac or white cotton, stiffly quilted in front to shade the face, and gathered into a frill behind to protect the neck. Forlorn survival from somebody's wardrobe is an incredibly small and narrow pair of women's bootees (still in their holland case) and four pairs of white cotton stockings, worked in cross-stitch with a number and the monogram *S.W.* (? Sophia Williams). And of course we come on fans and shawls of various kinds, especially paisley shawls in silk or wool.

How we wish we could see these ladies at work with their equipment. Who owned this mahogany work-table, with its deep cloth bag which slides out from underneath, and who wore two beautiful pairs of sewing-pockets? These, designed in a most convenient shape, hung from your waist to hold your needles and thread, etc. One is gaily embroidered in coloured wools (9), while the other is decorated in fine white work like the little caps. The tools raise all sorts of questions as we turn them over. This little wooden object, with a circle of pins round the top, must have been used for some kind of weaving, such as children do on pins today. Netting-tools of wood and bone can be identified, some so large that they would make fish nets – perhaps garden nets in Bratton? The lace pillow and bobbins explain themselves but it needs the expert[1] to identify the stilettos and tambour hooks used for

[1] I am grateful for help from the staff of the Victoria and Albert Museum in identifying these things.

white work, the latter to pull up the tiny stitches into a puckered effect which looked like quilting. And this chased-steel tool turns out to have several uses: it is a bodkin with various sizes of eye, and a stiletto, but at the other end – surprise of surprises – the ear can be cleaned out with the tiny scoop. Then there are emery cushions for keeping needles rustless and many pin-cushions, some for show and some for work. One takes pride of place: it is of grey satin, embroidered all over with a delicate shell pattern on which a curving flower-pattern border has been super-imposed and a wreath-encircled monogram at the centre. Another one (perhaps later) is decorated with sprays of leaves and a motto, 'The God of Love bless thee and make thee a blessing', all pricked out in pins. Everything that might be useful has been saved in little boxes and bags: cotton-reels, buttons, ribbon, lace, materials, fringes and feathers.

Boxes galore. This is one of the impressions left from sorting family possessions. Things were treasured (the word 'expendable' had not yet gained its modern connotation) and things to keep must have worthy receptacles. Hence the many polished and inlaid mahogany boxes. One is a Bible box; one or two open out into writing-desks; others are jewel or sewing boxes and some are simply boxes for treasures. Small tortoiseshell ones were probably for snuff and a silver-mounted mother-of-pearl one for some lady's purpose. Two cardboard boxes, decorated on the outside with flower designs and inside the lid with engravings, are interesting because they come from France, although the trade-marks are English. One, with a view 'À Perpignan', bears the mark of W. Clark & Co., and the other of A. Oswald & Co., with a picture entitled 'Départ pour la Chasse'. Both came from Bordeaux – what did they hold originally? Now, one, as we have already seen, contains sets of children's card-games, while the other harbours one of those chance collections of trifles that bring the past back with a tinge of melancholy. There is a set of silhouettes in black, with cut-outs made from them; a tiny case for the points of scissors; some cards with engravings of great men from Shakespeare to Walter Scott; a green net purse with a little cut-out paper pattern attached to it on which the Lord's Prayer has been inscribed in minute writing; a charming little 'housewife', complete with tiny reels, pin-cushion, needlebook, and a little packet of superfine needles in fine grit to keep them bright.

Writing had its own paraphernalia and when, like Jeffery Whitaker, you started by making the ink – not to mention the pen – it was a serious business. Inkstands and pots of various kinds have accumulated. A battered pewter one may have belonged to the school, while a more elegant Sheffield plate inkstand has the candle sconce for sealing wax. There are a number of seals of departed Whitakers to go with it. Other kinds of literary tool have turned up: ivory writing-tablets, paper knives of ivory and wood, tiny ivory containers for what seem to be small pencil-leads, ivory and pearl-handled pen-knives to cut quill pens, and spectacles for dim eyes or dim lights. These are steel-framed and usually small, some with the half-glasses which allow you to peer over the top; some seem to require a very narrow face. Letters in those days were mostly written on large sheets of thick paper, folded and sealed without envelopes. The art of folding was intricate, and woe betide the modern investigator who does not master it properly. They were fond of putting down their thoughts in little homemade notebooks and they scribbled jottings everywhere. One curious relic from an earlier age is a little bone tag attached to a ring which looks small for the keys of that date. On one side is carved: 'Your Servant Sir i am Your Deter' and on the other 'Winter is Good but Summer is Beter. 1686'. And another odd find was a minute notebook containing 'A Short-Hand Alphabet, 1797'.

In some ways it is the small scraps of paper that speak most vividly of family life. One has instructions on how to 'plat' 4 or 5 strands and here is a laundry list:

3 shirts	1.0.	2 pillow tyes	1.
2 shifts	4	1 apron	1.
3 sheets	8	1 cap	$\frac{1}{2}$.
1 bolster case	1	1 hand towel	$\frac{1}{2}$.

There is a doctor's bill which includes 'bleeding 1.0.' and a 'sedative 2.0.'. Another piece is headed enigmatically: 'account of people who had Yeast March 2nd, 1795', with a list of about 40 familiar Bratton names and, in addition, 'the tall woman'. One small scrap simply reads:

4 marks of an hypocrite from wc^h I w^d say 'Lord deliver me'$_z$ 1st He seemeth to be w^t he is not 2^{ly} He professeth to have w^t he hath not 3^{ly} He pretendeth to do w^t he doth not 4^{ly} All that he doeth he doeth it to be seen of Men'.

Strange things turn up: a little envelope contains simply an 'assignat' of the French Revolution. Now how in the world did *that* reach Bratton? Another piece of paper reads: 'My papa was born May ye 27 1691. My mama was born the 15 of July 1710'. This list continues with Attwater relations and goes on to 'Philip Whitaker was born Saturday at Eleven o'clock in the forenoon March 1 1766 – Anna Whitaker born Thursday Morn between 6 and 7 1 Dec. 1768 – Mary Whitaker Friday between 7 & 8 o'clock March 19 1773 – Thomas Whitaker born ye 11 Nov. at 5 o'clock in the afternoon 1776 – Ann Jane Whitaker born Aug. 25 1784'. A piece of paper which belonged to Jane Blatch has a curious medley of writing: it starts with a list of relations who are all dead, ending with:

Maria Attwater – niece ⎫ we three spared
Mr Joseph Goodenough Blatch ⎬ hitherto ye Lord
Jane Blatch ⎭ hath helped us.

Below is a prayer:

... prepare us O Heavenly Father to meet ye spirits of ye just made perfect in a world of bliss and glory – In the same way in which they Entered may we now be travelling and thro' ye Blessed Redeemer find a joyful admission to perfect Felicity when Time shall be no longer with us.

A perfect prayer for Jane's end, but overleaf we descend to the banal in a note: 'Tea 2.6 Snuff 1.4. Calico 3.9.'. and on the back of the folded piece, an account for materials (tape $3\frac{1}{2}$, $1\frac{3}{4}$ yds of linen at 10 p.y., neckerchief 1.0., 6 yds dimity costing 3.3. and so on).

What is the story, one wonders, behind the following little letter?

Dear Miss Whitaker,
   I beg my affectionate concern and desire to return my best thanks for what I received by Mrs. Blatch. I hope it will not distress you when I say if it had been the Lord's will I would rather had but one Gown to put on than to have been deprived of such a dear and valuable Friend, whose loss I feel severely. I had no other Friend on Earth to make know my Troubles to . . .

Another letter is headed 'The Humble petition of Martha Elkins' and tells a heart-wringing story of stark need, concluding: 'My request is now to you, Hon^d Sir that you will permit me to share in the bounty wch you Liberaly bestow on my fellow sufferers peculilarly at this part of the year . . .' On the back someone has scribbled a draft with many corrections which begins:

Treating a little of the solemn scene that lately I was spectator of, I mean the funeral solemnities of your dear departed Aunt, shall for a few moments reflect on what we have lost in her, a faithful Monitress . . . and experienced guide and director . . .

It is like listening to fragments of conversation from the past to read through these scraps of paper.
   A later letter of gratitude to Caroline Whitaker (addressed 'With Speed To the Aged Mrs Whitaker Mr Philip's Mother') also demands to be quoted:

William Norress have Written to let you Know my Dear Christen brethren and Sisters in Christ Jesus that I have received the Lord's blessing From your hands by the Carer . . . which Consisted of two Pound Noates and A Shift And A Shroal And A Leeg of mutton for this blessing I Adore His holy Majesty who is the Holy Creator of Every Good both for Time and Eternity . . . in his book of life I hope your Names are Everyone written . . . Amen let all know I received this blessing.

Among the letters is a long, quaint allegory entitled 'A Letter to Miss W. advising her to take Care of her House'. The House is the body and the allegory elaborates on the globular turret on top with two crystal windows:

It will therefore be necessary to lay a strict Injunction on your two Porters . . . in liveries of the deepest Scarlet just without the Ivory Palisades. I have seen some people paint the two Pannels just below the Windows but I would advise you to the contrary for your natural Colors far exceed all the Decorations of Art . . .

And it continues in this strain for some time. Finally an intimate letter from Jane Blatch to her sister, Caroline, must be quoted:

My Beloved sister,

This is the first day for many weeks that I have not been fav^d with ye sight of my valued Friend but knowing you had a superior attendant in your dear Daughter, I gave way to the calls of Self and took some medicine which rendered it not too convenient to go out this stormy weather hope you will excuse it & be assured it is not for want of sincere affection to my 2 beloved relatives but from ye real cause of *Frequent avocations.* I think I heard you express a wish for a tooth-pick – forgive this clumsy attempt to produce one till you can procure a better. I hope you and my dear Niece have comfortably Enjoy'd Each others society this stormy day. O my dear sister what tranquility of mind does it afford me that you are thus Favoured . . .

The clumsy toothpick has disappeared, but the delicacy of her allusion to her state of health remains.

What books did they read? Bibles survive in abundance, and copies of Isaac Watts' hymns. A 1778 edition of *The Pilgrim's Progress* is what one would expect to find, as also Foxe's *Acts and Monuments* which Jeffery was reading in 1739. But what was in those boxes of books he had fetched from Devizes? Perhaps one was *The Life of William III,* published in 1703. Philip Whitaker owned Milton's *Paradise Lost* (ed. 1789) and *A Complete History of England by Question and Answer* which ran from Julius Caesar to 1788 and was 'adorned with cuts expressive of the principal events'. *Letters containing A Sketch of the Politics of France* for the years 1793 and 1794 suggest that the French Revolution did not pass unheeded. *Sentiments on Education Collected from the Best Writers* by John Ash in 1777 was perhaps a guide to Thomas and Caroline in bringing up their children, though its headings display a curious hotch-potch:

On Female Accomplishments, On Modesty, On the Government of the Passions, On epistolary Correspondence, On Subordination in Society, On Behaviour in social and civil life, On Love and Marriage, On the Management of a Family, On Religion.

One of Caroline's books was *Letters Moral and Entertaining in Prose and Verse by the Author of Friendship in Depth*, published in 1733 and given to her in 1764. Its letters from 'Aleander', 'Silviana' and so on, interspersed with poems such as 'A careless translation of Tasso's Enchanted Forest,' give us another example of the neo-classical style so popular in her circle. In 1788 she gave it to her daughter Mary. On the business level, besides a book on calculating interest to a farthing, we find *The Court and City Register or Gentleman's Complete Annual Calendar for the year 1792*. This belonged to 'M.Whitaker', but what did Mary want with this? More suitably, she also owned *The Remarkable and Surprising Adventures of David Simple* and *The Christian Character Exemplified from the Papers of Mrs. Margaret Magdalen A – S* (1791).

It is the odd and curious which is sometimes most intriguing and so our final exhibit of family possessions shall be a bit of flotsam found wrapped round a bundle of letters. It is a local paper called *Salmon's Mercury, or Entertaining Repository*, published in Bath on Friday, 23 February 1781 (vol. iii, no. 119). It is a most curious production, beginning in Arabian Nights vein with a serial story about Hassan and the Caliph, followed by 'Letters of a Turkish Spy to the Venerable Mufti, Prince of the Religion of the Turks', then mixing in a touch of eighteenth-century pastoral in a poem, 'Damon and Phyllis', and concluding with 'A Man to my Mind (Wrote by a Lady)' and 'An Elegy'. If this represented fashionable Bath taste, it does not sound like the Whitakers and one wonders who read it. But one of them (surely Mary) has left her mark on it in a dashing little pen sketch of 'Mrs. Thumper', with a large crinoline, pin-point waist and huge feathered hat. The ghost of Mary who died at 28, seems to flit through these family relics both as child and woman, while a fragment of family history, written by an Attwater relation, tells us that when she died she was 'ripe for glory – the world was not worthy of so great a blessing'.

5 Farmers and Farm-workers in the Nineteenth Century

In 1800 Philip Whitaker and his younger brother Thomas between them held a great deal of land in and around Bratton. Whitakers were probably the leading family in the village at that time. Aldridges and Ballards had almost disappeared from Bratton; Drewitts no longer appear as landowners; Joseph Goodenough Blatch was a person of consequence, but later the Blatches also disappear. Besides the branch represented by Philip and Thomas, there was at least one other landowning branch of the family, probably descended from William the Elder whose will was proved in 1665. This branch was characterized by the recurring name of William. At the end of the eighteenth century the William of that generation was a younger son who had to fight for his inheritance at Crosswelldown Farm, while his elder brother, John, held the Court House, Bucks and Whites from the Marquis of Bath. William's melancholy diary has been edited by Mrs Jean Morrison.

Philip Whitaker lived at Bratton Farm, the Manor Farm of today, while Thomas, after his marriage with Sophia Williams, settled at the Yew Trees. There were no children of this marriage and we know little about Thomas's activities, apart from a beautifully lettered 'Statement of Lands and Premises in the parish of Westbury belonging to Mr Thomas Whitaker with the Amount of Rent Charge in lieu of tithes ... 1841'. This shows a holding of considerable size. He died in 1857. In the other family, however, three successive generations – Philip, Joshua, John Saffery – have left us, by great good fortune, an almost continuous set of farm records from *c*. 1810 to 1915, when John died. This is fortunate but not fortuitous: all the Whitaker characteristics of a liking for records, a meticulous attention to detail and facility in clear penmanship were brought to bear on their farming affairs. The most important records are in vellum-bound ledgers, mostly long and narrow, the heavy paper adorned with elegant copper-plate headings and flourishes. But before we turn to the main records, we have a chance to see how a boy of eleven was taught to keep accounts.

Joshua Whitaker was born in 1801 and in 1812 he started his own cash account, duly heading the first double page 1812 Cash D^r and Per Contra, C^r. His income consisted of 'gift from my aunt £10' and 'interest' on various sums. His expenditure was mainly on digging, weeding and stocking a plot of ground he calls the Nursery. He bought three turkeys but also spent £1.5.6. on books – 'Franklin's Works'. This was an augury of future interests. At the end of the first page he could only balance the account by 'money borrowed from my father'. On the next page we discover that he had a yearly allowance of £1.6.0. and that he bought himself a chess-board and men for 17s. Alas – the record soon descends to spasmodic entries and peters out finally in 1821. There is, however, an intriguing fragment of a 'Sparrow Account', from which we learn that a dozen sparrows cost *c*. 6d, and a 'Fowl Account' for 1814–15. After these boyish efforts, the young man of 22 started a proper cash account to which we shall return later.

Turning to Philip's earliest extant record, we find that this is, significantly, a Corn Book running from 1810 to 1827. At this time, arable farming dominates the scene. The first double page carries the headings: 'Barley of the harvest 1810 Winnowed' and 'Account of Barley Sold and used on the Farm for Seed or otherwise of the Harvest 1810'. The winnowed barley is recorded in quarters and bushels under the heads 'Best' and 'Tailing'. After Barley comes the all-important Wheat, similarly recorded. Like the barley it is carefully located in ricks on the various farms, a detail which enables us to visualize the end-of-harvest scene in places we can still identify: Home Barn, Grants Farm, Thorncombe Barn and so on. 'The long Rick near the Staddle Barn' reminds us of the use of staddle-stones and caps (stone 'mushrooms') for building barns and ricks above the damp and the marauding activities of rats and mice. On the sales side, besides recording the individual customers, uses on the home farm are set down: 'Tailing used for Horses and pigs', 'Family Tails', 'House use tailing'. (How *did* the household use tailings?) 'Grists' were sold more cheaply. Everything is accounted for, even the 'tuckings of ricks'. The ledger continues on this pattern. It is a mine of information on land-utilization, on quantities and prices, on customer farmers. Rye, Oats, Vetches, Beans and Peas are sometimes recorded and the pea crop was occasionally sold to the Parish for the Poor House, or, more frequently, 'Measured to servants'. Wheat was, of course, most valuable: in 1811, for instance, it brought in £1,830 as against barley £640.

The same recording routine continues year by year. Sometimes straw is sold, or Hay Grass Seed, while in the 1820s the crops are more diversified. At this time some meticulous mind has thought up a new idea: a tally of sacks sent out with corn, with the dates when they were returned. (This reminds us of that careful Angevin king, Henry II, who wanted to know what had happened to the chestnut bags.) A surprisingly large proportion of the sacks were, in fact, returned. Values fluctuated a good deal in this period: the peak year for wheat was 1812 when the crop realized £1,940 – part of the war boom, no doubt – but in the 1820s the value could drop to £600 (1821), yet rise again to £1,670 in 1825. Of course several factors affected these takings: good or bad harvests, area under cultivation, national price trends. The fluctuations, however, bring home the precariousness of farming in an age that was moving from conservatism to change.

This book runs to 1825, the last pages being used for odd jottings. An account of 'Cottage Building at Grants Farm 1828' records a construction of mud-wall and brick for about 26s. There is a note of Faggots sold and of an apple crop in 1837, when fallings were sold at 2s per sack, cider apples at 3s 6d and main crop at 6s. The second Corn Book (1826–32) stayed too long in an outhouse and is only partly legible. At the end is a statement '1841 Summary of In-comings on my little Farm' and 'Outgoings on the same'. The main income was derived from wheat, apple-cider and dairy produce, with rents and wages to set against this. On a total income of £144 the profit was £37. The third Corn Book (1832-7) is only the first part of a ledger afterwards used by John Whitaker as a time book.

The fourth Corn Book runs in beautifully clear hands from 1838 to 1876, thus spanning two changes in manage-ment, from Philip to Joshua and Joshua to John. There are gaps in 1848-9 and 1864-7 when the estate must have been in the hands of executors. There are also unaccountable gaps in 1851-3 and 1857-9, followed by low amounts of corn grown in the early 'sixties. Did Joshua Whitaker let the account-keeping slide or was he bored with farming? Over the period values still fluctuated, the peaks for wheat being 1844 (£1,800) and 1847 (£2,110) when the highest price was 30s a sack. It is for the economic historian to relate these figures to the abolition of the Corn Laws in 1845. Wheat and barley were still the main crops but a new feature of the record is that the types of seed are given, such as Butler's Imperial, Chevalier, Moldavian barley, Talavera Black or White, Tartan Oats. When the record was resumed in 1868 the wheat values were lower than at any time since 1810 and remained so until 1876 when from £430 the value jumps to £1,430. But the area under cultivation also jumps up. We are able to ascertain this easily because of a significant ad-dition to the account-keeping in 1869 when the total acreage of wheat and other corn is given along with the total yield in sacks. This soon develops into a calculation of the average yield per acre and the average price per acre for the crop. From this point onwards the calculation of the total and average yield per acre and the average price obtained are regularly given. Now, in 1869 John Whitaker was 29 years old and had had time to assess the farming situation since his father's death. We may deduce that he saw times were difficult and decided that up-to-date records were needed. No one had previously tried to sum up the year's harvest, indeed they had not even totalled the takings as a rule. John wanted to see in comparative terms how he was doing.

And well he might wish to do so, for Wiltshire farmers like others were moving towards the worst period, perhaps, in their history. In the 'seventies there was a general trend to bring more land under arable cultivation and John's farming reflects this: in 1873 he had 67½ acres of wheat, in 1874, 150. But prices remained low. In 1875 wheat averaged 21s 8d a sack. Farmers took a lower profit than they had expected and when the disastrous harvests and deep depression of 1879–80 hit them, they had little with which to buttress themselves. The story of corn farming from this point onwards was one of increasing difficulties and vanishing profits.

The farming picture in the first half of the nineteenth century can be rounded out by various other records. In 1819 Philip Whitaker started a new ledger with the flourishing title 'Stock on the Farms, December 30th, 1819'. It begins with Sheep, differentiated in categories, such as 'Ewes 2 Teeth out wintering', 'Lambs out wintering', 'Lambs at home', 'Rams', 'Ram Stags', 'Ram Lambs'. The total value is £2,993.6.0. and the whole flock numbers 1,578. The next entry under Horses evokes pictures of ploughing 'on the top', of a string of cart-horses plodding slowly homeward down White Cleaves, of Whitakers riding round in the early morning. Here is the list:

Home Stable	Captain £15		Colonel	£25
	Whitefoot £15		Duke	£18
	Short £22		Rose	£35
	Diamond £28		George	£15
Grants Farm	Smiler £15		Smiler (mare)	£18
Stable	Whitefoot £35		Short	£25
	Drummer £12		Tucker	£20
	Sergeant £9		Duke	£9
	Blackbird £12		Thumper	£5
Nag Horses	Chestnut Mare	£35		
	Gig Mare	£24		
	Joshua's Mare	£30		

Altogether the horses are worth £422. 'Horned Cattle' are divided into two categories, one of Hereford Oxen and Devon Heifers (20 worth £343), the other of Dairy Cows with names like Cherry and Myrtle. They are worth £75, while seven pigs worth £20.5.0. complete the animal stock. Corn is recorded by carefully located ricks, totalling wheat £784, barley £585.4.0., oats £135.6.0. There are also ricks of Beans, Peas, Grass Seed and Hay valued in all at £724.7.0. After this comes a valuation of crops in the ground and of fields lying fallow (the latter 116 acres at 10s an acre). We shall return to the fascinating inventory of farm implements later. Waggons and carts are carefully differentiated, while harness, shovels and pickaxes, bags and wheelbarrows are all included. There are two thrashing-machines, complete with sacks and winnowing-sheets; there is a cider-press, a bean-mill and a chaff-cutter. Staddle-stones are valued at £50, the 'Pump Head Trough' at £10 and oddments like Corn Bins, Cow Cribs and Hen Coops at £5. There are 1,517 Fleeces which, with Tail Wool, are worth £323.10. The stock-taking ends with 35 Hogsheads of Cider at 40s ('Barrels for family use not reckoned'), estimates of grain in the granary and 'Hurdles and Cribs' £20. The totals are summarized and added up to a grand total of £8,442.11.10. All this conjures up a visual picture of the farm at work in settings we still know, although equipment has changed radically. At that moment sheep were the most valuable economic resource, grain came next and dairy farming last. Horses and oxen for ploughing were still more valuable than machines – except for the thrashing tackle. The total is high compared with figures later in the century, indicating a prosperous going concern.

This annual stock-taking – so illuminating in its detail – was only continued until 1825. For these years one can follow the ups and downs, even the performance of the dairy cows – Cherry, Myrtle and the rest – and the fate of poor old Thumper who soon disappears. Potatoes and Turnips were added to the crops, but in 1821–2 the total value drops below £8,000. Recovery is evident in 1823 and by 1825 the value goes up to its highest level at £9,506.8. This meticulous work seems typical of the Philip Whitaker whom we have seen carefully gathering together family documents. We do not know what made him stop in 1825. After a gap in the ledger it continues in 1837 with 'An Inventory of Farming Stock at Grants Farm at Michaelmas 1837 made over to Joshua and John Whitaker'. Obviously Philip was settling his two sons in a business of their own. Nearly 40 acres at that time were given up to turnips, with only 54 acres of wheat. The flock numbered over 1,000 sheep and there were eight horses. The valuation was meticulously carried out, totalling c. £3,000. There are no more stock-takings in this book, which was later used by the careful John Saffery Whitaker to record Tillages for 1911–13. Another Stock Book however, begins with 'Stock taken December 1827'. This is a smaller affair and may refer only to Grants Farm. There is a similar stock-taking in 1831 and then larger ones in the 1840s, ending in 1847 with a valuation of £7,849 which must apply to the main farm business. These spasmodic efforts are much more difficult to interpret than the beautifully consistent records of the 1820s. Once again, the rest of the book was used by John Saffery for Particulars of Flocks (1904–13).

The impression begins to emerge that Philip was a beautiful book-keeper who perhaps slackened in later years; that his son Joshua was not so interested in record-keeping; that it was left to his grandson, John Saffery, to revive a systematic record. This is, on the whole, borne out by a ledger of accounts with various customers which starts in 1834 with the fine hand we can attribute to Philip but lapses after 1839 until 1881 when a much more systematic use begins lasting until 1901. In this latter part the neat, purposeful hand of John is easily recognizable. We also possess a casual memorandum book begun by Philip Whitaker in 1846 and carried on, again rather haphazardly, by Joshua. The most interesting parts are the detailed records of harvesting and sowing which again take one round the fields where the work is in full swing and bring back to the imagination an almost lost landscape in which groups of ricks formed an essential feature, as in the following:

1846 July 23rd. Talavera Wheat in Garston ricked in Home Farm.
July 28 Early vetches carried G.F. (Grants Farm)

July 29 Rye carried from Furzedown.
July 30 Peas carried from G.F. and ricked in Thorncomb yard with Peas from Measles put in two ricks and finished August 5th storm having interrupted.
July 30 Marigold wheat from West 6 Acres ricked 15 Loads in little Staddle under Sycamores ... 15 Loads Mixed and White Wheat ricked in Coomb on Staddle next east one very dry.

The wheat harvest goes on with ricks located in many places. Lammas wheat at Summerdown was ricked in the field on August 10, and finally, on August 14 Mersey wheat was ricked 'in piece Pitts'; August 15 Black Tartan oats were taken from New Bake and on the 17th they were ricked at Grants Farm. But the record then goes straight on to the next page.

Burrell Wheat sown in middle field Summerdown Sept. 25 & 26 with Mr. Neate's (?) seed ploughed in 5 sacks and 2 bushels sown in 10¾ acres ... Marigold Wheat drilled in East furlong Measles Field Oct. 27, 28 & 29 about 22 acres with my own seed from Middle Ridge taken from Mr. Ingram's seed. 11 sacks 1 bushel.
Clover Red Wheat drilled in South furlong Middle Field G.F. Oct. 27, 28 & 29 about 14 acres with Mr. J. W. Brown's seed of Uffcott. Remainder of the furlong drilled with the same Nov. 5 & 6.
Marigold Wheat chopped in Portway upper piece Oct. 28.

The sowing season ends with 'Marigold Wheat chopped in at Coleman Nov. 6 to 11 – my own best'. Notice that a great deal is still sown broadcast, then to be ploughed or chopped in, although a drill is also used. In such a record we see the revolving farm cycle: from harvesting to sowing, with the implication of the next harvest ahead.

Interspersed with this record, which continues unevenly until 1851, are odd little accounts for Apple Picking and sales of Pigs, Sheep and Faggots. There is an interesting little note on the 'Measure of New Cottages Grants Farm':

Front and sides	73 ft. by 10 ft. 3 ins.
Back	33 ft. by 5 ft. 10 ins.
	Wash houses
Sides	15 ft. by 7½ ft.

Back	19 ft. by 4 ft.			
Mudwalling	48 perch at 1/6	£3.	12.	0.
„	20 „ at 2/3	£2.	5.	0.
Plastering			8.	0.
		6.	5.	0.
Day Work		6.	10.	6.

Philip Whitaker must have been the grand old man when he died in 1847 at the age of 81. He had long been a man of affairs, administering charities, handling Baptist church business, promoting good causes. As a young man, he has revealed his inner thoughts to us. Joshua is more elusive. He may have been overshadowed by his father, and he had a shorter run on his own – only to 1864. He became a kind of legal adviser to the village and in one legal case was referred to as 'a very leading member of the Baptist congregation and a person of highest standing'. When he died there was a magnificent funeral oration. Yet we do not get inside his mind very easily. What we have got is a sequence of Petty Cash Accounts which reveal his tastes and habits in a remarkable way. In 1823 he started his adult accounts in the same book as his boyish efforts and he carried them on until 1859. Some notebooks have been lost and some are now disintegrating, but we can pick out many fascinating details. In 1823 he was getting a quarterly allowance of £6.5. He sets himself up with a watch, watch-key, ribbon and seal. From 'Blackford' he buys two pieces of nankeen and four pairs of stockings for £1.5., later selling one piece of nankeen to his mother. Blackford's also supplies him with hats, gloves, handkerchiefs and shoe-ribbons for 12s 10½d. He pays 2s 9d for tooth-powder, 8d for a nailbrush, 5s 6d for an umbrella and 2s 6d for a toothpick. His hair-cut costs 3d, but by the 1840s is 2s 6d. Later we meet such items as 'Stock, Collars & Crape 8s', Pencils 1s, Sealing Wax 4d, Soap 6d, 'Scizzors for Anne 2s', Hairbrush 5s 6d, 'Boot Top stuff 9d'. In 1846 he buys 15 postage stamps for 4s 3d. There is a wealth of information on personal habits recorded in minute detail over the years. Occasionally we meet an intriguing item such as 'Show of wild beasts 1s'.

Two things are particularly noticeable: the large proportion of items dealing with religious matters and his book-buying. He regularly enters collections, especially at the 'Ordinance', i.e. Communion Service, and subscriptions, which appear on the credit side when he collects them from others. He buys and sells Bibles, hymnbooks, catechisms and tracts. As for his reading, carriage of books is a regular item, as thus: 'Scammell one $\frac{1}{4}$'s carriage of books from Devizes'. He gets *Paradise Lost*, Young's *Night Thoughts* and Watts' *Logic*. A little later he buys Beveridge, *Private Thoughts* (4s), Lock's *Conduct of the Understanding* (1s) and Thomson's *Seasons* (1s 6d); later still, Doddridge, *Rise and Progress of Religion*, Butler, *Analogy* and a book of Spanish poetry. He pays a regular subscription of £1.4s. to 'the Book Society' and we meet a payment for bookbinding. 'Paintings at Phil. Exhibition 2s' suggests a visit to an art exhibition. Once he records the expenses of an outing: Cheddar (2s 3d), Wells Cathedral (1s 6d) and Wookey Hole (1s 6d).

In the later accounts there is less about personal expenditure and books, although the subscription to the Book Society goes on and in 1850 Joshua pays £1 for the 'concluding numbers of the Rural Encyclopedia'. The mingling of religious and secular business is characteristic. Thus in a single transaction he collects from his mother subscriptions to the minister's salary, the Mission and the Sunday School, and payment for a bottle of brandy. In this connection one cash book provides a trap for the unwary. It is labelled clearly on the cover 'Home Mysion Treasurer's Account 1824' and inside, 'Philip Whitaker, Treasurer to the Wilts and East-Somerset Home Mission Society'. It starts with the 15 guineas collected at the society's inaugural meeting in 1824 and goes on recording subscribers, collections and expenses as one would expect, to 1831. When entries are resumed after a few blank pages one could easily assume that this is still a religious account since items such as 'subscription to the Minister' appear regularly. It is only when the eye falls on 'Biscuits, Cocoa Pods, Fowls, Eggs' that one realizes that this has become Joshua Whitaker's petty cashbook for 1849–57 – fitting exactly between two other cash books. The quaint mixture of religious and domestic matters continues. We can pick out only one or two odd items: 1s for oranges in 1853 and 5d for a newspaper in the same year. And what did he do with 19s 10d worth of soft soap and arsenic in 1851? Involvement with the chapel appears continually and we note subscriptions to Sunday School treats, money for 'the children's boxes for Patna'[1] and 'buns for the School'. Subscriptions go to such causes as 'the Translation Society', Bristol Baptist College, the British School and in 1854 'Patriotic Fund £2' – was this latter connected with the Crimean War? The whole set of these petty-cash books is a mine of information on commodities, prices, local tradesmen and family buying, and to accompany them we have an unusual collection of receipted bills which we shall look at in a later chapter.

But at the moment we are still in search of Joshua, and his book-buying sends us to an anthology of readings which he made for himself. These homemade anthologies seem to have been characteristic of the Whitakers, for several of them survive in exercise-books. Joshua called his 'Poetical Extracts' and began it on 15 December 1823, in a hard-backed notebook with good paper, for which he paid 2s 3d. He eventually filled three of these. He wrote in a uniformly fine, small hand which is beautifully legible. Starting with a poem called 'The Voice of Spring' by I.H., he selected poems on nature, on departed friends, on pious hopes. Wordsworth and Cowper suited his taste, but rather surprisingly, he twice turns to Byron's *Childe Harold*: perhaps he was the owner of the nice edition of Byron's complete works found sitting a little uneasily next to Isaac Watts' *Hymns* on one of the bookshelves. His anthology ties up with his accounts, for he quotes from the book of Spanish poetry which he had bought. Sir Thomas Brown fits a melancholy mood; Southey finds a place several times, as also Henry Vaughan. Some extracts suggest unusual reading – from Milman's *Martyr of Antioch* or Sheppard's *Tour on the Continent*, from Ben Jonson, from 'Russian Poetry'

[1] See Chapter 9 for the Bratton involvement in the Baptist Mission to India.

101

and 'Lines written in prison by Anne Askew 1546' – although much naturally comes from minor religious poets of the time. He usually gives the source, sometimes the date. He ends with an 'Old Latin Hymn'.

So we do, after all, get a glimpse of the tastes of this serious-minded young farmer. He appears quite fastidious in his habits, studious, and anxious to extend his knowledge by regular reading. Perhaps there is a hint of an artistic streak, and this might be linked with some clever pen faces doodled on an envelope addressed to him. In 1821 he bought Wheatstone's *Collection of 32 Popular Dances, Waltzes etc. for the Flute or Violin*, a miniature book of elementary pieces. So perhaps he played one of the flutes found at the Yew Trees. We know nothing about his own education but, as we shall see, he took care to send his two elder sons to a first-class school. He took over some responsibility both in farming and the Church at a fairly early age and in time became a leading Nonconformist figure, pillar of the Bratton Baptist Church, secretary of the Caleb Baily Trust, involved in running local charities, such as the Honeybridge, on the Board of Guardians, and so on. Perhaps farming was not central to his interests. His granddaughter remembered her father (J. S. Whitaker) shaking his head and saying that *his* father had been no farmer, but, all the same, he won a silver mustard pot in 1838 'for the best Plough' and was often called on to judge sheep at the Bath & West Show. Perhaps he was too soft-hearted. Another story relates how, in the 'hungry forties', he said to his bailiff: 'You must go today and sell the corn at market. I cannot go and sell barley at 5s a sack with the people eating black bread'. In his last years he poured out his inner religious thoughts in yet another notebook, with all the eloquent introspection so characteristic of the Whitakers. He died suddenly from a fall from his horse in 1864.

John Saffery (1840–1915) was the last of the farming Whitakers (except for his son Philip who died prematurely in 1917). At his father's death he had unexpectedly to take on a big responsibility for his family and the farm, and he came into a hard inheritance. A valuation of land and stock made in 1865 shows such a fall in value – a total of about £3,300 compared with over £7,000 in the 1840s – that some part of the estate must have been excluded. This was almost certainly Grants Farm (II) which had been made over to John in his father's lifetime. But, in any case, the farm records show John struggling to make the farm pay in a period in which profits were growing smaller and smaller.

The fifth and last Corn Book runs steadily from 1877 to 1913 – almost the bitter end of Whitaker farming. Throughout, the clear, business-like handwriting of John Saffery (modern as compared with his grandfather's flourishes) and his beautifully formed figures remain unchanged. But the contents grow sadder. He continued the practice of totalling and averaging the corn output in terms of yield and cash value. In 1877 he had 157 acres of wheat, yielding 1,076 sacks, but the average price was only 24s 11d and the total value of c. £1,340 did not match the earlier peak years in spite of increased acreage; the market was glutted. In 1878–9 the price slumped, averaging 19s 6¾d. Thus, although he produced nearly 1,200 sacks, his takings sank to £1,170. 1879 was a disastrous year for the harvest and, although he had 155 acres under wheat, he only reaped just over 633 sacks and his takings only totalled £569, for the price, affected by the influx of cheap American corn, fell to 17s 11½d. Some recovery is apparent in the 1880s but the average barely rises above £1 and the total takings for wheat only once exceed £1,000. Again there was a disastrous harvest in 1888 when the average yield on 176 acres was just over 4 sacks as against a normal 6–7, but cheap foreign corn drove the price down to 11s 3d a sack and the takings were only £433. After that the price seldom rose above 16s. Perhaps because the trend was so disheartening John Whitaker stopped his totalling and averaging. In the 'nineties the price sank to the 10s level until 1896 when a good harvest produced an average of 9 sacks per acre and the average price went back to 15s. In that year John had the heart to do his sums again and so he does also for the 1897 and 1898 harvests. What is very noticeable here is that the total acreage under wheat has dropped drastically to 60–70 acres, while the average yield is good, 11 sacks in 1898. In the very bad years John had probably gone on too long growing a large acreage of wheat (176 acres in 1888), but by this time he had adjusted to the need for more diversification and corn-growing became a shrinking part of his production. I have merely attempted here an amateur's outline sketch of the picture which only an economic historian can properly interpret. But what was happening to corn was an essential factor in John Whitaker's life – a hard reality which he could not, and did not, try to escape. Of course some corn-growing was essential for the horses that were an indispensable factor in the farm economy of such widely scattered lands. In the oats account particularly the large amount they consume is most noticeable. 'Grants Farm horses', 'Bratton cart horses', 'Nags' appear again and again munching through the money, and we also meet 'Moses with foals', and 'Old Smiler' who consumes a guinea's-worth in 1883.

The latter part of John Whitaker's life did indeed coincide with hard times for arable farmers. This was widely recognized. In his account with the Marquis of Bath John records in 1891: 'Donation from Lord Bath in consequence of bad times £15'. This was in fact a deduction from the rent and a similar item appears in 1893 and 1894. At the same time John himself was showing generosity to others, entering on the credit side of his account: 'Mr. Thos. Sharp of Westbury £70 for four orchards of fruit' and on the debit side '£10 allowed off in consequence of bad trade'.

Diversification of crops was one obvious answer to the situation, and the record of the Corn Books shows that this line was increasingly followed. For the last period (1909–13) we have an interesting record of Tillages showing field by field 'over the top' (in Winklands, Ridgeway, Grants Farm, etc.) what was sown, how it was cultivated and what fertilizers were used. Swedes, turnips, rape and vetches are common, while superphosphates appears as fertilizers alongside the time-honoured method of folding sheep on the land. We also have a little book of John Whitaker's Notes of Farm Work from 1894 right to the time of his death in 1915. It records the crops meticulously, as sown, fertilized and harvested, each cycle ending with the dates of the beginning and end of harvest – generally between mid-August and the end of September.

Perhaps John Whitaker put much faith in his flock which became increasingly important in his latter years. In the back of an earlier stock-book he kept a close record of it from 1904 to 1913. From this we learn of the movements of the flocks on the downs, of the various operations, such as lamb-tailing, washing, heddling and riddling, and of the casualties among ewes and lambs from various causes, including 'pining'. We also have six volumes of the *Hampshire Down Flock Book*, published by the Hampshire Down Sheep Breeders' Association to which the Whitakers belonged. In 1906 his flock is recorded as consisting of 419 Ewes, 119 Tegs and 4 Rams, with the note 'Established many years since by the late Joshua Whitaker and passed to the present owner by valuation in 1867'. These figures correspond to those in his own records. The size of the flock remained much the same to the end. The lambs were usually sold either at Westbury Hill Fair in early September or Warminster Fair in October, except those which were killed at home or given to one of the shepherds. In 1911, 50 fat lambs were sold to Messrs Garlick & Sons, Trowbridge butchers, and from a fragment of an account with Garlick we find that the price was 8d per lb and that they averaged between 50 and 60 lb. The same little book contains a wool account with Messrs J. & T. Beaven of Holt for 521 fleeces sold in 1912 for £129.8.10. Unfortunately it is only from these odd fragments that we glean anything about the economic return on the flock, for the 'Particulars of Flock' which record so carefully the ewe that died of indigestion or giddiness give no prices at all.

The sheep – alas – certainly did not 'pay for all'. But they were one of the pivots round which the farm revolved. The shepherds were the aristocrats among farm-workers and, at lambing time especially, everything gave way to their needs. At this season they stayed out on the hills in the little movable shepherds' huts which were once a feature of the downs. For much of this period the two shepherds were

Benjamin Coleman and Frank Whatley, well-known figures walking the downs with their flocks and their dogs. There is a legend that Frank Whatley, for a wager, got his dog to collect 20 sheep on the eye of the White Horse at once (the number in the story varies). During a bad lambing season anxiety mounted: 'Oh maister, it'll kill I', large Ben Coleman (10) is reported to have wailed in one such crisis, and the mournful way in which the 'Particulars of the Flock' records the death of lambs day by day in a bad season, subtracting one each time, tells an eloquent tale. The other crisis came at sheep-fair time, when all the sheep seemed to be gathered from miles around on Westbury down and the great question was: What price? Sheep behaviour added to the tension – the occasion when the lambs John Whitaker sold jumped their hurdles en route for their next abode caused deep gloom. Jumping sheep were bad sheep. But normally Whitaker sheep had a good name. The flock has long since been dispersed but a few of the original sheepbells still ring gently on the hillside.

Another line which John Whitaker tried was developing his dairy farm. From 1895 to 1915 we have a Dairy Account Book. Fat calves were sold regularly to Garlicks and buttermaking for sale seems to have started in 1897. Each week the amount made, the price and the sales are recorded. In 1897 eight cows produced an average return of £14.7. per cow. In 1902 the figure goes up to £16 per cow, in 1907 to £21 average return and it stays above the £16 level to the end. In 1907, 1,547 lb of butter was made and the dairy brought in altogether £126. This little concern was the one bright side of the farming business. Perhaps the effects of education were more apparent here than in more traditional areas, for the local Butter School was held seasonally in Bratton at the old mill on the Edington Road. After they left school, both John Whitaker's younger daughters attended these classes and we still have Jane Whitaker's notes and answers written in the *Practical Guide* for 1895, though the classes were held during the winter of 1898. Besides butter-making itself, they covered some general milk science, a little on breeds of cows and, above all, hygiene, proclaiming: 'Principal Things to be attended to in the Dairy are: Cleanliness, Temperature, Light, Ventilation'. Their later text-book was the *Wiltshire County Council's Handbook on Practical Dairying* by I. J. Moir (1901). The dairy at the Yew Trees farm was probably quite up-to-date for that time, with separator, big hand-worked churn, shining milk pans, slate shelves and flagged floor, yet it belonged to the era of Tess of the D'Urbervilles rather than to the age of the milk-factory.

Another little enterprise of his last years was selling eggs commercially, which John Whitaker recorded, characteristically, in a used notebook labelled 'Cheverell Chapel'. They were dispatched first to Messrs Besant and Fry, London, and then to a Mr J. Huntly. From a ledger of accounts we trace a few more of his dealings. Against the rent of Grants Farm which he held from C. N. Phipps he set a regular fee for gamekeeping as well as such items as: '14s for 14 Partridges' nests saved'. In the 1880s he was doing business with Mr George Brent, owner of the revived woollen mill at Luccombe, regularly providing – amongst other items – 'horse labour' for 'setting engine and machine'. To Ushers', the Trowbridge brewers, he supplied straw for the great cart-horses which drew the brewers' drays all round the countryside; in return he sometimes took barrels of ale. With the family doctor, first E. P. Shorland and then G. G. Parsons, he also did business by barter, supplying oats, hay and straw for their horses and setting medical attendance against this. Thus in 1897 he had only 12s to pay on a year's medical bill for the family of £5.6.6. This ledger also provides a good example of the habit of mixing up business and philanthropy in an account with Mr A. Pocock:

To 3 Tins Fly Powder	By 12½ qurs. barley
„ 2 bags Manure	„ Service of Bull
„ 4½ bushels seed wheat	
„ Subscription to Imber British School	
(and other items)	

John Whitaker clearly gave a good deal of his mind to farming and appears to have been the most methodical farmer of the family. His calculations of yield show that he sought to

107

discover just how he was doing. But a real attempt at a profit-and-loss assessment appears nowhere in these accounts. One has the general impression of a farming family with clear, orderly minds, sometimes with a passion for detail, so that they will record the one sack of good beans from a spoilt crop, or the oats eaten by an old horse, but with no idea of a balance sheet. John was, of course, only too conscious of the depressed situation: his daughter recalled her father coming home from market saying: 'There seems to be no money anywhere.' Yet making or losing money was not so very important. He cared very much more about the well-being of the farm. His habit was to rise early, make a cup of Nibb Cocoa from the pot which stood on the hob of the kitchen range and ride round all the hill-farm lands to see the men starting work before he came home to breakfast. His granddaughters remember his upright figure on the horse waving good morning at their nursery window on his way home. But he had a great deal more on his mind as he became increasingly involved in public affairs. Leaving aside for the moment his deep devotion to the Church, we find him collecting the secretaryships (or trusteeships) of the Caleb Baily, Gaisford, Honeybridge and Haynes charities. In 1865 he was elected by the parish to represent it on the Westbury and Whorswelldown Union as Guardian and Rural District Councillor. Later he became chairman of both the Board of Guardians and the Rural District Council, completing 50 years' service in all. A presentation silver salver records this service with solemn dignity. In local government he ended as County Councillor and J.P. To complete the variegated list we must add that he was actuary to the Warminster Trustee Savings Bank, on the board of Trowbridge and District Isolation Hospital, for 50 years treasurer of the 'Loyal Castle' Lodge of Oddfellows in Bratton, and involved with both the Clothing Club and the Bratton Friendly Society.

Most revealing of the variety of activities in his incessantly riding life are the fragments of diaries he wrote in 'Collins Scribbling Diaries' for 1885, 1887 and 1893. Some extracts will illustrate this:

Memo, from 1886. Night of Dec. 26th, there was a fearful storm of wind and snow, the worst I can remember since January 18th & 19th, 1881. Many of the sheep were buried. 3 tegs trampled to death, but there was no loss amongst the ewes. Snow very much drifted roads impassable in many places. The next day beautifully fine and frosty.

Thursday the 30th. W. H. Brinkworth lectured to the Mutual Improvement Society on 'Character'.

Friday 31st. Watchnight Service was held. After the snow storm we began giving the ewes some hay once a day.

2 January. Sunday. Week of Prayer.

3 January. Mr. Drew conducted the missionary prayer meeting.

4 January. Sophie[1] and I went to Trowbridge market – fearfully slippery.

Reuben Ashley conducted prayer meeting tonight.
        (prayer meetings go on all the week)

7 January. Special Assessment Committee Meeting at the Board Room at 10 a.m. – very long sitting – I did not get home until 5.30.

8 January. Went to Market – wheat rather lower.

J. S. W. conducted prayer-meeting tonight.

11 January. Not very well – did not go to Board of Guardians' meeting. Settled up Sunday accounts with Benjamin (Coleman) this evening. Mr Jeffries came to go into Club Accounts. Polly[1] and Sophie had their Sunday School classes to tea.

13 January. Pollie, Sophie and self went to Station to see Pat and Archie on their way home from Bristol. Mutual Improvement Society's Concert – such a row!

15 January. Went to market – sold 'White Challenge' wheat at 17/6 – wheat lower again ... Mrs. Keevil died after only a day's illness.

16 January (Sunday). Mr. Aldis preached this evening. I called to see Mr. Keevil after evening service.

17 January. Sophie, Edith[1] and Phil[1] went on the hill with me and had some skating at the upper tyning pond. Finished thrashing 'Bromwick' wheat at sheep pen.

18 January. I rode on the hill – queer riding – Toby rather fresh – I managed to quiet him. Went to Friendly Society meeting at Westbury Leigh in the evening ... a very good meeting.

19 January. Annual Meeting of the Trustees of the Honeybridge Charity at the Vicarage, Westbury – only Rev. W. P. J. Bingham and myself present.

20 January ... Harry (Dermer) and I went to the 'Mutual' to the debate on Sunday Closing (of public houses).

[1] Polly = John's wife; Sophie, Edith and Phil = three of his children, see Chapter 8.

21 January. Special Meeting of the Assessment Committee at 10 a.m. very late home. Church Meeting.

22 January. Did not go to market on account of Mrs. Keevil's funeral. Went on the hill first. A fine day. Moved 6 cows from Sheepyard to Lower Farm.

24 January. Children began school after the Christmas holidays. Went over to see David White in the afternoon and found him fairly well.

25 January. Board of Guardians – rather a long day with Highway business. Meeting of the Committee of the Mutual Improvement Society this evening.

26 January. The deacons came to tea – audited the various accounts in the evening – we had a pleasant meeting.

27 January. Mutual Improvement Society's meeting – Lecture on 'Pompeii' by Rev. W. P. J. Bingham – only a poor attendance.

28 January (Friday). Pay night. Sunday School Teachers' Tea-meeting. I went up (to the chapel) soon after 7 o'clock and stayed till the end.

29 January. Went to market with Mr. Pocock – sold Barley at 18/6 – Wheat at 14/6.

30 January (Sunday). Went to Tinhead this evening (preaching) – T. Millard taking Ashton for me . . .

8 February. Board of Guardians – very long sitting on account of Assessment Committee work – such a number of appeals – left the Workhouse at 6 p.m. quite tired out – had a cup of tea at Eden – rode home and found folks at home somewhat anxious.

14 February. After prayer meeting I heard of the death of William Bigwood's wife.

15 February. Rode over to Coulstone to see William Bigwood – found him better. Saw David White as I returned – found him ill in bed – a touch of bronchitis. Went on the hill in the afternoon . . .

17 March. A most severe frost – some persons registered 28 degrees of frost – a great comfort there is such a covering of snow to protect vegetation. I walked on the hill – very heavy walking – came home to dinner very tired and very late. I found the sheep and lambs quite as comfortable as can be expected. While we were at dinner G. Walter came in to say old Diamond had dropped dead in Court Lane – no doubt she has had heart disease for years. In the evening we had a Public Meeting to consider the question of removing Infant Schoolroom and making it a Public Room in commemoration of Queen's Jubilee.

21 March. The snow is melting. I walked on the hill and found sheep and lambs pretty well. Went to meet Mr. Rouse (mission-

ary) after dinner ... A capital Missionary Meeting – a first-rate address from Mr. Rouse and a good collection.

22 March. Went to the Board of Guardians' Meeting, taking Mr. Rouse to station first – home to dinner soon after two o'clock – a very rapid thaw and plenty of wind.

23 March. G. Walter quite laid up. I went on the hill early and started 10 ploughs on Highdown ploughing in oats – sheep all right – busy all day – went three times on the hill.

24 March. Went on hill before breakfast – finished ploughing in oats on Highdown and began working in grass seed. Intended going to Freshford this afternoon but it came on to rain and I felt quite poorly. In the evening attended Jubilee Committee at Messrs. Reeves's Office. Estimate cost of removing, repairing, fencing, enlarging and furnishing the room £130. It will probably not cost so much.

27 March (Sunday). Went to Ashton in the evening (to preach) – took Edie and Phil with me – a good congregation – a beautiful drive home – Philip Smith came down to say two horses were unwell.

28 March. Went early on the hill – found the horses better but not fit to work. Sowing oats at Sedcomb – broadcast and scarrified behind – more couch than I expected – wheat looks up nicely. One of the heifers I bought at Chippenham on the 11th inst. calved today – a very good calf – heifer doing well ... Prayer meeting, afterwards choir practice.

29 March. On the hill early – a lovely mild morning – sheep all right finishing off Sedcomb oats ... Went to Board of Guardians' Meeting – only Messrs. Bigwood, Doel and myself there. Quarterly cases were considered – rather a long sitting. We finished about 2 o'clock. I rode home calling at Eden Vale and going down to pastures to the men hedging – in the afternoon Mr. Bull came to buy fat cow but we did not deal.

These entries, selected over one period of a few months, portray a way of life that speaks for itself. It should be noted that although only here mentioned twice, John Whitaker was also out nearly every Sunday preaching in one of the villages. As we shall see, he kept a separate record of these. Nor was his preparation perfunctory, for a thick pile of sermon notes in his neat handwriting has also survived.

The great army of farm-workers who upheld the social and economic fabric of society is often viewed as anonymous and faceless. In this Wiltshire village they were certainly not anonymous and often not faceless either. This is due in the first place to the splendid series of Parish Registers in which we read the tale of the families in terms of marriages, births and deaths. And the same families march on from generation to generation: Smiths, Newmans, Meads, Hobbses, Holloways, Callaways, Snelgroves, Cooks, Colemans, Drewitts. It appears a very stable society from the seventeenth to the nineteenth century. Secondly, for a certain group of these we have the Whitaker 'Servants' Ledgers', running from 1830 to 1876 and some other bits of information from the Whitaker papers. Thirdly, as we shall see shortly, the Baptist records bring some of these people to life.

When we open the first of the ledgers (1830–45) we are at once aware of hard work and hard living. Each page is headed in the familiar flourishing hand with the name of one of the farm-workers and records his wages. When the page is full the account is continued on the next blank page. Two points first strike the eye: the men are apparently only paid about once a month, and against their wages are set the bushels of flour or barley and the sacks of potatoes which they buy. The prices they pay for this stuff look favourable, but we do not know the quality. The 'take-home pay' is often under £1 and seldom over £2. The numbers employed mostly range between 10 and 20, with seasonal variations, occasionally dropping below 10 and once or twice in the 1840s going above 20. The consistency with which the same names and same families go on year after year reinforces the impression of an almost unchanging society. Sometimes a name drops out, or there are two for a time – Senior and Junior – before one disappears. The ledgers read like a roll-call of old Bratton families. There is, of course, a whole clan of Newmans – James, John (senior and junior), Benjamin, Joseph – and another of Smiths, in which Henry Smith (milkman) has to be distinguished from Henry Smith (thresher), and George James Smith from George Smith. There are several Burgesses and Callaways, there are Meads, Prices, Hobbses and Sculls. The Walter family served the Whitakers over a long period: we meet George, Thomas,

James and Jonah, and there was a second George who was John Whitaker's bailiff. The Whatley family – famous for its shepherds – is represented in the later years by Charles and Robert. George and Lewis Snelgrove are important figures; once a Reeves – Alfred – appears for a short time in 1849. In the ledgers there is only one woman – Sarah Cook in 1831 – but we shall meet some more later. It seems likely that relationships between master and men were good, since during the agricultural riots of 1830–31 Philip Whitaker gave his men 1s a night to watch his ricks by turns.[3]

The staple diet in these families appears to consist of corn in some form and potatoes. In 1830 a bushel of flour – to these men – cost about 10s, so if the average wage was between £1 and £2 for about four weeks, there was little left over when the two bushels which most families seemed to need had been paid for. But the number of days and weeks worked varied greatly and obviously some of these men must have been working elsewhere simultaneously. They also grew or reared part of their own food: there are mentions of chicken and eggs and occasionally a pig. During most of this period wages rose only a little: in the 1860s a man's wage for four weeks was still only about £2 or £2.8. for the more skilled. But the standard of living seems to be rising slightly, for, while in the 1830s and 1840s they buy little but flour, barley and potatoes, in the later years we meet the occasional piece of meat, peas, butter, apples, walnuts and cider. But it is the staple bushels and sacks that go steadily on.

One point is obvious from the ledgers: the children and lads work alongside their fathers and what they earn is firmly gathered in, as a rule, under their father's takings. In the 1830s a 'little boy' earned about 4s for two weeks' work, sometimes specified as 'bird-keeping'. Combined labours at harvest time could produce larger wages, as for instance in November 1831 when James Newman, with his sons Ben and David, totted up £3.7.4. His 'little girl' apparently earned only 4s for eight weeks' work. In 1848 Jacob Newman had his son Esau working with him, but sometimes

[3] I owe this information to Mrs Morrison.

113

the lads get a page to themselves, as, for instance, 'Bristowe's Boys' in 1834 who earned between 2s 6d and 5s for variable weeks but also once brought in 8 lb of beef to the family. Again, in 1844 'Jane Callaway's Boy' is paid over 2s a week for long spells lasting 14, 18, or 22 weeks at a time. It is clear that the children's labour was a vital part of the family economy. No doubt the adult workers disciplined them well. Two little stories survive from John Whitaker's days. Discussing a rather unsatisfactory shepherd's boy one day, Ben Coleman said to his master: 'Oh he always were a caddlin' little to-ad!' On the other occasion, the boy leading the ploughing horses was observed to be crying. 'What be th'matter?' said the ploughman. 'Horse trod on my foot,' whimpered the boy. 'Well, next time thee tread on his'n', was the only reply he got.

One factor which must have helped to make life viable was that of extra payments. The most important of these was the 'harvest money' and extra earnings for threshing. Harvest money could bring in something between 10s and £1. There was also extra money for lambing, sheep dipping and shearing, while turnip-hoeing seems to have been paid separately and quite well. There were also regular payments for rat and mole catching, reckoned by producing the tails. A year's mole catching could bring in £1, while a boy could get 2s 8d for 65 mice. There were occasional perquisites: in 1839 Jesse Grant is allowed 10s 6d smock-frock money; in 1867 Isaac Burgess gets half his dog licence paid; throughout there are credits for harvest suppers reckoned in.

There are only fragments of evidence about the women at work. In a ledger of accounts there is a little scribbled memo for 1847 which records apple-picking by five women and two men. There seems to have been no standard rate, for Betty Newman got 11s for 17 days' picking, while Mary Grant got only 8s 6d for the same period. After the series of servants' ledgers has ended, however, John Whitaker's 'Reaping and Tying Account' (1882–96) brings in the women as 'tyers'. In 1882 the reaping was done by 12 men who earned altogether just over £23 for 43 acres. At the tying stage six women were at work in various places. For instance, Ann Millard, Sarah Grant and Lydia Smith were tying at God's Hill, Lousy Corner, Pitts and Ridgeway. They were paid according to the area they covered, earning between £2 and £5 for the work. The same pattern is recorded for the following years, where other well-known Bratton names appear, such as Couldrake, Merritt and Cox. Incidentally, this record gives us many interesting field names, such as Paul Ridge, Swakley, Diggle Shoot, Sunny Corner, Quarry Piece and Pewitt Piece, in addition to those already mentioned.

Apart from the ledgers we have one precise little picture of the farm men at work in the mid-nineteenth century. On 8 December 1853 John Whitaker, then aged 13, wrote a letter to his father, Joshua, who was away from home. It is written on carefully ruled notepaper in a very careful schoolboy hand – perhaps copied out, since there are few mistakes:

My very dear Papa,
    I went up on the hill Tuesday, and as you desired me, I wrote down what the work people were about. Three horse and two ox ploughs at work in the barley stubble – two horses at harrow in Pitts – Lewis with one horse at odd jobs – four men in the barn thrashing. Thos. and Isaac Burgess mending sheep troughs – Sheep's eye better. Prior cutting out gutter at Coomb – George Smith chopping headlands, filling stepples etc. five men at the swedes on Portway – Daniel Walter in Parish Court – Coomb horses timber carrying in the morning – in the afternoon two men and two horses getting out muckle up to Portway and George Walter went after bricks.
Wednesday – The sheep's eye 'keeping better' – but I am sorry to say that one of the ewes, (not a first-rate one), got on her back in the night and was found dead. Three horse and two ox-ploughs again at work in the barley stubble, and two horses at work in the same place with the presser – two boys and a horse at odd jobs – Thos. and Isaac Burgess mending sheep troughs – 13 men and 4 women at work in the swedes on Portway – Daniel/Walter in Parish Court – George Walter took a load of manure down to Mr. Anderson's in the morning and then Philip Smith went to Coleman with three horses to plough the headland, and begin ploughing that strip under the White Horse – George, with one of the horses, got some sand and dirt to mix with it, for J. Carr, and was not out in Coleman till about two

o'clock – then they sowed the headland, and followed on with the Zig-Zag, Thursday. I have not been up hill today, but George Snelgrove tells me that they are again at plough and at work with the presser in the barley stubble – they are carrying the swedes on Portway, and there are 22 people at it, including men, women and boys. I think I have no more to communicate.

Believe me dear Papa,

Your loving son,

J. S. Whitaker.

After 1876 little record of the farm-workers remains, except John Whitaker's Time Book from 1903 until his death, but this only gives days worked and does not tell us much. At some point the system of payment was changed from a monthly account to a weekly pay day on Fridays. We have the tangible evidence of this in a set of smooth wooden bowls in which the various denominations of coins were ranged when the men came to John Whitaker's little counting-house at the west end of the Yew Trees to be paid. His daughter remembered that it was one of their treats as children to go and watch while the rats' and moles' tails were being counted out. She also recalled that before Christmas a sheep would be killed and cut into joints which were allotted according to a strict hierarchy among the farm men. It was the children's privilege to go and put the labels on each joint.

John Whitaker's kindnesses to his work-folk mostly go unrecorded, except for chance references in his diary. But there is one rather unusual letter, written by Lewis Snelgrove to John Whitaker in 1874, which must be quoted in full:

My dear Sir,

Allow me to Say how Amazed I am at the step you are about to take, Involving such Trouble and expense. (I hope your servants will know how to appreciate such amazing kindness) as for myself I am no less amazed at your kindness towards me, all being well I shall accept the offer so kindly made Hoping it will be a success in every respect, and you dear Friend greatly blessed in your deed; I must be allowed to say (and that without flattery which I sincerely hate) that I feel increasing respect for you sir and for Mrs. Whitaker and all your friends, to whom under god I have ever owed very much, that has contributed to

smooth my path through life which is now drawing to a close.
Praying gods blessing to be ever with you Dear Friends
   I heartly and gratefully append my worthless name
      L. Snelgrove.
Mr. and Mrs. Whitaker.

We do not know to what action of John Whitaker's this refers.

6 Bratton Ironworks

In 1774 Robert Reeves, bachelor, married Eve Pepler, spinster, in Bratton Church. While many could only make their mark in the Register, both these could sign their names, though in uneducated hands that do not compare with the Whitakers'. In 1786 'Reeves the blacksmith' was employed when the Baptist Meeting House was enlarged. In 1799 William Whitaker recorded in his 'Expences': 'R. Reeves for mending Plump at Smarts 30 Aug. 1/6'. Peplers were a well-known family in the vicinity; Reeves was a new name. It looks as if Robert Reeves came to the village from Dilton Marsh, where he was born c. 1750, set up a blacksmithy, and found a bride. A receipted bill of 1799 shows us his son, Thomas Pepler (born in 1778), also doing a blacksmith's trade of shoeing horses and mending tools. We do not know where the first Reeves workshop was. In 1808, however, a lease was drawn up on the lives of Thomas Pepler Reeves and his two sons, Thomas, aged 6, and Horatio Nelson, aged 2. Thomas Pepler is there described as a blacksmith in occupation of a messuage with garden and orchard of about one acre, part of a tenement called Harts', and Deanly. Harts' was almost certainly the site in the middle of the village where the Ironworks stood until demolished in 1973.

Not much is known about Horatio Nelson – echo of Trafalgar enthusiasm – except that he is named as one of the 'lives' for the lease of land to the Meeting House Trustees in 1817. This suggests that the Reeves family was already connected with the Baptist Church. The younger Thomas continued the trade of blacksmith, at one time in Westbury, but Thomas Pepler's two younger sons, Robert, born in 1810, and John, born in 1815, seized the chance to branch out into a wider business. Guy, the youngest, worked in their blacksmith's shop, but never acquired a share in the business. There is, unfortunately, little evidence to bridge the gap between 1808 and 1846, when the first surviving ledger begins, but this shows that an account with J. Flower, a Bratton farmer, had been allowed to run on from 1828 to a total of £215, while a catalogue of 1859 claims that the firm has been celebrated for its corn-drills for 30 years and as ploughmakers for 40 years. Robert was the carpenter, while his father and his younger brother carried on the blacksmith's work. The ledgers suggest that Robert's side of the business had become the larger and that he was the enterprising member of the firm who developed the carpentry side and started the Foundry, for which he bought the equipment 'at Moody's Sale'. At any rate, there was a flourishing business when the stock was valued at Thomas Pepler Reeves' death in 1849. The smithy had 5 bellows, 4 sledges, 6 anvils and 3 sets of shoeing tools; the machines listed included 5 vices, 4 lathes and 2 drilling machines. The foundry had a steam-engine and boiler valued at £110, besides other equipment, and the valuation included $51\frac{1}{4}$ cwt of new pig iron, 87 cwt of new castings and 133 cwt of cast scrap. The valuation also lists the 'upper yard', paint shop, saw-pit and other buildings. So already Reeves's was astride the main road, occupying what is now the garage and petrol station as well as the main site. This was very far from the simple rural smithy or carpenter's shop: by a process of which we have few traces machines had arrived in Bratton, though no one seemed to notice it and no one could prophesy where the machine age would take people. A bill-head of 1864 shows that it was now officially Bratton Iron Works, though to the villagers it was always the Foundry – the institution whose time governed their time, and whose prospects governed, to a considerable extent, their prospects for 125 years.

This is not the place to analyse the slow process by which farmers were turning to machinery more sophisticated than the simple implements which one sees – more or less unchanged – in illustrations from Anglo-Saxon times down to the seventeenth century. We can, however, use Philip

Whitaker's stock-taking inventories to get an idea of what may have been going on at Reeves's in the first half of the nineteenth century. In 1819, besides ploughs and rollers, Philip Whitaker had three pairs of drags, ten harrows, two 'sowing machines', two threshing-machines valued at £100, 'winnowing tackle' valued at £15, a bean-mill and a chaff-cutter. In addition there were, of course, waggons and carts, wheelbarrows, hand implements, feeding troughs and other items of carpentry that would keep Reeves's busy. A little later a presser and horsehoe are added to the list, but otherwise it hardly varies from year to year. In 1823 a 'drill plough' is specified and in 1831 a turnip harrow. In 1836 the drill plough has a manure-box and in 1841 this has become '12 Drills with manure boxes', while there are also more kinds of harrows. In 1843 we hear of 'hay knives' and a turnip-cutter. Thus, over the period covered by the inventories (1819–47), basic farm implements changed very little, only increasing in number and becoming rather more specialized in function. The only direct evidence that Whitakers were dealing with Reeves's before 1846 comes from one partially illegible bill sent by Robert Reeves to Mr P. Whitaker in 1841, but when the series of surviving ledgers begins in 1846 Whitakers take pride of place, running long accounts for repairs to equipment. In the 'forties the breakthrough in agricultural manufacturing was, however, on the way. From these ledgers we can trace the transition from wooden to iron ploughs: in 1845 they made 28 wooden ploughs and two iron ones; in 1846, 24 wooden, two iron; in 1847, 13 wooden to 27 iron ploughs; in 1848, 31 iron to 12 wooden; in 1849, 66 iron to eight wooden. During the 'fifties the number of ploughs made or sold is triumphantly totalled each year: they are virtually all iron, rising in number to 113 sold and 66 remade or altered in 1857.

Why did the oldest agricultural engineering works in Wiltshire start in a village like Bratton? One would have looked for it in a county town, and indeed its next competitors were Toone's and Titt's of Warminster and White's of Devizes. The foundry, with its tall chimney, the whirring saw-mill and the activities along 'Carpenter Shop Lane' must have been something of an intrusion into the changeless pattern of a farming community. Accessibility to raw materials and markets was not good. There was no railway until the Wilts, Somerset and Weymouth line reached Westbury in 1848, while the main G.W.R. line was not completed until 1900. The turnpike road connecting the village with Devizes and Westbury was probably quite good, but all haulage was, of course, by cart and horse. Iron mined at Westbury may have been used at one time, but coal had to be hauled from Radstock until the advent of the railway. It seems that this development happened because the Reeves family caught the moment when farmers were just awakening to the possibility of a wider range of implements. In this remote area of villages and isolated farms on the Plain there were as yet no competitors. When William Cobbett rode from Westbury to Devizes in 1818, he might have commented on the strategic position of the small business he passed on the way, but he only says:

My road was now the line of separation between what they call South Wilts and North Wilts, the former consisting of high and broad downs and narrow valleys with meadows and rivers running down them; the latter consisting of a rather flat enclosed country; the former having a chalk bottom; the latter a bottom of marl, clay, or flat-stones; the former a country for lean sheep and corn; and the latter a country for cattle, fat sheep, cheese and bacon; the former by far, to my taste, the most beautiful; and I am by no means sure that it is not, all things considered, the most rich.

It was to supply the dual needs of Plain and Vale that the Reeves business came into existence. Thus a ripe local market seems to have been the start of their good fortune and on this rising tide they were carried forward into national trade. Perhaps most important of all in this growth was the factor of personality: the drive and inventiveness of Robert Reeves. He probably had little education, for it does not seem that the family bothered much about this. The 1799 bill sent out by Thomas Pepler Reeves is mis-spelt and badly written. In 1826 Jeffery Whitaker's charity for educating poor boys paid out 9s for half a year's schooling for

'Reeves's boy'. This was probably John, not Robert, and, in any case, was only intended to give a grounding in the three Rs. Robert probably had no more than this.

After Thomas Pepler's death, the brothers, Robert and John, paid off their eldest brother, Thomas, and formed the partnership of R. & J. Reeves which appears in the earliest extant catalogues of 1853, 1859 and 1863. Now began the period of growth, both in range of manufacture and widening markets. In 1848 they exhibited at the Royal Agricultural Show at York, gaining a silver medal. They gained a licence to make Chandler's Patent Liquid Manure Distributor and patented improvements, producing over 20 of these annually in the 'fifties. In 1857 they won several prizes for their Patent Manure and Seed Drill and Manure Distributor. They developed new models for ploughs, land pressers and harrows. They began making water-carts and portable shepherds' huts, so essential for farming on the Plain. They exhibited assiduously at regional and national shows and early catalogues carry illustrations of the medals awarded. Some of these are still treasured: a bronze one from the Great Exhibition of 1861; three silver ones of the Royal Agricultural Society; an undated one for a 'Patent Weeding Paddle or Thistle Destroyer' and awards for a Dry Manure and Seed Drill (Salisbury, 1857) and cheese-making apparatus (Chester, 1858). The Yorkshire Agricultural Society gave them an award for a water-cart at Thirsk in 1867 and medals were won in Paris in 1855 and at the Concours International at Lille in 1863. A bill-head of 1864 bears the proud legend: 'Patronised by His Royal Highness Prince Albert'. The two brothers were setting their sights high for a village firm (13).

Both Robert Reeves's sons, Thomas and Henry, came into the business, but his flair seems to have been inherited chiefly by Henry. By 1871 manufacture in Bratton reached a new level of sophistication when the Iron Works began to make the Andrews Elevator under licence from William Andrews of Melksham. This was designed 'for ricking Hay, Corn or Straw either by means of a one-horse Gear or to be driven by a Thrashing Machine'. Henry Reeves quickly saw

122

and patented an improvement which he sold to Andrews in 1873. The 1890 catalogue claimed that 'it will elevate a wagon-load in five minutes', and trade was brisk. For a small village it was quite a feat that, between 1871 and 1898, 305 Andrews Elevators were built. The Bought Ledger of 1871-8 shows a surprisingly large quantity of raw materials purchased: 622 tons of pig iron (mostly from Scotland), calculated to produce over 200 tons of new castings a year; 117 boxes of tin plate (estimated as 10 tons) which in expert opinion was a 'tremendous amount'; plough plates for about 250 ploughs a year and seed-cups sufficient for a total of c. 5,000 drills.

But the Andrews Elevator was a wooden machine and in 1896 Henry Reeves went one better in designing and patenting the 'Advance' Steel Elevator which went into production in 1897.[1] Its price in 1900 was £44 and it was the chief pride of the firm. Parts were made during the winter and assembled as the orders came in. At the peak of production about 40 of these would rumble out of the yard each summer, and there would be a sense of excitement and achievement about their departure, even occasionally a little last-minute painting on the road. New methods in feeding sheep and cattle also brought a response from Messrs Reeves. From 1896 onwards they were manufacturing Andrews Patent Combined Lamb Creep and Shelter. In the advertisement for a similar Meikle Lamb Creep there is a kindly, solicitous note declaring that it 'makes provision for the return of the lambs without injury when from their increased size after feeding . . . they can only with safety return through a larger opening than that which just sufficed to let them out'. The widening market for these machines is clearly traceable from the ledgers. In the early ones the accounts are mainly local and many pages list little but small repairs, horse-shoeing and odd jobs. In the 'fifties the wholesale business in machines begins to appear: in 1859, for instance, Messrs Proctor & Ryland of Birmingham bought 45 Chandler's Drills. The picture given by the 1862 ledger differs strikingly from that of 1846. Now, the biggest

[1] It still, however, had a timber frame.

accounts are with wholesale dealers all over the south and midlands, even going as far north as Aberdeen. Ploughs, drills, manure distributors and, finally, elevators are Reeves's 'line'. But the long accounts for small repair work go on as well: this double role was the essence of the business.

One facet of the Reeves success was surely their versatility as craftsmen. Thomas Pepler remained a blacksmith to the end and his sons all worked with their hands. They must have attracted and trained the kind of village craftsmen who combined skill and patience with a liking for individual jobs and time to do them solidly. The firm acquired a reputation for turning its hand to making or mending almost anything. During the harvest season in particular Reeves's men would be all round the countryside tinkering with machinery *in situ*, while in the Works hours were spent – often uneconomically – trying to make something go. They attended to pumps and wells, put in water supplies and heating apparatus, built greenhouses, soldered kettles and pans, and made almost any piece of domestic equipment to specification, even cages for parrots. They made coffins for the village and acted as undertakers. On one occasion they supplied 'straining apparatus' for a soup kitchen. In 1864 they made the wrought-iron chandeliers and candlesticks for Steeple Ashton Chapel. In a later ledger we find the unusual entry: 'To man's time only, clearing Bats from Belfry, using gas. 7/–'. Robert Reeves was even willing to turn architect and builder. He built cottages at Grants Farm, and the Jubilee Hall out of material from the old Infant School. He directed the building of the Ashton Chapel and after him his son, Henry, did the same for the Cheverell Chapel.

This variety of business provided a good seedbed for craftsmen talent and, as it expanded, the village changed its character from a timeless community of farmers and farmworkers to one of diversified skills, rising standard of living and changing circumstances. The Census returns of 1851 and 1871 shows that craftsmen had been coming from the Midlands, Wales and Ireland to work at Reeves's. Unfortunately information on wages is very scanty. On the smithy side of the business we know that in 1846–7 three shillings was paid for a day's work, making a weekly total of about 15s. 'Wages of men and boys' totalled £105.11.3 for 1847, indicating that perhaps two men and two boys were employed. In addition, John and Guy, both working in the smithy at this time, received £39 p.a. and £22.2 p.a. respectively. In an inventory three smiths are named: Dale, Bazley and Orchard. As in farming, wages did not shift much during the next 30 years: in 1870 the average wage for a twelve-hour day was still only about 14s a week, but this, of course, compares favourably with a farm wage of £2 for four weeks.

If our information is lacking on wages, we can at least gain a picture of conditions in 'The Foundry' from *Rules to be Observed by the workmen and Apprentices of R. & J. Reeves & Son, Bratton Iron Works*, printed by W. Michael of Westbury in 1871. The working week was 56 hours, i.e. five days of ten hours each and six hours on Saturday: everyone was paid by the hour. During the winter months the working day was from 6.30 a.m. to 6 p.m. In the summer months they arrived half an hour earlier and left at 5.30. Saturday work was from 6.30 a.m. to 1.15 p.m. all the year round. Meal times were allowed, for breakfast from 8.30 to 9.15 and for dinner from 1.15 to 2 p.m. 'The Whistle shall be blown exactly at time for working, and all persons not on the premises at the time will be considered as late'; unless he produced a reason 'satisfactory to his Masters' the laggard was fined the amount of half-an-hour's time. There were fines for many misdemeanours, such as:

for entering the premises by any other way than the main gates 3d.
for taking time off for Luncheon or Tea 6d.
for overstating his time fine: twice the amount of the time overstated; for Idling or Wasting his Time 6d.
for neglecting or absenting himself from work 6d.
for cursing, swearing or using obscene or profane language 1/–
for throwing at another workman, interrupting or annoying him 3d.
for damaging an article or machine, wilfully or carelessly, fine, sufficient to replace the same
for 'wasting' materials 6d.

for making tools or doing work for themselves, or taking away
any materials, firewood or shavings without permission 1/-
for leaving his lamp or candle burning after work 3d.
for smoking on the premises 6d.

There were special regulations about beer: any workman
could bring in one pint for himself alone at mealtimes, but
the penalty for bringing in beer or any intoxicating liquors
at any other time was a fine of 1s. Equal fines were exacted
from anyone leaving his work to go to the Public House, or
coming on the premises in a state of Intoxication. Anyone
who did not inform his Masters about another breaking any
of these rules was liable to the same fine as the offender. All
the fines were deducted from wages and put into the Sick
Fund, but the Masters reserved the right to reduce the fines
for Boys or Apprentices. Finally, Rule XXIII reads: 'All
Workmen before leaving shall give One Week's Notice . . .
on the Saturday previous, and in like manner all Workmen
shall receive One Week's Notice from the Masters before
being discharged excepting for improper conduct to the
Masters or Officials, for such they will be liable to Instant
Dismissal.' These rules surely speak for themselves of an
industrial discipline now almost forgotten. But the Masters
were not quite without care for their workmen.

A Sick Club was started in the mid-century for which the
books survive for the period 1863 to 1913. Men, and boys
earning 6s a week upwards, contributed 1d a week to the
Fund whilst all workmen's fines were paid into it. Benefits
began modestly but soon increased to such an extent that
the Fund ran into debt in the 'seventies, although by 1871
there were about 40 contributors. In 1880 the deficit was
£8.5.5. and there follows the entry: 'This account was squared
by the balance owing being given by the Old Firm.' In spite
of this clean start, the Old Firm had again to pay off a deficit
of £27.19.4 in 1891. The inability to remain solvent was
probably due to the length of time Sick Benefit was allowed to
run, in some cases even up to 25 weeks or so. In 1891, however, a fresh set of Rules was drawn up and the Fund placed
on a new footing. The Rules are set out in a new Account
Book which runs from 1891 to 1913. The Fund is to be

under the management of a committee consisting of the Masters and five workmen chosen to represent the Moulders, Fitters, Blacksmiths, Carpenters and Painters respectively. The Masters are to be the Treasurers of the Fund and have power, with the Committee, to raise the contributions above the 1d a week level if necessary. The Benefits are laid down carefully as 5s a week for six weeks and 2s 6d for a further seven weeks, in any one year, with no further claim to be made for six months. No one is to receive sick pay until he has contributed for six weeks. Fines and gratuities are to go into the Sick Fund. When a member dies, all the other members are to pay 6d each towards the expenses of burial. These rules give a stark picture of what sickness could mean in the days before national insurance. In 1898 we meet the entry: 'From this date R. & J. Reeves & Son agree to contribute £2 at the end of each year to this Fund in lieu of the donation which had been given to the Workmen's Outing Fund.' The club remained solvent under the new rules until the end. In 1912 there were 62 members. On 1 March 1913 the account was closed and the balance of £1.0.11d was handed over to the Cottage Hospital: State Contributory Insurance was taking its place. A sombre footnote must be added. The Sales Ledgers often have an end-page for 'Labouring Men's Accounts' and one notices how many items are for coffins, especially for children – price 2/6d.

The Reeves family prospered in a modest way and went on doing well even when agriculture was starting on the downgrade and the competition of large-scale machinery was seeping in. It was probably the diversity of their business that saved them for so long. They catered for both animal-rearing and arable farming, for the Vale and the Plain. They made equipment for other purposes than farming. For instance, their water-carts were also used for road work. In August 1881 they actually sent 9 water-carts to Egypt and there is a famous story that Harold Bryant, the Works clerk, met up with one of them in Cairo during World War I. With good contacts in various parts of the country, Messrs Reeves collected agencies for the type of larger machine that would eventually stifle their own manufacturing work. In 1891, for instance, they were advertising McCormick's Improved New Steel Harvester and Binder – 'the King of Harvesters'. Above all, they maintained an essential repair service all round the district. Robert's two sons, Thomas and Henry, came into the business in due course, and after them, Thomas's two sons, Oswald and Nelson, and Henry's only son, Robert John. We know nothing about the education which Thomas and Henry, with his engineering skill, received, but all three boys in the next generation probably went to Keyford School, Frome, where John Whitaker's son, Philip, also went. The families spread themselves around the Works. Henry bought an older house, the Butts, which had been built by the Seagrams. Thomas built his house just across 'Butts Path' and called it the Beeches (now The Wilderness). A little lower, but still within sight of each other, Nelson built Lyndhurst (now Tynings), while in 1900 Henry Reeves built The Elms for his son Robert. If the Whitakers presided over the lower end of the village, the Reeves family tended to dominate the upper part and – rather untypically – the Seagrams at Bratton House, who were the real squires, played a lesser role.

Besides higher wages, the Iron Works brought certain social benefits to the village. In 1892 Messrs Reeves were instrumental in getting a telegraph service for the village. When the Westbury Gas and Coke Company were contemplating development, it was the guarantee of a certain consumption by the Iron Works that induced them to lay a three-mile pipe out to Bratton in 1904. So it was the first of this cluster of villages to become gas-minded. Three years later another 'modern benefit' was on its way – the telephone. Six subscribers had to be guaranteed: the doctor, the Iron Works and three Reeves households agreed, so the story goes, to pay the vicar's subscription between them in order to make up the six. The street-lighting scheme in Bratton was actually suggested by the Baptist minister, Rev. Carey Sage, who thought the dark lanes were detrimental to the moral life of young people. But it was promoted and largely run by Messrs Reeves. The first committee meeting

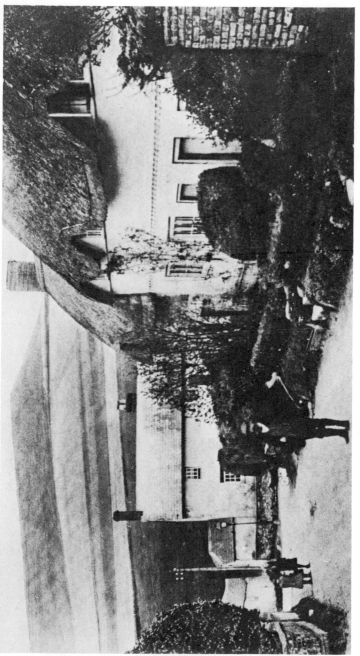

1. Bratton village, between the Plain and the Vale.

THE

Proteſtant Tutor,

Inſtructing YOUTH, and Others,

In the Compleat Method of

Spelling, *Reading*, and *Writing*

True Engliſh :

Alſo, Diſcovering to them the Notorious

ERRORS, Damnable DOCTRINES

and Cruel MASSACRES,

OF THE

Bloody Papiſts;

Which *ENGLAND* may Expect from a

Popiſh Succeſſor,

With Inſtructions for Grounding them in the

True Proteſtant Religion.

To which is Added,

The Preamble to the PATENT, for Creating the Electoral Prince of HANNOVER,
a Peer of this Realm, as Duke of CAMBRIDGE.

London, Printed and Sold by *B. Harris*, at the *Golden
Boar's-Head* in *Grace-church-ſtreet*. 1713.

---

2.   An eighteenth-century lesson book: propaganda with education.

3. The cult of curves in a hand-written arithmetic book used at Mr Whitaker's Academy.

4. Anna Jane Whitaker's embroidered map of Europe.

5. Dolls of various periods – and varying condition.

6. Toy carriage.

7. Trick puzzle, 'Courtship and Matrimony'. If turned upside down, the picture tells a different story.

8. Well-used kitchen utensils: (*left to right*) brass pestle and mortar; mahogany lemon-squeezer; brass roasting-jack; brown earthenware roasting pot; sugar cutters. (*Drawing by Mrs Deirdre Wheatley*).

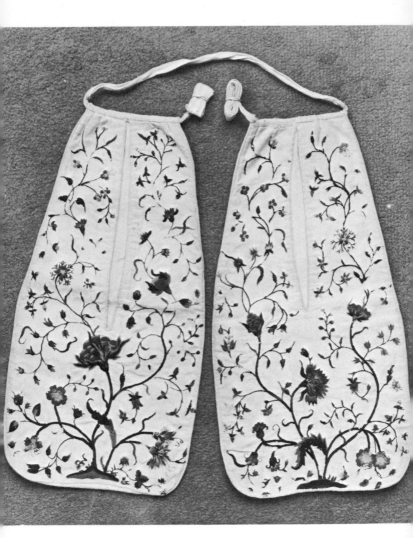

9.   Eighteenth-century sewing pockets.

10.   (*Opposite*) Ben Coleman the shepherd.

11. Sheep-shearing at Grant's Farm.

12. One of the forges at Bratton Ironworks.

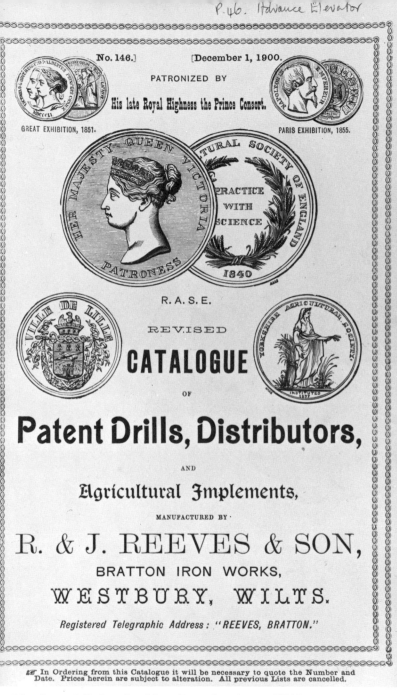

No. 146.] [December 1, 1900.

PATRONIZED BY

His late Royal Highness the Prince Consort.

GREAT EXHIBITION, 1851. PARIS EXHIBITION, 1855.

R. A. S. E.

REVISED

CATALOGUE

OF

Patent Drills, Distributors,

AND

Agricultural Implements,

MANUFACTURED BY

R. & J. REEVES & SON,

BRATTON IRON WORKS,

WESTBURY, WILTS.

Registered Telegraphic Address: "REEVES, BRATTON."

☞ In Ordering from this Catalogue it will be necessary to quote the Number and Date. Prices herein are subject to alteration. All previous Lists are cancelled.

13. A proud display of medals on Reeves' catalogue of 1900.

ESTBURY COAL DEPOT, WESTBURY RAILWAY STA

June 30

J Whittaker Esqe

Bought of ESAU NEWMAN.

Date.	Description of Coals.	Weight.			Price per Ton.		Am
		Tons.	Cwts.	Qrs.	s.	d.	£
63							
null	7 To Load Best Coal	2	0	0	13		1
11	To Load Walshoppe	1	6	0	do		
2	To Load Best Coal	1	2	0	do		
y	7 To Load '' ''	1	4	0	do		

14. The railway comes to Westbury. Billhead of 1863.

15. Association Meeting at Bratton Baptist Chapel, 1894.

16. Up-to-date equipment – even gas – on Hill's billhead of 1862.

17. Baptist worthies at the opening of Cheverill chapel: John S. Whitaker; A. Pocock; Rev. Charles Hobbs; Henry Reeves.

18.   Cycling-party at Stonehenge before the turn of the century.

19.   Family picnic at Grant's Farm, *c.* 1909. John Whitaker (*right*) has his youngest grandchild in his arms.

20.   Aunt Tillie (Matilda Brinkworth), *b*. 1835, *d*. 1939.

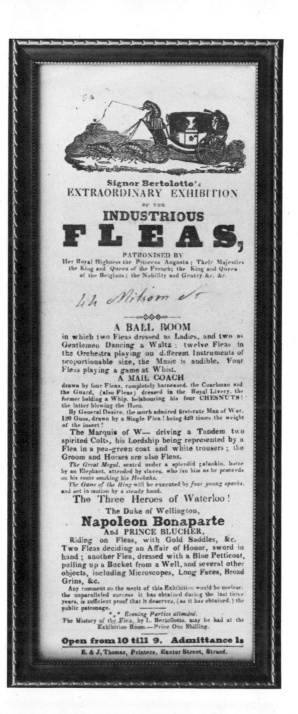

22. Robert Reeves marries Edith Whitaker: photograph taken at the Yew Trees in 1900.

21. (*Opposite*) Handbill of a Flea Show found wrapped round a bundle of letters.

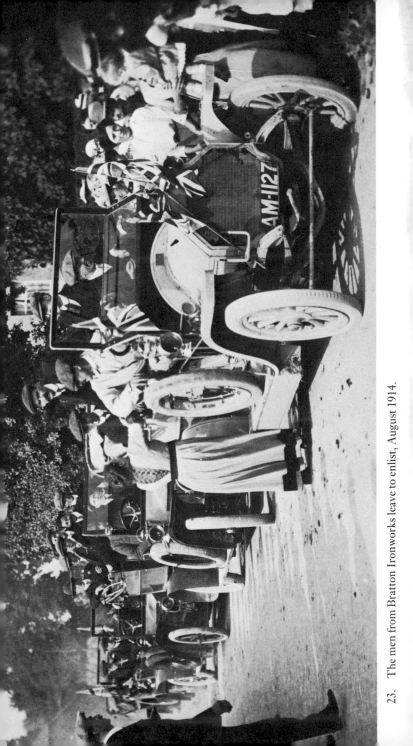

23.   The men from Bratton Ironworks leave to enlist, August 1914.

was held in their office in 1901, when Henry Reeves was made Treasurer and Robert John Secretary. Our information comes from a Minute Book among the Reeves papers. The scheme went forward, with collectors soliciting subscriptions from all the inhabitants. Messrs Reeves provided lamps at 24s each and cast-iron pillars at 28s each. They also provided the oil for the first lamps from 1901–4. These six were lighted from Michaelmas to Ladyday on the nights when there was no moon. The lamplighter, Edwin Whatley, got 6d a night. In 1905 the Gas Company's offer to light them at 17s 6d a lamp for about 120 nights was accepted. The little scheme seems to have worked pretty well, though people grumbled about subscribing if they did not have a lamp right outside their door. There would probably be other views now about the 'benefits' of the new housing which Reeves's brought indirectly. The White Horse Cottages and Spring Gardens were the first signs of worker demand for something more modern than the traditional cottages. So the Bratton of the early nineteenth century began to disappear and terraces of modest red-brick houses replaced the cottages, whereas in Edington the older housing was preserved until the era of cottage-conversion by the more affluent. So now, in reversal, Edington seems the more élitist community, whereas in the nineteenth century Bratton tended to look down on Edington as a poor neighbour. Finally, mention must be made of Bratton's own fire-engine, a little hand-manipulated affair which was housed for years in a corner of the Works and which the Works men operated. There are legends about that little fire-engine and its exploits. Once it galloped down to Dunge and put out a fire before the big Westbury engine could arrive on the scene. Once it missed the bus altogether because the man with its key was asleep in his taxi, waiting to fetch Works men from a late spree. It has found a final home in a Canadian museum where only a few years ago a one-time local resident was thrilled to meet it again.

Reeves's politics appear to have been generally Liberal from the mid-nineteenth century onwards, but not, perhaps, as consistently as the Whitakers'. In 1868 the *Wiltshire*

Times reported a meeting, held on Messrs Reeves's premises, which was addressed by the Conservative candidate, Mr J. L. Phipps. Robert Reeves was voted into the chair and explained disarmingly that he had been accustomed to stand on 'the other side of the house' and, indeed, he still considered himself a Liberal, but he found that the Liberals had become Radicals and the Conservatives had become Liberals (cheers). This change evidently met with disapproval, for among the correspondence we find E. M. Bratton: 'A man who acts the hypocrite and turns his coat in the manner this Baptist Deacon has, deserves censure.' A white silk handkerchief with a broad blue border long survived as a relic of this flutter among the Conservatives, but by the end of the century the Liberal candidate was secure in the patronage of the two presiding Bratton families. At the Liberal Dinner to celebrate John Fuller's victory in 1900, John Whitaker and Henry Reeves figured prominently and Robert Reeves made an 'eloquent little address'.

In the early twentieth century 'the Foundry' was still a central feature in Bratton (12). The Works clock was the village time-keeper and people set their watches and their meals by the Works whistle. The ting of its steam-hammer struck an up-to-date but not unpleasant note. Its activities fascinated the children: the boiler-man leaning out of his little window on the main street to get a breath of air, the whirring saw-mill eating through a tree-trunk, and especially the ceremony of bonding wheels. This took place in the yard. The men would heat the iron rim in a special wood fire, lift it, red-hot, with tongs, drop it over the wooden wheel positioned horizontally, and then run round with cans of water to prevent the wood catching fire, while sizzling steam rose and the iron bond slowly tightened. The team, by custom, got the wood ashes from the fire as their 'perks'. The great store of patterns was a wonder of exact craftsmanship in wood, preserving parts of machines that went back for years. So when some antique drill or harrow slowly rumbled in for repair they could always fit the old lady up with a new set of teeth, or whatever. Equally fascinating was the moulders' shop where these intricate patterns were translated into exquisite moulds in a mixture of sand and soot, superior to any sea-side castleing. To watch the molten steel being poured into these moulds, while white-hot metal bubbles fell around and sparks flew, was an awe-striking experience. Some of the men were great individualists and masters of their arts. When timber was to be bought, for instance, the expert carpenter, who would know at a glance what he wanted, would be taken to view the trees. The Iron Works was a meeting-place of old and new, of traditional village skills and attitudes and the advancing machine age. An episode just prior to World War I symbolizes the fact that they sometimes clashed. Messrs Reeves bought the first motor-car in the village and sent Joe Stiles away to learn how to drive it. He returned and drove round the village in triumph, everyone watching. But coming 'up street' he ran into one of Reeves's horse-drawn water-carts proceeding home at its own pace.

It would be a mistake, however, to view Robert and John Reeves and their descendants as just successful businessmen. Lacking the culture, and perhaps the introspective self-expression of the Whitakers, there is, none the less, ample evidence from the mid-century onwards of their religious fervour and devotion to the Baptist Church. Thomas Pepler Reeves's children were all baptized at the Parish Church, but the lease of 1817 already noticed suggests an early connection with the chapel. Robert Reeves joined the Baptist Church in 1836. In 1840 John Reeves was paying for a pew-sitting, although we do not know about his church membership. In 1840 Robert was already contributing to the minister's salary, in 1843 to the 'Chapel Case Fund' and in 1844 to the building of the British School. The level of subscriptions is interesting: to the Chapel Case Philip Whitaker gave £2 and Robert Reeves 5s, while to the grand effort needed for the British School the former contributed £25 and the latter £10. To an unnamed cause in 1858 Robert Reeves gave £25, his brother John £20, while the senior Whitakers contributed £35, £35 and £25. Meanwhile we find Robert Reeves signing in quite a good hand as auditor of the Chapel Trustees' Accounts and continuing to do so in succeeding years. In 1847 he was elected a deacon and from this time onwards he was involved in Sunday School affairs, buying the *Juvenile Herald* (missionary magazine) and 'reward books', and collecting money for treats and tea-meetings. Soon he was taking an active part in property maintenance and building projects. He was responsible for building the British School in 1844, while in the 'fifties and 'sixties the Trustees paid a number of bills to Messrs Reeves. Later, his son Henry prepared specifications for improvements at the Manse and acted as architect for Cheverell Chapel, while the Firm carried out the work on the new baptistry. By 1890 Robert, John and Thomas (in the next generation) were all trustees. When there was a crisis over the lease of land at the back of the chapel, it was John Reeves who this time put his hand in his pocket to redeem the freehold, not John Whitaker. When John Reeves died in 1893 he left £200 'to augment the minister's salary', although, apparently £25 of it was later used to bring gas to the chapel. Henry Reeves became a trustee at this point, and later chairman of the Trustees. At this period Whitakers and Reeveses between them managed the affairs of the Baptist community in a kind of grand alliance that becomes amusing as one meets it in minute after minute. For instance, J. S. Whitaker had for long managed the 'bread money' charity founded by Jeffery Whitaker. In 1891 the Trustees decreed that he should confer with one of their number about the recipients and promptly appointed Robert Reeves to this office which a Reeves held for a number of years following. The increasing affluence of the Reeves family is seen by comparing the level of subscriptions once more. Thus in 1894 the total Reeves contribution to the new baptistry came to £30, whereas John Whitaker, sole remaining Whitaker subscriber, gives very modestly: £1. In the locality as well as the Church the Reeves position is extended, so that we find Henry becoming chairman of the Parish Council and in 1912 a Justice of the Peace.

The involvement of the Reeves family in religious affairs was, however, not only at the level of practical ability and financial support. For the first generation there is only the evidence of one undated letter: from Robert Reeves to Joshua Whitaker, expressing sympathy – perhaps on the death of Joshua's mother – in genuinely pious terms and signed: 'I am My dear Brother Yours Truly in Jesus, Rob.Reeves'. In the next generation, Henry became an active local preacher, appearing in a Preachers Plan for 1897. But especially he devoted himself to the Sunday School, presiding over it as superintendent for many years. His son, Robert John, followed him in most of his offices. Not only the good order of chapel affairs but also the quality of religious loyalty in the Church owed something to three generations of the Reeves family.

7 At Bratton Farm

In the nineteenth century Whitaker territory was in the lower part of Bratton. Philip Whitaker and his wife, Anne, lived at 'Bratton Farm' (the present Manor Farm). When his son, Joshua, married Jane Saffery in 1835, they went to live at what had been the old Ballard homestead in Bury (still called Ballards). At the Yew Trees, on the Lower Road, Philip's brother, Thomas, resided with his wife Sophia (née Williams), through whom the house came back to the Whitakers again. Thomas died in 1857, leaving his wife to reign alone in a large house, since they had no children. Thus when Joshua's son, John, married Mary Brinkworth, 'Aunt Thomas' invited them to make their home at the Yew Trees. Here John Whitaker's children were brought up and here the youngest of them, Jane Saffery Whitaker, collected the family material on which much of this book is based.

The Whitaker ladies of the nineteenth century were mostly long-lived, surviving their husbands and leaving an impression of influential personalities in family and village affairs. They were prolific letter-writers and it is from her letters that Philip's wife Anne comes to life again. We first discover her as a young, unmarried woman of very definite views, writing to her sister, Maria Grace, in the early 1790s. Here she is, fulminating against politicians:

... the Mushroom Sages of the present day, whether their ambitious vanity enlists them under the Puissant Banner of Modern Patriotism or teaches them to emulate the sounding Titles of Loyal Subjects, Bullwarks of the State, Pillars of the Throne ... Miserable Nation that shall rest on such deceitful strength, and surely that seat of Majesty however glorious that shall be supported by such bruised reeds must experience an inevitable fate. Witness the unfortunate Grand Monarque.

How she enjoys the pomposity of words! But then Non-conformist sentiment comes uppermost and she sets the Crown Rights of the Redeemer in contrast to earthly ones: '*Our* King is not an Ahasuerus who hardly may be approached without danger yet we should do well in following the example of Esther ... The Golden Sceptre of Heavenly Mercy is sure to be extended to every emploring Supplicant'.

In courting her, Philip obviously had rivals, for she writes to her sister:

Last Saturday Mr. A. brought me from Town a very handsome Dunstable Bonnet and fashionable Cap call'd the Prince of Wales's Night Cap which together cost him 30 shillings, for my comfort they were both unexceptionable as to neatness and propriety. I endeavor'd to appear obliged and gratified but it was hard work. I had reason to be thankful for his attention but when I viewed these trifles as part of the price offer'd for my integrity I rejected them with scorn. I assure you I have some ground for these suspicions. I had a very narrow escape of a White Beaver with yellow Feathers ... which would have quite metamorphosed your Sister Anne ...

It would have been nice to see her in that White Beaver, but Philip Whitaker offered something more permanent than yellow feathers and they settled down to a stable married life in the low-roofed, rambling farmhouse at Bratton.

Anne believed in self-discipline; she wrote that it was necessary 'to preserve a suitable celerity of motion in the lazy Wheels of my corporeal frame' and also in her 'mental machine which ... frequently stands in need of friction to rub off the rust'. She certainly had no chance to rust after her marriage in body or in mind, for she had a family of seven boys and two girls to bring up, and lively ones at that. When there were only four boys, Alfred, Joshua, Edward and Philip, an Attwater relation described them as 'four lovely sensible engaging boys that was ever beheld at that age may their parents and friends be kept humble'. The girls, Emma and Anne, were born in 1805 and 1807. Then came John (1810), George (1811) and Edwin Eugene (1814). What a bustle when they were all at home! Yet Anne managed to keep up her correspondence, commenting in letters on sermons, books, public affairs and social welfare. She even ran a little school in Bratton which we know only from her own reference to it. Her main attention, however, was focused on her children. The eldest, Alfred, was sent in 1804 to be educated in Salisbury under the care of her sister, Maria Grace, now Mrs Saffery. Anne's pen flowed at great length in letters of warm affection but daunting language for a *six*-year-old:

My dear little Boy' (she wrote on Oct. 3rd, 1804)
A convenient opportunity presenting itself, I have sent you a present of such trifles in the eatable way as used to please people of your age and size, desiring at the same time that your Cousins may enjoy all due participation. The satisfaction of distributing your little treasures among your playfellows is one into which I wish you fully to enter ... A selfish person is at once the object of our contempt and pity ... You will perhaps think I have said a great deal on ... so trifling a circumstance as the disposition of a little Cake and fruit but I can assign a very sufficient reason – young as you are your Character is now forming – what you are at present you will doubtless very much resemble in future ... accept for yourself the tenderest love of a Mother who is perhaps too devotedly Yours, Anne Whitaker.

A year later she is wondering if she will find her little boy 'commenced Philosopher ... since I find he is engaged in reading Sturm's *Reflections*'. She wants him to be well-acquainted with English History: 'there is scarcely any species of ignorance that will let a Man down more in Company than an ignorance of Geography and History particularly that of his own Country'. In another letter she writes of her pleasure because his aunt has 'indulged him with a sight of Wilton House', where, she supposes, he was astonished and delighted with the beautiful works of art. 'Which of the Sister Arts do you most admire,' she asks, 'Sculpture or Painting?' And then she plunges in a big way:

But I have another question to ask – Which pleases you most on reflection – the various beauties of Nature so agreeably combined and diversified as they are at Stoke Park, or the labor'd but admirable productions of Art at Wilton House? I wish you to admire the ingenuity of Man but I hope when your taste and judgement are more form'd that you will give a decided preference to the sublime and exquisite works of Nature.

136

'As an expression of her views on education and on taste, these letters are fascinating, but it is almost impossible to conceive that they are addressed to a six/seven-year-old, yet it must be so, for they are clearly addressed and dated.

Anne is at her most eloquent when she feels that little Alfred must be reproved, as in a letter of 20 September 1805:

... when I consider the extent of your natural capacity and the skill and attention of your instructors, I am ready to anticipate a most agreeable and evident progress both in manners and information – but when I reflect on your prevailing errors: your natural indolence, your want of docility and a propensity too frequently discover'd to exchange one bad habit for another equally unpleasing, my fears are again excited ... Self-knowledge is the most important and useful of all knowledge ... Do you conceive the reason why I think so much of your faults ... it is because I love you so much – You hear how vigilantly our Government and our great Sea Officers watch over the movement of the French with a design to prevent them from doing us any injury – so do I watch over the predominant errors of your disposition I consider them as the cruel and inveterate enemies of my beloved Child who will if not observed, if not guarded against, both devise & accomplish his ruin ...

This, written in the year of Trafalgar, puts a different slant on the use of 'the French' in education – most usual was 'The French (or Boney) will get you!' Anne does not threaten, and ends in deep affection:

Good Night my dear Child, it will be many many years before you will be able to form any just idea of the love your Mother feels for you, who can scarcely think on your name without breathing some secret desire on your behalf ...

We have only a few elusive clues on the schooling of the other children. Perhaps they started at what remained of Jeffery Whitaker's Academy which ran until c. 1820. But some, at least, went to boarding school. 'My George has left me for Frome,' writes Anne disconsolately, 'and my little boy has commenced for the winter quarter at Mr. E's'. We do not know who Mr E. was or how Edward Eugene fared in his establishment, but George's prowess at Frome Grammar

School is celebrated in a treasured little pamphlet of verses to be recited on 15 June 1826. The subject was King David and George's long, spirited poem won a prize. The back page of the pamphlet tells us that George was in the top class of *Praepositi*. We also have a letter of 1829 from a Mr Scott of 'Gawcott' which must apply to Edward Eugene. He acknowledges payment of £35.3.0. for fees and reports to Philip Whitaker as follows:

If your son (to whom I beg to be kindly remembered) apply with even moderate diligence, he may not only maintain his ground, but make progress which will amply repay his exertion. Some young men labour hard and make no progress, but this will not be the case with him; and he may by *steady* and *moderate* reading do enough to secure his success at the university without pressing forward with such eagerness as to sacrifice his health. Many dangers and temptations must, of course, attend a young man in college. True religion is the only safeguard that can be relied on; next to that stands diligent study and where the two combine their influence ... the young academic will find delight and profit in that very place which is ruinous to thousands.

This gives us a good idea of the *milieu* in which the Whitaker boys were educated. It is disappointing that we know nothing about Joshua's education. We know his bookish habits and can imagine that he might be the one to hanker after the university, but perhaps – for all their love of learning – these staunch Nonconformist parents would not risk it. As for the girls, it seems likely that they went to their aunt's school in Salisbury, but the only two bits of evidence point elsewhere. One is an advertisement for Miss Vine's school, The Vineyard, at Westbury, where young ladies were boarded and educated at 20 guineas p.a., 'parlour pupils' being 'genteely accomodated'. The second is a letter of 1822 with a Worcester post-mark, addressed to 'Mr. Whitaker, Bratton' by M. M. Sherwood, relating to his daughter at boarding-school. Philip had requested that she should not study the Church of England catechism, and this reply promises that instead she shall 'devote her spare hours on the sabbath to sacred history'.

We have, however, quite a lot of their school books. Dictionaries and Latin Grammars were, of course, foundation stuff and a guide to Scriptural pronunciation must have helped them over many sticky places. Although only one tattered French Grammar survives, by 1815 Joshua was reading Fénélon's *Télémaque* in French. Nothing strikes the mind more than the intense belief at this period in the moral value of biography. A good example of this is seen in *The British Nepos; or Mirror of Youth: consisting of Select Lives of Illustrious Britons who have distinguished themselves by their virtues, talents, or remarkable advancement in life, with incidental practical reflections. Written purposely for the use of schools, and carefully adapted to the situations and capacities of youth* by William Mavor (2nd ed, 1800). In the frontispiece 'The Genius of Biography' directs 'British Youth' to the Temple of Honour, in the path of Industry and Perseverance. The two eager scholars at the foot of the mountain have to climb from Alfred the Great to John Howard before they reach the temple at the top. A broadening of the curriculum towards 'universal knowledge' is reflected in *A New Geographical, Historical, and Commercial Grammar and Present State of the several Kingdoms of the World* (1805). In two stout volumes it dealt with (amongst other things):

The Figures, Motions and Distances of the Planets, according to the Newtonian system ... The grand divisions of the Globe into Land and Water, Continents and Islands. The situation and extent of Empires, Kingdoms ... and Colonies. Their climate, Air, Soil, Vegetable Productions, Metals ... The Birds and Beasts peculiar to each country ... The History and Origin of Nations ... The Genius, Manners, Customs and Habits of the People. Their language, learning, Arts ... The chief cities, Structures, Ruins and artificial Curiosities ...

This, we remember, was the period when young men were seeking their fortune in the east and bringing home those 'curiosities'. The attraction of the orient appears in one of Edward Eugene's books: *China: A Dialogue for the use of schools: being Ten Conversations between a Father and His Two Children*, by an Anglo-Chinese (1824). 'The young mind should early be led to view all mankind as one family', says the preface, and right at the start the queer habit of the

139

Chinese in wearing long tails is rationally explained to 'Mary Rebecca'. The new science is represented by *A Grammar of Chemistry* (4th ed, 1810), with pictures of experiments as a substitute for lab. work, while we find the young Whitakers imbibing their literature from two copies of *The Speaker* which gave them their 'gems' first in short sentences and then under headings such as Narrative Pieces, Didactic Pieces, Pathetic Pieces. The girls were thoroughly catered for in Dr Gregory's *A Father's Legacy to His Daughters* (1801), with a charming frontispiece of three daughters seated in a row. He instructs them on Conduct, Amusements, Love, Marriage and so forth, revealing incidentally a typical male prejudice:

I have no view by these advices to lead your tastes; I only want to persuade you of the necessity of knowing your own minds, which, though seemingly very easy, is what your sex seldom attain on many important occasions in life, but particularly on this of which I am speaking (marriage) . . .

They also had T. Gisborne's *Enquiry into the Duties of the Female Sex* which was an all-purposes manual on women's education, and *Utility or Sketches of Domestic Education* (1815) in which a little of everything was learnt through stories and conversations.

Something on a more credible level than Sturm's *Reflections* is Alfred's model geometry book in which he laboriously copied angles and triangles. Joshua's beautiful hand-writing must have been formed on these pattern writing-books, and the flourishes which all the Whitakers loved would have been practised on the enscrolled angel face which adorns this copy:

When health forsakes us, and when friends are few,
When friends are faithless, or when foes pursue,
'Tis this (i.e. religion) that wards the heart or stills the smart,
Disarms affliction or repels its dart.

Most curious among these children's exercise-books is a set of pictures on English History. Each page carries a group of emblems and dates representing major events and people from 54 B.C. onwards. Among some puzzling early ones we recognize Arthur's Round Table, Cnut's throne beside the waves and the death of William Rufus. The exercise, no doubt, was to identify the symbols and then copy the whole page which one of the children has done quite competently. By this pleasant method they proceeded through English history, enlivened by such suggestive images as a skeleton pointing to a map of Asia for 1349, a barrel of Malmsey for 1478 and red and white roses sprouting from a crown for 1485. We end with a page on famous men and events in 1800 and two triumphal pillars representing Nelson and Wellington. As a visual aid this must have been highly successful.

They must have been a lively crowd when they were all at home for the holidays. There were large family parties. Anne, writing near Christmas to Mrs Saffery to request a visit from her daughter, Jane, says: 'My great boys will be home shortly and will be glad of the addition of females to their society'. (No wonder Jane married her first cousin, Joshua). There were winter evenings when they sat round the log fire guessing New Puzzles (published in 1801), cards which set you picture-conundrums, like a large red hat (hatred) and a cat inside an O (Cato), or playing with a set of Animal, Vegetable, Mineral cards. Education was never far off and so we discover in a little leather trunk slips of cards with nouns and adjectives to be matched up (e.g. Rugged – Mountain), and a set of moral questions and answers, in which, for instance, to the question: What is it makes a death-bed peculiarly terrible to rich men? you must find the answering card with an anecdote about Dr Johnson and David Garrick.

No doubt Anne read to the little ones from some of the lively little books which survive. There are *Rural Scenes or a Peep into the Country for Good Children* (1805) and its companion *City Scenes* (1809). Here the imagination was startled and the heart wrung by vivid pictures of the poor:

The Garret. What a dismal place! However, it may do us good for once to see such a wretched sight. Let us wait at the door and observe them. See this poor mechanic and his starving family. His hands are so benumbed with cold that he can hardly

141

grind his rusty tools. His wife and children seem stupified with cold and hunger; they sit motionless and appear given up to despair. There is not a spark left in the grate, and the last morsel of bread has been devoured.

Then the moral is driven home relentlessly: 'let us remember this unhappy family and learn to be grateful and content'. The virtue of honest toil is also inculcated:

The Match Boy. This little boy has been used from his infancy, to hunger, thirst and raggedness; . . . He works hard and lives hard too; and therefore, for his industry at least, is a good example for those little gentlemen, or great gentlemen either, who consume many times more than he does, without doing any good by their existence.

Moral education is tackled by an ingenious method in another of their books, *The Mother's Fables in Verse*, 'designed through the medium of amusement to convey to the Minds of Children some useful precepts of virtue and benevolence'. Here various children do or say foolish things and are reproved by Mamma's fables. Here is a sample:

The Self-Conceited Little Man
If I were king and I could rule,
I'd not go back again to school,
Mamma, I've read my books all through
And now I must have something new . . .
Sometimes I make the scholars stare
For I know more than any there . . .
Well, Edward, then I do suppose
Your education here must close,
Since you're beyond your master's reach
And nothing's left for him to teach.
But, Edward, if you did not know
'Tis ignorance persuades you so! . . .
O Edward, hide that foolish face,
And from a fable learn your place.

And then there follows a story of a conceited young partridge who flew too high.

As they grew up, one member of the family, at least, thought they argued too much. Edward writes to Alfred:

I would advise a total abstinence from all controvertible subjects and more especially from those which I was sorry to find

142

had got into black and white in the shape of epistolary correspondence. Differences of opinion I think among relations cannot be kept too much out of sight, for when they come to be clearly defined and understood they will always . . . produce an unpleasant separating feeling.

But they also played music together. We have the actual flutes they played: one of ivory, a rarity by Thomas Cahusac, dated 1780–1800, and two of boxwood, dated between 1800 and 1820, by Goulding and Astor respectively. Joshua was probably a flautist for in 1821 he bought *Wheatstone's Collection of 32 Popular Dances, Waltzes etc. for the Flute or Violin.* Alfred played the bass viol and to accompany they probably used an upright piano which can be dated to the early nineteenth century by its brass inlaid trade-mark: 'John Broadwood & Sons. Makers to his Majesty and the Princesses'.

With their background, however, it is not surprising that these boys took chiefly to the pen to express themselves. Alfred and Edward went to London to be articled to a solicitor in Gray's Inn Road, and the young men's letters to their mother reveal much about family life. Boxes of laundry and other things are sent up from Bratton and in 1817 Alfred writes that 'The shirts were not starched near so well this time, so that they would not wear so long. I hope the next will be stiffer. I have a deficiency of pocket handkerchiefs – had I better get a silk one?' He thinks 3 shirts, 3 cravats, 3 pairs of stockings and 3 sets of underwear will be sufficient each week. Sometimes he gives an account of his expenditure and grumbles once about the additional expense of mourning clothes. But he writes about less domestic matters too. He visits the British Museum, but finds it all fossils and stones and not very interesting. He asks to have his bass viol since he has found someone who plays the flute and 'I miss my music very much'. Obviously he develops an interest in politics. When he first arrives in London in 1817, he describes the political scene in some detail, concluding: 'All the opposition papers except Cobbett's speak against Hunt and revolution.' On 25 June 1817, he tries, but fails, to get into Westminster Hall for the 'State Trial', and sends home three newspapers because he thinks they will be interested. Dovetailing very nicely, we find in Bratton five numbers of *Bell's Weekly Messenger*, between 1817 and 1823. Lining an old trunk, there also came to light a fragment of newspaper reporting Queen Caroline's trial. Was Alfred not responsible for these? As for Edward, we have already quoted his strictures on arguing, but he was capable of quite violent views himself. 'I have just been looking', he writes to Alfred on one occasion, 'at Southey's ridiculous if not prophane Poem ("vision of Judg.") . . . I shall never like him more'.

In 1820, on his 54th birthday, the three younger boys presented their father with original poems – no doubt urged on by their literary mother. John, aged ten, was perhaps not very clever. He cannot always make his verse scan, but he is honest:

They think I'm a booby and do not know more
Than twice one makes two and twice two make four
But I know very well there is nothing so clever
As to have a dear Father who will love one ever
And who though we're naughty will always forgive
And do nothing but good to us while he shall live.

George, aged nine, was already aspiring to literary distinction:

If my little brother pay
In artless strains the votive lay
How can I forbear to say
What I wish on this blest day . . .
O that Israel's God may shed
Rich blessings on thy reverend head
And long preserve the brittle thread
Which keeps thee from the silent dead.

Little Edwin Eugene, aged six, produced this – perhaps with his mother's help:

Though I am a little boy
Dear Papa I wish you joy
For this day when it is o'er
Mamma says makes you fifty-four
This seems a great while to me

144

> But I hope you yet will see
> Many happy days and years.

Perhaps Anne had a special feeling for her 'Benjamin', since we have a touching little poem written 'To my little son Edwin Eugene on his birthday, June 22nd 1829'.

One of the most surprising and entertaining discoveries was some numbers of an original magazine entitled *The Budget*, first issued on Friday, 1 July 1831 and brought to an all-too-rapid decease on 22 July. It is a holiday frolic, written in high good spirits. In the first number the editor asks for contributions:

I should not wish that the present number should be taken as a sample – articles of a more serious nature are wanting in consequence of my incapacity to furnish them ... I shall receive them most gladly from others and will take care that they shall not be put in awkward juxtaposition with anything of a frivolous nature. Nevertheless I should wish the production to retain a light and unpretending gaiety, as I conceive that by so doing it will run much less risque (sic) of miserable failure.

There are imaginary conversations, riddles, titbits. Among the advertisements are:

Wanted immediately. For family use a dilution of the book of Psalms. Want situation in a Gentleman's family, Two geraniums in bloom. For particulars enquire at the hot bed. The Country would be preferred. Wanted immediately – a cook without incumbrance. Apply at the Budget office.

The second number ridicules sentimental poetry in a mock review of 'Verses to Nightingale, lamenting her absence' purporting to be published in the new *Baptist Miscellany*:

... Lackadaisical indeed he must have been to have blubbered solus among the 'hallowed shades' but we should say Lackadaisical to a fault to have gone deliberately home – stalked into the parlour – called to his youngest for pen and ink – and spoiled a nice sheet of paper ... Lackadaisical indeed not to have observed the loud tittering of the family when the aforesaid youngest peeped over his shoulder and reported to brothers and sisters that papa was writing to a nightingale.

Was this a skit on a recognizable family scene? We then

plunge into a splendid mock-heroic poem, 'The Expedition',
recounting a trip to Erlestoke, turned back by rain:

With many a weary step and many a groan
The Charioteer ascends his proper throne; . . .
Seated aloft he guides an awful car
Filled with embattled forms and female war.
There each ascended wrapped in shining arms
Whilst each ascent the groaning steeds alarms
Still more and more upon their aching backs
The weight descends – the steaming harness cracks
Till the sage driver o'er the coursers' head
Lent the long lash and the swift chariot fled.
Along the plain its rapid wheels were rolled,
Bristled the dreadful arms and blazed the gold,
But darkness came and fled the cheerful ray
Clouds upon clouds shut out the source of day.
When thus the seer – 'In vain – in vain we rise
To break the purpose of the hostile skies' . . . (they turn back)
But oh despair not – still the day shall come
O'er eastern hills shall break a cloudless sun . . .
Again the wondering tribes of earth from far
Shall watch the progress of our coming war
I see the (?) coach – its wheels are rushing fast
Thy walls O! Stoke – have shaken as they passed,
That day thy children shall remember well,
And sire to son the wondrous story tell
How on thy peace the joyous tumult broke
And Bratton poured in dazzling pomp on Stoke.

The third number includes an essay 'Of Eating and Drink-
ing Superstitions' and 'Proceedings of the Society for the
Suppression of Cats'. It also contains the following gem,
'Prayer at the Holcombe National School':

Beheld the bigot's cell – the infant knees
Hard pressing on the rough uneasy floor –
Eyes – all contracted with a nervous squeeze,
Hands – clenched as hands were never clenched before.

Meantime the mistress stalks the chamber round
Arranges duly every errant thumb,
Rebukes with savage speech and darksome frown –
Till all alike are blinded, stiff and dumb.

Those eyes will open! and that hand must part
From its small fellow's close embrace. For lo!

146

A fly upon his front has fixed its dart.
'Crush it!' cries Passion, Wisdom answers 'No' . . .

But hark! their tongues are loose – they join the song
Loud and louder break their voices out,
Their gladsome lungs each syllable prolong
Till comes the great Amen with joyous shout.

And this surprising piece of irreverence is capped by the following:

On Sunday next two Sermons will be preached at the Baptist Meeting-house by Durtee Crater – a Convert from the Hottenpot Faith – he will introduce many important particulars respecting this eccentric nation of peculiar interest to the Christian world. We are authorised to say that this descendant of Hottenpot has not been guilty of any gross immorality for some years past and is therefore fully qualified to exercise the duties of a Christian pastor. We respectfully inform the public That Durtee Crater has after much solicitation given up the Hottenpot method of hairdressing.

The final number heralds 'the end of the Bratton season' and finishes with the 'Dying Speech of the Budget', deserted by its friends and done to death by prussic acid. This is an astounding production for a pious Nonconformist family and says much for the tolerance with which Philip and Anne viewed the capers of their young. Who was the author of these irreverent skits? I think it was the little-known George. He has already appeared as the literary member of the family who wins a verse-prize at school, and we shall later meet him helping his cousin and sister-in-law, Jane, with another magazine, *The Village Rill*. We know something about his later education and the unexpected fact that he eventually became Provost of Trinity College, Toronto.

Though starting life so energetically, much child-bearing must have wearied Anne. After Philip's death in 1847, she went to live in an unidentified house called Underhill, where she kept in touch with her children and grandchildren, by letter in the case of the distant ones. There is much about illness in these later letters, but also much expression of sincere piety as she neared the end of the road. She gradually fades out of our sight, although she did not die until 1865,

147

nearly 20 years after her husband, and outliving her two eldest sons.

Anne and her sister, Maria Grace, almost repeat the pattern of Caroline Attwater and her sister, Jane, in the previous generation. After Anne's marriage, Maria Grace came to stay with her at Bratton Farm. There one of the most dynamic Nonconformist ministers in the west of England – the Rev. John Saffery of Brown Street Baptist Church, Salisbury – came courting her. We have a revealing letter from Philip Whitaker to Saffery reporting on the state of play with his sister-in-law. Eventually she accepted him, they were married in Bratton Parish Church in 1799 and she returned to Salisbury to play an impressive role, backing up her husband in his manifold activities and running a highly successful girls' boarding-school which drew pupils from all over the south of England. We have grateful letters from former pupils and parents and occasionally news of their circumstances, as in the case of Sarah Dear who is earning a salary of £25 p.a. residing with a lady of the highest piety and good manners. Amongst her papers is one setting out the conditions under which a governess ('the Lady') is to look after two girls:

She has a large bedroom and a 'Dressing Cabinet' to herself, but one of the children must sleep with her. Parlour breakfast is at 8 a.m., but before this the Lady must superintend dressing and hair-plaiting, and also take her turn in conducting family prayers. Morning school is in the schoolroom, and after lunch the Lady accompanies the children in walking or playing in the garden, till dressing for dinner at 3 p.m. Then needlework till Tea. This is at 5, after which some light exercise of the Body or Mind for the children till 8 p.m. when they go to bed (again supervised by the Lady). She sits with the family till 9 p.m. when the Tray comes in with the Servants to family worship. At 10 everyone may retire to his or her own room.

The parallel with Jane Attwater appears in her literary gifts. Mrs Saffery achieved quite a reputation as a minor poetess and we still have her purple velvet copy of her *Poems on Sacred Subjects*, published in 1834. More interesting still is the unpublished volume of her *Lyra Domestica*, handwritten in her own fine small hand and illustrated by delicate little pen drawings. She remained in Salisbury after her husband's death in 1825 until her daughter Jane married Joshua Whitaker in 1835. She then gathered together all the Saffery papers and came to Bratton where she lived until her death in 1858. Many of her poems were written in Bratton and the poetess in their midst must have stimulated a new generation of Whitakers to literary efforts. In the *Lyra Domestica* we have moved a long way from eighteenth-century classicism. These are charming, whimsical and intimate verses written for family and friends – for a birthday, or an album, to a friend, on a death – some light, some serious. She addresses verses 'To Margretta Macdonald for whom I could not find a flower on a winter-day due to her for personating the Lady in Comus' and composes 'On a Butterfly taken asleep on Sunday', with a charming little picture to go with it. Accompanied by a neat sketch of scissors, thimble, etc., we have the whole philosophy of charitable bazaars expressed most gracefully:

Addressed to the Contributors of an Infant School Bazaar
... At stately hall or cottage door
    Sweet charity prefers her plea
    Just as the Bee collects her store
    From flowers of high or low degree.

    But chiefly from the World apart
    Where leisure claims the skilful hand
    And Culture guides the thoughtful heart
    She seeks her tributary band.

    Ladies, we thank you in her name
    For all your graceful works of Skill
    'Twas hers these gentle arts to claim
    'Tis yours her purpose to fulfil ...

A quaint little verse 'To an affectionate Domestic in the family of a friend with Spectacles once my own' begins:

Kind hearted Maiden, deem not I advise
Ought that might look like seeing through my eyes.

Queen Victoria's accession inspires several poems, but the most delightful group are the poems for children, including one 'To a Child one year old with her first alphabet'. For

Rosalie Anne Green on her fifth birthday, 6 March 1839, she wrote:

Dear frolic Rosalie, one word
In token of this birthday meeting
Don't fear – I will not be absurd
And teaze thee with a formal greeting.

In truth I might as well prepare
Thy Pussy for a cloak and bonnet
As meet thy pretty gleeful air
With grave salute of sober sonnet.

The tail-piece of 'Pussy in a coat and bonnet' is delicious. Rosalie belonged to a family of relations at Holcombe who often exchanged visits with the Bratton Whitakers.

Jane Saffery – Mrs Joshua Whitaker – comes across the years as something of a *Grande Dame*. She was a prodigious writer and receiver of letters. We still have her polished rosewood writing-desk, with 'Jane' inscribed on a brass plate on the lid, and the surviving letters she received fill a large box. Earlier ones are on large sheets, folded, addressed on the back and sealed; later ones are in small envelopes with charming little motifs on the flap. When separated, she wrote almost daily to a close friend, Miss Salter ('Salter' to the family) and they expected letters to arrive quickly. She attracted admirers: before marriage one of these in particular wrote at great length from the island of St Helena, while an intriguing find was a later effusion to 'Mrs Whitaker' in the form of a chivalric poem about Sir Conrad and a maiden with deep blue eyes, written on notepaper with blue forget-me-nots on it and accompanied only by the card of a Mr John Bullar of Lincoln's Inn. Her brother Philip Saffery wrote constantly to 'my precious, precious sister'. She pursued books and culture ardently, visited friends and relations all round the country, yet managed to run an Infant School in Bratton and dominate the village scene. We have now moved into the era of Photography and are able to view her, dignified and silk-gowned, face framed in ringlets, seated reading at a table – characteristically.

Her reading notes of the 1820s – in an imposing vellum-bound volume – give us a remarkable glimpse into the reading tastes of an intelligent young lady. She is reading about the continental scene, starting with *Scenes and Reflections during a Ramble in Germany* by Major (blank) whom she criticizes for 'skimming over the surface of things – seldom seeking after the why and the wherefore'. As regards the matter, she is particularly touched by the melancholy devotion of the King of Prussia to his dead wife ('This in an absolute Monarch is very touching'), and the way the Elector of Hesse consoles himself for the loss of the larger part of his dominion by leading his own orchestra ('tho' some may call it *unmanly* – or at least *unprincely* I could not help sympathising'). How nicely she catches British prejudices in these remarks. Next she sets out to read Mme de Stael on German literature, and a 'very masterly work by Mr Russell', *A Tour in Germany and . . . the Austrian Empire . . .* 1821–3. Here she starts with a long extract on the King of Prussia and the late Queen Louise, because 'it places the character of the Germans in a very amiable light'. She wishes all kings were like Frederick ('*Oh si sic omnes*', she sighs) and compares him to George III. Her pages of extracts on government and economics, etc., include exclamations of horror at the police system in the *free* country of Austria under Prince Metternich. Having read Russell's two volumes twice through, Jane sums up her judgement in a four-page review, commending Mr Russell as 'a very superior man'. The Court of Weimar draws her enthusiasm particularly, with its literary coterie which included Schiller and Goethe, and this moves her to extol the effects of good literature 'in doing away with those narrow-minded and illiberal prejudices which a want of culture ever betrays'. What passionate disciples of culture these literary ladies were. After all this she turned to science – to Francis Bacon, to an introduction to Euclid and a Table of the Sciences.

Even pocket-books were designed to cultivate taste. Poole's 'Elegant Pocket Album' for 1824 probably belonged to Jane and the 1828 edition certainly did. These contained 'A Variety of useful information Embellished with twelve Views and five Portraits of Interesting Characters'. The engravings of castles and mansions are delightful, while the

151

'characters' are an extraordinary mixture, ranging from Mrs Fry to the Duke of Angoulême, and Maria Edgeworth to the Duke of York. Popular dances are included, with 'The Der Friedschutz Quadrilles for the Pianoforte or Harp' reproduced in facsimile in the 1828 number. All kinds of surprising items turn up in these and other similar productions which probably belonged to Jane. She could learn about 'Travels in the Subterranean Regions of the Globe', or 'The Enormous Appetite of a Siberian Child', or enjoy the tale of 'Dr Bossy and Richardson's Parrot'. Enigmas and charades for home amusement find a place and popular music is important. For 1829, indeed, she had 'The Harp, or New Musical Pocket Book', featuring Handel's Monument and his life at the beginning. Here practical information is reduced to a minimum, while the range of verses, extracts, engravings and music gives a vivid idea of the tastes to be cultivated in polite society. T. W. Lloyd's 'Valentine and Original Hastings Quadrilles', as performed at the promenade, are reproduced in facsimile. The very flavour of the elegant danceroom is communicated. Lloyd advertises himself as professor of music and dancing at the Athenaeum of Arts and Sciences, 'where thirty Professors and Female Teachers give Private or Class Lessons in every Branch of the Arts, Sciences, Languages and Accomplishments to the Genteel Class of Society'.

We have an unusual opportunity to picture the bride settling in at Bratton, for on 29 July 1835 Jane wrote to her 'Sweet and precious Mother' describing her arrival at her new home. She is already in love with Wiltshire's 'fine hills and fertile valleys' and finds 'many soothing influences here – Nature with her ever cheering aspect – dearer still human sympathy and kindness – dearest of all, I need scarcely say, the companionship of my dear Joshua'. She describes her welcome as a 'homish one' and gives amusing glimpses of their varied reception 'from Dr Seagram's judiciously worded desire that we might have everything we *ought* to wish for ourselves, to old Thomas Callaway's more definite and emphatic prayer, "I wish 'ee peace" – other rustic salutations have been very grateful to my heart ... a poor woman assured me I should have a "downright good husband" ... She had been accustomed to say that if Joshua married he ought to have an angel for a wife! ... We have been performing ceremonies this week and I am happy to think that "sitting up days" are now closed, though they have not been particularly appalling. All the Bratton coterie have called ... We have only now, I suppose, to expect straggling visitors from a distance.'

Once settled at Ballards Jane could hardly pursue the opportunities offered by the metropolis, but she kept the flag of culture flying. Soon after her marriage she started a lending library which was 'an unparalleled success', in her own words (scribbled in the 1829 'Harp' which she used for 1836). She tells us that new subscribers were coming in and she regularly records 'attended library'. She went to lectures in Devizes on Egypt and Palestine, and read books 'with Mamma' or 'with the Circle', implying the existence of a literary group in Bratton.

In her diary for 1849 she gives us a list of books read which include the Hulsean Lectures for 1846 by R. C. Trench, Mme D'Arblay's Diary, Milman's *Fall of Jerusalem* and *The Last of the Plantagenets*. At a humbler level, she started what became known as 'Mrs Joshua Whitaker's Infant School'. We shall return to this later.

But rural life had its attractions too, and these ladies walked much, more than we often think they did. Jane records walking with 'dear Mamma' or with Joshua, to 'Eddington', to Westbury, up to the White Horse before breakfast, in the fields to hear nightingales. She picks primroses and violets and goes with Mamma to see the lambs. Social life is continuous, drinking tea or dining with the other Whitaker households, receiving or paying calls, entertaining relations. These seem to pour in, during 'the season' especially. There were expeditions and picnics, even 'a rustic feast on the lawn'. They really were gadabouts, these ladies. Jane's letters and diaries are full of visits to relations at Bodenham, Salisbury, Holcombe, Bath and elsewhere. Trips to Trowbridge, Frome and Devizes are mentioned as a matter of course. Visits to London are quite frequent, even before the advent of the railway. It gives one a start to re-member that all this travelling was done by coach, carriage or on horseback. Their surviving wicker-work cases and light dress-baskets remain to witness to the mobility of these constantly visiting ladies. In London, Mrs Joshua was just as energetic, walking from Peckham to the City and out to Bethnal Green, going to hear famous preachers, calling on friends and relations, as well as doing the inevitable shopping.

Joshua Whitaker preserved all his bills, carefully dock-eted in yearly bundles, so we can take the lid off the Ballard household, as it were, to see how it was ordered. Groceries came from Wilkins of Westbury and Brodribb of War-minster. Wilkins was also Draper, Hatter, Hosier, etc. Sugar in 1836 still came in a loaf of 17 lb at 11d per lb. There was much buying of spices, currants, 'muscatells' and so on, which suggests many puddings. In December they bought 'French Plumbs' and Turkey figs. It seems that they did not bake much bread at home, for there is a regular account with R. Snelgrove, baker in Bratton. On the other hand, meat bills are few: one with T. C. Smith in 1837 came to only £7.2.9½d for nine months; they must have relied on home supplies. Tea, coffee, cocoa often came from S. Ben-nett of Bath, while they bought sherry, brandy, port and other wines from William Griffith of Frome or Giddings & Ellis in Devizes. Perhaps because of his recent marriage, Joshua started to re-furbish the house. W. Taylor of West-bury, Painter, Plumber and Glazier, re-decorated the par-lour for about £5, while Chapman, a stonemason, put in a new marble chimney-piece for about the same amount. For furniture they shopped at N. Newton's in Bath, 'General and Fancy Cabinet Maker. Manufacturer of Writing Desks, Ladies Work and Trinket Boxes and Dressing Cases of every description'. Joshua had his best clothes made and repaired by Stephen Gishford who supplied him in 1835–6, amongst other things, with a swan-down waistcoat (13s), a best black coat (£2.18.0) and a brown frock-coat at the same price. Humble repairs were done by Robert Stevens who would alter trousers for 9d and mend a coat for 4d – he could only make his mark when receipting the bill. Similarly, the high-class shoemaker was Sloper of Devizes, but Nathaniel Snelgrove would mend footwear for anything between 2d and 1s 8d.

Bill-heads form a fascinating social study. Even country tradesmen at this time were aware of the far-flung British Empire. William Payne of Warminster, 'Dealer in China, Glass and Earthenware', features Britannia seated on a wharf with sailing-ships departing to the ends of the earth with her china treasures, and a belching kiln behind her. S. Taylor of Westbury has fascinating engravings on his bill-head: on one side, a tea-clipper, a Chinaman and cases advertising 'Teas of the first quality'; on the other, a curious chemical scene with the caption 'Genuine Horse and Cattle Medicines'. Another attractive bill-head is that of J. K. Saunders, Watch and Clock-maker of Warminster, which figures Britannia and her lion, with a pair of balances and the motto: 'Be just and fear not'. An invaluable tradesman was R. E. Vardy of Warminster who in 1836 was chemist as well as stationer, bookseller and bookbinder. By 1841 S. L. Vardy is there as chemist and druggist, offering 'Every Galenical and Pharmaceutical Preparation of the purest quality. Teeth carefully extracted. Prime well-seasoned Woodville and Havannah Cigars'.

Many of these were old established tradesmen. But the bills tell a story of both continuity and change. In 1837 Joshua was sending goods to London by 'Expeditious Fly Waggons – From Frome to London in 46 Hours'. By 1863 he was buying coal from the Westbury Coal Depot at the railway station and receiving a bill with a delightful little toy train at the top (14). The new technology was also reaching the ironmongers. One of the most informative bill-heads is that of P. L. Hill, Furnishing and General Ironmonger of Silver Street, Trowbridge, whose bill of 1862 tells us all sorts of things. He offers 'Baths on sale or hire' and shows an up-to-date kitchen range to heat the water. He sells powder, shot and caps which, strangely, appear above a new-style canopied bed which has replaced the four-poster. There are 'experienced workmen on the premises' mending kettles and teapots. He proclaims himself a Bell-hanger, Locksmith, and – most important – Gas-Fitter (16). But this was 50 years before gas reached Bratton.

The ladies usually had their own accounts. They bought materials in quantities to be made up by local dressmakers. In 1838 old Mrs Saffery was buying 13 yds of 'Black Gro.' for £1.11.5d and 12 yds of flannel at 1s 10d per yd. But she was extravagant on trimmings, for 6 yds of fringe cost her 5s and 'shawl-bordering, bobbin-lace, border net and ribbon' ran up the bill a lot. She bought her stockings in quantity: nine pairs at 1s 9d a pair. On the same bill her daughter, Mrs Joshua, was buying two sheets for 8s and blue print at $5\frac{1}{2}$d per yd. Another of her bills, with James, Fox and Co. of Devizes, shows similar shopping: materials, trimmings (including Brussels lace), needles, pins, buttons, etc. Perhaps Joshua paid for the extravagances, since bills from Charles Roach, Devizes, are addressed to him, but contain items for both. An 1837 bill has '1 Rich Silk Stock', but also a parasol at 15s 6d. By 1855 Roach was extending his business, advertising 'Wholesale and Retail Warehouse for London and Paris Hats, Furs, Hosiery, Gloves, etc. etc. Funerals Furnished'. The 'Ariel' and Satin ties on this bill were no doubt for Joshua, and the cloth caps; kid gloves, perhaps, too, and handkerchiefs (silk at 1s 9d and 'Monteith' at 1s – quite expensive). Undoubtedly, on Mrs Whitaker's account were '1 Imitation Sable Queen Boa and Cuffs, 1 fine Paris Hat, Braganza flower cloth' and 6 pairs of Ladies Merino Hose. But whose was the '1 Brown Sham Hat 3s 6d'?

A large packet of funeral mourning-cards and another bill from Roach bear witness to the solemn importance of such occasions in the family. (We remember that Alfred grumbled at the cost of mourning clothes.) Large numbers of relations and friends gathered for the funeral and the minister was expected to 'improve the occasion' by preaching at length on lessons to be learnt from the life and death of the departed. The physical signs of grief were the deep mourning clothes which everyone assumed and the heavily black-edged paper and envelopes which the bereaved used. The custom still survived of presenting the nearest mourners with gloves and scarves for the funeral. So, in 1838, Roach presented his account – with a tactfully muted bill-head showing a funerary monument – to the executors of the late Miss Whitaker (Anna Jane). He lists all the 38 ladies for whom he provided 'best funeral Kid Gloves at 3s a pair'. They include – besides Whitakers – Safferys, Seagrams and Blatches. Similarly with '33 Gents. Ditto at 4s'. There were also 12 pairs of Women's Silk Gloves at 2s a pair. Were these for the servants?

Jane Whitaker's first child, Anna, was born in the year of Anna Jane's death, and after this the children came in steady succession: John (1840), Joshua Cecil (1842), Mary Grace (1844), and Alfred Thomas (1846). There was less and less time for literary flourishes. But she had, at least, seized the chance before the children were upon her, and in collusion with her cousin, George Whitaker, had produced, in 1836, *The Village Rill* (a more genteel periodical than the boisterous *Budget*) of which numbers 1 and 2 survive, 'printed at the Alfred Press, White Horse Valley'. Notice, Anglo-Saxon attitudes again. The first number we have as copied into Jane's vellum notebook; the second is beautifully produced in meticulous handwriting on quarto sheets. The mannered style of a literary lady is splendidly demonstrated in the first number:

From the editorial: The Editor of the Village Rill confesses an anxious desire for an easy flow of its noiseless stream through the channels of communication into which it may find access.
It is hoped ... that the simple current as it glides along may, at least, refresh the intellectual without danger to the moral system: resembling some favoured, or rather fabled stream on whose banks are found the beauty and fragrance of flowers and the virtue of salubrious herbage, unmingled with the distasteful and pernicious weed ... (The Editor hopes) that the unpretending pages of this rural visitant (will) supply thoughts and feelings that may introduce into our village homes a smile of guileless fancy to cheer the fireside of the winter parlour or a sentiment of moral beauty to heighten the picturesque enjoyments of the garden seat.
From the news: The sittings of our provincial senate at Westbury Hall during the last few months have promised to rival in urgency and depth of discussion the parliamentary labours ...

of St. Stephen's Chapel . . . We beg to call the attention of our readers to an advertisement in another part of our paper which announces that a Literary Institution has been established in the metropolis of our district under the immediate patronage of the nobility, clergy and gentry of Bratton and its neighbourhood. The object . . . is to awaken and cultivate a taste for Literature in the several departments of science, morality and religion; and we hope it will meet with all the support which the boasted 'March of Intellect' authorises and anticipates.

The second number has an editorial in which *The Rill* goes on 'murmuring' and 'prattling' beside cottage bowers and pursuing its 'playful meanderings' through the pastoral scene. There is a paragraph on the 'opening of the Bratton Season', a letter complaining of the bad state of the village lanes, a piece on the 'Origin and Progress of Albums' and, in Poet's Corner, a touching Plea for Infant Schools which concludes:

Sunlight and dews refresh the herbage wild
As freely as the gayest garden flow'r,
So freely let Instruction's genial show'r
Light on Life's spring buds in the Cottage bow'r
And bless the home of every little child.

Here she catches the essence of the charitable ladies' concern for education which she put into effect in her own Infant School. At the end of this number the Editor advertises rather desperately for writers on 'Moral, Natural and Experimental Philosophy – Village Statistics and National Improvements – also Agricultural, Horticultural and Meteorological reporters'. Poor Jane! Her vision of a Bratton Athenaeum 'to awaken and cultivate a taste for Literature', her picture of *The Rill*, enjoyed by every fireside and on all the garden seats of Bratton, her expectation of a cohort of writers rushing to pen on those intimidating subjects – how unlikely they were. *The Rill* trickled out. In 1837 the indefatigable editor produced *The Village Quarterly*, with a fanciful foreword on the demise of *The Rill*. It is beautifully penned and very earnest. The Editor asks for any vagrant ideas lying around, offering to provide 'a receptacle for trifles of every description' and a storehouse for 'all our village Observations on Nature – all resolvable and unresolvable phenomena . . .' She then serves up such items as 'Wisdom and Knowledge – an allegory', 'A Tribute to the Memory of the Rev. Dr Carey', 'The Habit of Reflection', 'Insect Habitations' and 'Poetry and Practice – The Bard and the Blackbirds'. How marvellous it would have been if she had succeeded in creating a storehouse of observations. But she was ahead of her time, and it appears that *The Quarterly* petered out like *The Rill*, as also, no doubt, did yet another periodical, *News from Parnassus*, whose three surviving numbers are devoted to selections from authors such as Washington Irving and Mrs Hemans.

After these high cultural endeavours, Jane, perhaps, settled down to a more realistic view of the needs of Bratton society. And then there was the education of her own children, an absorbing interest to which we shall turn in the next chapter.

8 'Ballards' and 'Yew Trees'

We can now actually catch a glimpse of the Joshua Whitaker household through the eyes of one of that army of domestic servants which upheld the Victorian family, though I fear she wears rose-coloured spectacles, for she is reminiscing years later:

In the year 1863 I went to live in the family of Mr. Joshua Whitaker, a straightforward upright Christian Gentleman and Mrs. Whitaker, one of the gentlest of Ladies, where I lived for 17 years. The family consisted of two sons and two daughters who all married while I lived with them. A Godly family; family prayers morning and evening when the Maids took their place, where the Sabbath was kept by the family and Maids. No cooking on Sundays, earlier Breakfast on Sundays, so that the family and Maids could go to the Baptist Chapel to the service at half past ten. The Master died when I had been with them about a year and a half and all the other members of the family have crossed the line and gone to the glory land, and God has spared my life to see their Grandchildren, greatgrandchildren and great greatgrandchildren. 'The Memory of the Just is blessed'.

There is a solemn sense of the passing generations in this, and indeed each generation thinks of itself as one of extreme change. Anne Whitaker, writing at the beginning of the century, felt this:

What a world of change do we inhabit, how unstable does everything appear, mutability and change characterise every object, every desire, every arrangement. Well – there is One who changeth not...

Yet materially the interiors of the Whitaker houses do not seem to have altered much throughout the century. The tall secretaires, mahogany tables and wing-armchairs still furnished their parlours and dining-rooms. The same grandfather clocks chimed. The beaded bell-pulls beside the Adam-style fireplace still summoned the maid to the drawing-room. The same oil lamps were cleaned daily and lit at night from handmade spills. In the kitchen a large range was now installed, with a special place for heating the heavy flat-irons at one side. Their heat was tested by holding near the face, or even by spitting on them, and, rubbed with beeswax, they ironed the great starched linen tablecloths and the Master's shirts marvellously. Cooking, pickling and baking went on with the time-honoured utensils, for the day of aluminium and non-stick pans was still a long way off. In the cellar stood the big tubs for curing sides of bacon, which had to be turned and rubbed with saltpetre at intervals – not a pleasant job in winter, with chapped hands. The slow and dignified rate of change which consorted so easily with continuity is something we do not know today.

Four out of the five children grew up to happy and busy lives. Everything was carefully ordered for their intellectual and moral progress. We have the tattered remnants of a lettering book which begins with 'William the Conqueror invaded England 1066' and then jumps to the Battle of Inkerman. Obviously most of English history has been lost in between. After this we have the Lord's Prayer, lettered phrase by phrase in curious and elaborate styles and increasing size until we reach 'for Ever and EVER, AMEN'. Another writing book intended for *Mulhauser's Method of Writing* has been used for a Calendar of Nature in which the migration of birds (with their Latin and English names) and the appearance of flowers (with Linnaean and English names) are meticulously recorded month by month in beautiful copper-plate. Probably the little ink-pot in the form of the globe belonged to one of these children. They made a neat little collection of shells. A bundle of scraps of paper shows us Cecil writing out texts in 1851, while Gracie was doing the same every Sunday in 1852. One little bundle, in which the child has printed texts by following dots, is labelled 'Tommie's texts 1851'. This was Joshua's youngest son, Alfred Thomas, then aged five. He was a merry little chap and it is sad that he died at the age of eleven as the result of an accident in 1857.

Joshua and Jane's children, we are not surprised to learn, were well furnished with books from the outset. John received his *First Present for Very Young Children* at the age of three, but he seems to have chewed it all up except the covers. Parley's *First Steps to the Natural History of Quadrupeds* was also received with too much enthusiasm, for only the Lion, Dromedary and Guinea Pig won the battle for survival. Later he had the same author's *What to do and How to do it* – a wonderful book of moral teaching which starts from the proposition that every creature is made to be happy, and instructs the reader, not only on good and bad hearts, but also on how to settle disputes and on not being too positive. An undated present from Grandmamma Saffery gave John a delightful window on the World, *Papa's Log or a Voyage to Rio de Janeiro* (1845), as did Parley's *Tales of all five continents*. Another from this grandmother, so intent on his education, was a picture panorama of kings and queens from William 1 to Queen Victoria, while he also possessed an informative little sixpenny in *Grandmama's Easy Series*' on the Public Buildings of London. When John was nine he had to tackle *Learning to Think*, published by the Religious Tract Society, but still in the pleasant pictorial style of Peter Parley. When he was ten, however, he must have staggered under the ten volumes of M. Rollin's *Ancient History of the Egyptians, Carthaginians, Assyrians, Babylonians, Medes and Persians*, each volume inscribed 'John Saffery Whitaker from his kind Aunt Thomas'. Much more attractive was *The Boy's Book of his Own Country Written by Uncle John for his Youthful Friends*. This did a tour of England and Scotland in romantic style, and is matched by *Harry Brightside or The Young Traveller in Italy* by Aunt Louisa (1851), an enthralling mixture of quaint information and moral lessons, with a splendid coloured plate of Victorian travellers hauling themselves up Vesuvius.

When he was four, John's younger brother, Cecil, received from an aunt a tiny letter in its own small envelope and two booklets in the 'Infant Series', *The Avalanche* and *Little Peacemaker*. The letter laid down clearly, though with a delicate psychological perception, the whole duty of a four-year-old:

Though you are but a little boy, yet you know, I think that the way to be happy is to be good, so you must try to be very good, and ask God to help you. Only to think of your having another little brother. Are you not much pleased? You must be very gentle with him. I hope you will always be loving brothers and sisters. I send you a little book with three beautiful little psalms in it, which somebody will be kind enough to read to you. The last of them tells us how pleasant it is to love one another. When your dear Mama is well enough perhaps she will help you to understand it and teach you to say it ... Kiss *gently* the new baby for me and remember that you are much loved by Your very affectionate Aunt.

Anna, as a child, eludes us – perhaps she took all her treasures away on marriage – but Mary Grace (Gracie) emerges as a busy little girl, devoted to her big brothers and ready to do chores for them. Of her books we have one which must have been a mouthful when, at the age of eleven, it was presented to her: *The Early Choice. A Book for Daughters* by the Rev. Mr Tweedie. It begins at once on 'Woman – Her Sphere and the Means of Elevation' and produces the fascinating analogy that Woman is like the moss which grows on the north side of trees in Siberia and is a sure guide to the traveller. Similarly Woman is the barometer of society by which its elevation or depression can be measured. Gracie probably found *The Little Guide of Ardrighoole or How to be Happy* more congenial. In 1863 her grandmother Saffery gave her *The Flower of Christian Charity* by Mrs Lloyd – yet another collection of edifying biographies, with an odd selection of examples which range from the two St Bernards and Savonarola to Patrick Hamilton and Andrew Melville. But it is in opening her box of treasures that we really spy on Gracie. A small gilded box inside, holding a minute basket made of blue and white beads, has written on the outside: 'Mary Grace, Jan, 19th, 1850'; it must have been a present to thrill a six-year-old. Its pair, in a twin box, is a tiny jug. Among her other treasures are the remains of a minute tea-set in Bristol glass, a tiny ivory magnifying glass, a miniature sewing apron, like the eighteenth-century ones, with a wee housewife inside the pocket, two small silver baskets and two little silver stands mounting transparent pictures intended, I think, to be lighted from a tiny candle sconce behind. Were they night-lights or a form of magic lantern show?

With such a tradition of writing for fun in the family, we find ourselves expecting these children to seize pen, and so one of the most enjoyable treasures to be dug up from a box of letters was a production called 'The Hodge Podge' – eight numbers written between January and March, 1856. Anna, the grown-up sister, was on a long visit to relations in London, and Mamma (the literary Jane) got the rest going on a serial letter in which they all wrote what they liked to Anna. It was their hodge-podge pudding, compounded of many ingredients. Here we catch the children talking to each other and I make no apology for giving them their head. John (J.S.W.) was 16, Cecil (J.C.W.) was 14, Grace (M.G.W.) was 12 and Alfred (A.T.W.) was 10.

The Hodge-Podge No. 1. January 18th, 1856.
    Dearest Anna,
        Mamma has proposed that we should keep a sheet open for you, in which any of us might write what we thought would be interesting so here begins the first number of our family journal which we intend to call The Hodge-Podge. Having introduced the dish, J.S.W. makes his bow and retires ...
Yesterday afternoon Mary went to the school with me; there were 22 children; they were hemming some glass cloths ... I gave your love to them which they received with smiling faces. I went again today, very wet and dirty – only 13 children. Gracie. You should have seen me set off this morning to fetch Papa from Market it was very wet so Mamma arrayed me in a huge mackintosh of Papa's. I expect I looked very mature but it answered well and kept me dry. J.S.W.
Mr. Cross has removed to his new abode and we have this morning made our first purchase at the fresh shop – and what do you think it was? *Bacoy-pipes* ha! ha!! ha!!! You know how prevalent smoking has become in Bratton. J.C.W.
We were blowing soap bubbles today, dear Anna, so you must forgive me if I only blow you a kiss. Alfred.

164

The wise Johnson oracularly pronounces that a Hodge-Podge should be boiled – so, as Mother's love is at the boiling point, it is well ordered that she should complete the dish, which she hopes may be sufficiently savoury to afford you some enjoyment.

The Hodge-Podge, No. 2. January 24th.
Mother. 'Will no one prepare the Hodge-Podge'? Cecil. 'Truly Mother, I know not how to put in the first ingredients'. M. 'An' that be thy trouble, my son, throw in some crumbs of Table talk, or scraps of Village gossipry, and for as much as thou knowest that no dish is savoury without salt, strew the mixture with as many Attic grains as thou canst furnish'. I have accepted the challenge, fair sister, and proceed. First, I think I must throw in a little pepper, and if you find it too hot you must thank yourself for having wrought me into the hot mood by the vehemence of your accusations, which I must return, since you have vouchsafed no apology to your three brothers after receiving in the former Hodge Podge, the proof of the injustice of your charge . . . J.C.W.

The Hodge-Podge, No. 3. January 26th.
The boys decree that it is M.G.W.'s turn to lay the cloth – it is hoped that she will do it neatly, for it would be a pity that our Country Dish should not be *grace*fully presented. Enter Hodge-Podge bountifully garnished with love sprigs, laid around it by the hands of little Gracie.

Allow me to offer you a slice, dear Sister, you will find delicate suet in it supplied by three little lambs lately ushered into life on the breezy heights of Grants' Farm. A.T.W.
Dear Anna, I do not know whether any one mentioned to you that the Brown Pony fell down as Papa and I were coming home from Warminster . . . but she is able to work again now. I rode to the station yesterday with Cousin John (Attwater) – he rode 'Fanie', I 'Uncle'. I have been giving Tommie a lesson in riding this morning at which he was very much delighted . . . J.S.W.
I have been so deeply engaged with the Caxton family today that I must crave your pardon, fair sister, for having allowed their captivating influence to render me for a while unmindful of your stronger and dearer demand upon my time . . . I request you to blame Pisisatus, Vivian, Fanny, Blanche, Uncle Roland and, of course, the mercurial Uncle Jack, indeed any one of the illustrious set but oh, deal gently with your loving brother. J.C.W.

The Hodge-Podge, No. 4. January 30th (the two elder boys go back to school).

Sugar and Spice and many things nice lie waiting around till One can be found, who with skill and care, the mess shall prepare so with suitable aid, and attention paid, Tommie has *took*, the office of Cook, and here presents, with his compliments, and every best wish, the savoury dish. A.T.W.

Going away presently, dear Anna but I should like to add a sugar-plum to the Hodge-Podge first. Crack it and you will find it nothing but a lump of love from your affectionate brother J.C.W.

Parting words are so painful that I hardly like writing just now anything that reminds me I am going but I hope dearest Anna we shall all meet at home again soon and exchange our Hodge-Podge for a right hearty supply of home love and gossip viva voce. Adieu. J.S.W.

Yesterday morning Tommy and I went with Papa to Coombe where they were thrashing from thence we went to see the Church water it was lovely ... Today we heard from the boys; they are very well and tell us their schoolroom is being enlarged and that they have three new boys. M.G.W.

The Hodge-Podge, No. 5. February 4th.
Gracie. 'Really Tommy you and I must try and finish the 'Hodge-Podge'. Tommie. 'Well, I'll try what I can do – but my first morsel will taste of soot, for the chimney-pot fell off the kitchen chimney on Tuesday.' Gracie. And I will throw in a little of the fragrant caudle that was made that day, for what do you think, Annie? A new baby arrived that morning at Daniel Walter's – a little girl. Mrs. William Snelgrove had a baby the day you went away, but we forget to tell you of it ... Jane Smith and her baby girl get on very well ... Haven't we a nice lot of babies coming on?

> And now, Good-bye, our sister dear,
> For we've no more to say;
> And Mother thinks this Hodge-Podge queer,
> Had better go today. A.T.W.

The Hodge-Podge, No. 6. February 18th.
Do you ask for a Hodge-Podge rich, spicy and good? Do you say that we lately have sent you no food? Perhaps you may think our ingredients fail Well – listen to me, and I'll tell you the tale: Most of our Cooks have taken to books, and some altogether, through stress of the weather, have made their retreat to Learning's seat. While, of those left behind, they too are inclined by Hook or by Crook, to stick to their book; and what with Phonography – Grammar Ge-o-graphy – French and Arithmetic – Music (oh Fiddlestick) – History and Science – not

much reliance can we now place on Tommie or Grace ...
(? Mother)
Let me invite you to our garden, dear Annie, so gay with Crocuses and Hepaticas, and such lovely Snowdrops; how you would enjoy them. I do not think you have such sweet spring flowers in London. M.G.W.
And I will take you to the meadows, dear Sister, where the daisies are springing and the little lambs are frisking about. Papa has now about 300. Charles Whatley had a hut to shelter him by night, and last week it was burnt down it was a good thing it did not happen when he was asleep. 'The time of the singing of birds is come' – When will you come home and hear them? A.T.W.

The Hodge-Podge, No. 7. February 29th.
... At half past ten we started off
　The Pony had a little cough – ...
　You ask our party, by the bye,
　Papa, Mamma and Tommie and I:
　We laughed and chatted as we went along,
　Gailly as sings the lark his early song ...
　We looked upon the face of nature too
　As children wise should ever love to do;
　Took note of trees – the Oaks, the Ash, the Pine,
　The graceful Birch, and creepers that entwine,
　And Tommie talked quite wise and sentimental,
　About the useful and the ornamental.
　Arrived at Stoke – Mamma got out,
　You'll guess for what, I have no doubt: ...
　Again we're off – and soon in sight,
　The Park appears to our delight;
　The peaceful stream was gliding on,
　Bearing, as wont, the stately swan ...
　So on we went, with lively chat,
　Now struck with this and now with that, ...
　So, not to dwell on Times disguises,
　At half past twelve we reached Devizes ...
　We dined with Mrs. Roach and then
　Started away for home again.
　Tommy and I so very merry
　You might have thought we'd had some sherry;
　No, I assure you, not one drop –
　And so our journey ended, and I stop. M.G.W.

I have a few little items to put in our Newspaper:
1st. We have had four young rabbits, but *sad* to relate two died and one was killed by falling out of the house.
2nd. Papa has six young pigs at Coombe.

3rd. There are nearly five hundred lambs.

4th. One of your Cochin hens has been poorly and under hospital treatment better we hope.

5th. Gracie and I have nice bows and arrows and shoot at a Swede (poor fellow). I have no more to say, revered Sister, than that I am, with profound respect, Your loving little brother, Alfred.

The Hodge-Podge, No. 8. March 11th
Yesterday we really had *Roast Beef*: the first time since Christmas; a morsel of so rare a dainty should surely be put into the Hodge-Podge and let me add, for your satisfaction, that I hope by the time you come home, the larder will not always be sending forth *Mutton – Mutton – Mutton –* for we are devouring the last of the home-fatted sheep. M.G.W.

For all their literary aspirations, these children – like others – in the end get down to pets and food.

When schooltime came, both John and Cecil went first to Keyford Academy, Frome, and then to Mill Hill, Hendon, one of the leading public schools for Nonconformist boys. A bill for both boys from Edward Flatman, the Frome headmaster, tell us that for the half-year to Christmas, 1855, board and instruction came to £31.10s, with extras such as stationery and pencils, washing, seats at chapel, drilling and books, bringing the total to £40.9.9. John was fifteen and Cecil, thirteen. They were reading Horace, Tacitus, Greek Testament, Zoology and History. From the Mill Hill days there survive a prospectus, with a fine view of the school from the cricket field, bills and reports, and the letters the two boys wrote home to their parents – also a typical memo, of their mother's, scribbled on the back of an envelope: 'Memo: send Cecil 2 towels, 1 Clothes Bag, Books, Soap, Cloth Clothes, Socks.' Both the boys did well, but John's health was so poor that he went home without finishing his second year. None the less, he was placed in the list of *Optimi* both in 1856 and 1857. His course included, besides Religious Instruction, classics, ancient and modern history, geography, English language and literature, French, German, mathematics, natural philosophy and astronomy – not a bad education for a boy who would spend the rest of his life in a small Wiltshire village.

The General Observations of the Headmaster, Rev. Philip Smith, in John's report for 1857 clearly reveal the tone and outlook of the school:

I cannot better occupy these few lines than with a parting testimony to my dear young friend's admirable spirit, and to his unblemished excellence of character and sincere piety. May God give him health to 'serve his Will in his generation'.

From one quarter's account for 1857 we learn that John's board and education cost £7.17.6, travelling £1.3.3. and, with extras like shoe repairs and hair-cuts, the total came to £11.7.7. A separate bill includes the purchase of Cornwall's *Atlas and Geography*, Herodotus, and Wilson's *Chemistry*. John was then a serious-minded boy of seventeen who wrote home regularly rather anxious letters addressed to 'My dearest Father' or 'My darling Mother'. He was concerned about his own and his brother Cecil's spiritual progress:

Cecil's letter which I received today is a very nice one indeed. I think he seems to be getting on very well (i.e. at Frome) and continuing to go steadily forward in the Christian course and earnestly pursuing the only safe path – the narrow way – I trust I am doing the same – pressing forward and endeavouring to make some advance at any rate in the spiritual life . . .

When he became ill, his letters grew rather pathetic, though not without a rueful humour:

I had a mustard plaster on the back of my neck this morning to relieve my head, but it has not had any effect – My head is so hot and my feet so cold, and not being in contact the temperature of the two don't equalise . . .

Letters from the headmaster and housemaster show much concern for John's health and after the boy had gone, the former wrote in stately, though kind, style to his father:

I hope that life in the open country air will restore him and that, though the providence of God has clearly shewn that his life is not to be that of the Scholar, he may have much pleasant fruit from his studies as time and strength permit . . .

Cecil followed his brother in 1857. The headmaster was

pleased to have another member of the family and he did well, winning several of the impressive 'Optimi' certificates. Joshua and Jane Whitaker wrote letters of affection and solicitude to their sons, encouraging in reply an epistolary style far removed from modern schoolboy scribbling. Cecil enjoyed the art of letter-writing to the full, though once complaining that the scratch of a steel nib checked the flow of his ideas. Religious aspirations and schoolboy concerns mingle in his letters:

... I still hope to study for a still higher purpose, the work of the ministry. Mamma tells me that Johnnie has decided on joining the church at midsummer and I have been hoping to do the same ... I regret that last Christmas passed so badly but hope it will be a warning. I trust to my Saviour that he will keep me from disgracing his cause in such a way again ... Give my love to all at home – especially to dearest Johnnie ... Tell little pet Gracie that I think it was very good of her to write so constantly ... I intend now to make the most of the remainder of this half year and hope that I may give satisfaction to you and Mamma as well as to Mr. Smith and that my mind may be improved. Above all I pray that I may serve my God better ... I want you to ask Gracie and Johnnie to look after my silk-worms' eggs as I think it is time to start hatching them ...

He was disappointed that his parents did not come to the 'public day', though acknowledging that he did not have a speech or a prize, only four optimi. But his parents had decreed rather against his will, that he should return next year, and so he wrote:

If I'm here next half I shall have a good chance of the music prize. I'm glad to hear of the multiplication of the silk worms and I think there is not one too many. I'll take care of 1000 or even 2000 when I come home ... I think next year you ought to come up for Public Day and Mamma too. That would quite reconcile me to coming back, if you could come then to witness my triumphs ...

A letter after his return in October 1858 gives an entertaining schoolboy mixture:

Last Sunday in chapel Mr. Smith gave us a sort of astronomical lecture occasioned by the comet. It lasted for an hour and 10 minutes. He deludes himself into the idea that it was a sermon from the Epistle of Jude, v. 13. Under these circumstances all I could console myself with was George Herbert's lines

... 'When all wants sense
    God takes a text and preaches patience'
... Yesterday we had a whole holiday the morning of which I enjoyed very much in playing football. In the afternoon, however, I had a violent attack of toothache ... However about 5 o'clock I went down to Mr. Barclay's ... Well, out came the obnoxious tooth and from that time till now I have had no more toothache ... I should be glad if you could send me a little parcel – some apples or anything of that sort but don't trouble yourself if it is not convenient. Now I must come to myself and tell you my feelings. I am still on the whole happy, though I often have severe conflicts in my soul. Your last letter was a great comfort to me. I am still tried a great deal on account of my temper though I generally am enabled to subdue it. My greatest comfort is the support I obtain from communion with God in the night. My only regret is that I cannot keep awake longer ... I should like to tell you all my feelings but I cannot attempt to do so as it would fill volumes upon volumes ...

A little later he writes mysteriously to his mother. Thursday was 'character day' and he got his 'optimus', yet he was in very low spirits because of some circumstances which he promises to explain when he comes home:

In the afternoon I went for a walk with Carter and another boy and my mind's health was much improved. But just before tea I had all my care lifted off my mind by another part of the affair I referred to. Restrain your curiosity about this till I come home and I will spend pleasant hours then relating them to you. I know they will be scarcely less interesting to you than they are to myself. Yesterday everything went prosperously. I am so full of happiness and gratitude for that happiness that I cannot find words to express it. Then your letter was a most delightful accompaniment to all this ...

He caps this letter with a slightly ambivalent comment on Mill Hill:

You will be glad to hear that I am acquiring extensively that 'esprit de corps' which you wish in me. I am truly getting quite enthusiastically patriotic for Mill Hill. I think that in after life I shall think it an honour to have been here at school. Who knows but I shall be distinguished also as having been the schoolfellow here of some of the great men of the land. I say 'who knows', but I don't particularly care for this sort of fame.

We can imagine that comfortable conversation with his mother at Christmas about the 'circumstance' to which we have no clue. She urged him to write down his religious experiences and it was probably a very close relationship to her that made him so articulate about his states of mind.

Cecil's eldest sister, Anna, was also his confidante. Just before leaving Mill Hill he wrote her a letter which causes a smile when one remembers that he was seventeen and she twenty-one:

I do indeed remember the old times you speak of with sad yet pleasurable regret. Oh for 'the days that are no more'. My dreams are still wild sometimes when my imagination gets quite uncontrollable but for the most part I have quite sobered down to what is rational. You talk about the old habits with pleasurable feelings. My own sweet sister I still love the old habits as much as ever but my usual thoughts run in a different channel in as much as since those days 'old things are passed away – all things are become new'. My dreams are of a different sort to what they used to be. Now I see no visions of dreamy indolence in rural retirement . . . I hear, I think, a voice saying 'Go work today in my vineyard' . . . God is calling me to the work of the ministry . . . One thing I feel certain of. I *may* make a preacher, *I shall never make a scholar . . .*

And then he suddenly switches from pious dreams into a hot discussion of contemporary politics, telling his sister that 'the French are England's born enemies' and that Louis Napoleon is 'a very clever lying knave', writing a whole page on Gallic iniquities before he ends 'Ever your most loving brother'.

II

Perhaps the greatest Dame in the succession of Whitaker ladies was John's and Cecil's 'Aunt Thomas' (actually Great Aunt). She bestrode the century, really belonging to the previous chapter as much as this. Born as Sophia Williams in 1790, she lived until 1891, for decades No. 1 on the Baptist Church Members' Roll. She was evidently a good businesswoman, holding the lease of a shop and other property before her marriage, as well as her interest, through her father, in the Yew Trees. When she married Philip's brother Thomas in 1824, the Yew Trees came back to the Whitakers again. After Thomas's death in 1857 she reigned alone in the large house. So when John was planning to bring home a bride, Mary Brinkworth, in 1867, she asked them to make their home with her. Joshua had died in 1864, leaving Jane the mistress of Ballards. Thus the two gracious but formidable ladies confronted each other across the orchards and four critical eyes were focused on the new bride. Her mother-in-law told her in no uncertain terms what linen she must buy as suitable for John's establishment, and until Mrs Joshua's death in 1884, the 'other house', as they called Ballards, was a cause of considerable anxiety to Mary. On the other hand, although she had promised them a separate ménage, Aunt Thomas had her finger in most pies – as Mary's diary makes clear. Mary must have felt like Alice between the Red and White Queens. The last generation of Whitaker children was brought up under Aunt Thomas's eye. But the old and the very young are often happy together, and we shall meet Aunt Thomas again in the company of her young relations. One of John's children, born in 1877, could still recall in 1976, the year of her death, being called upon on Sunday nights to sing into her great-great-aunt's ear trumpet her favourite hymn: 'Grace 'tis a charming sound'. Between them they spanned the whole period from the French Revolution to the 1970s.

So we return once more to the Yew Trees, to John and Mary – or rather Polly, as she was always called – bringing up the family that was to be the last generation of Whitakers in the house. Polly Brinkworth belonged to a well-known Chippenham family with a musical and artistic strain in it. She herself sang and played piano and organ. She brought to Bratton a brass-bound Bible presented by the New Baptist Church in Chippenham 'as a mark of their appreciation of her valuable services among them', that is, as organist, and also a copy of Scott's poems given her 'in affectionate remembrance of the patient kindness with which for many years she skilfully discharged the duties of Musical Governess in the Establishment of her friend and cousin H.E.'. We can actually watch her becoming a bride and a wife, for in 1867 Philip Saffery (Mrs Joshua's brother) gave her a diary inscribed: 'Miss Mary Brinkworth With much love for another's sake and, by anticipation, for her own sake. P.J.S.' In it she scribbled many memos concerning her preparations, such as 'Articles to be brought from Chippenham'. Much of her activity revolves round 'dear John', but when it comes to 9 October she records simply: 'Married to my *dear* and *precious* husband in B.C. (Baptist Chapel) at 11 . . . reached Southampton at 7.' The honeymoon was spent in the Isle of Wight and soon she was back in Bratton, installed at the Yew Trees, receiving and returning the calls which were *de rigueur*. Her mother-of-pearl card-case and John's tortoiseshell one are still treasured.

Next year (1868) she had the same type of diary, the Scripture Pocket Book, published by the Religious Tract Society, writing at the beginning: 'Received this pocketbook from Uncle B. Last year I was a spinster and now What!!!!' By April she 'commenced to be busy with little garments', but there was no slackening of activity. She 'rode on the hill with John', drove here and there with 'Aunt T.', went shopping in Trowbridge and Devizes. On 25 August she was making calls, visiting the Infant School and driving to Westbury to shop. On the 28th she entered in her diary: 'My precious baby was born this morning. Tillie (her sister) and Nurse not here. All things ordered *so well*', and, in the margin, 'Bless the Lord, O my soul'. Then relations and letters descended from all sides and the usual round of visits moved into an orgy for a time. 'Baby' (named Sophia for obvious reasons) was carried round in triumph, travelling to Chippenham at a very early age. At the following Christmas we meet the first mention of a Christmas Tree, and on Boxing Day they all trooped off again to Chippenham. Baby was vaccinated soon afterwards.

Polly Whitaker's diaries (still in the leather-bound Scripture Pocket-books with a text for each day) give glimpses of a household regime in which she supervised two maids and

174

other women without being quite tied to the kitchen. She could spend a morning on embroidery or 'making bookmarks' and go on innumerable walks, drives, calls, tea-drinkings. Nonetheless she worked beside the maids. Spring-cleaning, begun in May, was a heavy time. There was redcurrant jelly and blackcurrant vinegar to make, and cowslips to be 'pipped' (her daughter remembered that each child had a small glass for cowslip wine). Her cookery book, now in pieces and well-singed at the edges, shows her collecting recipes from various quarters. 'Mrs Alfred Pocock's Powder Cake' brings back to memory a formidable Baptist lady who always had her own urn and her own place at Baptist tea-meetings. The recipe for making vinegar from a vinegar plant is written on the back of a summons to her husband to attend the Westbury and Whorwellsdown Technical Education Committee, while that for Rhubarb Blancmange is from *Home Chat*, May 1897. Someone recommends a preparation of lobelia for neuralgia, and someone else a concoction for polishing tables. Then comes a typical little Whitaker surprise: a section headed Original Poetry in the midst of recipes, quaint doggerel mixed up with directions for making Gingerbread and knitting a shell pattern. What really weighed on Polly's mind was the mammoth wash, inevitably linked with the weather: 'Preparing for the wash' (Saturday); 'Lovely day – commenced our 5 week wash' (Monday); 'Beautiful day for drying clothes' and 'Folding morning' (Tuesday); 'finished ironing' (Wednesday). Altogether Polly Whitaker comes through as a purposeful, capable woman, supporting her John in every possible way and playing a full part in the Church, including that of organist. Two small memories bring her back. One recalls her entering her daughters' bedroom in the morning singing briskly to a cheerful tune: 'My God who makes the sun to rise'. The other tells how at the end of family prayers one summer evening she was discovered under the dining-room table, because a bat had got in.

A little lady who hovers on the edge of the Yew Trees household until latterly she came to be a permanent part of it is Miss Matilda Brinkworth, Polly's sister Tillie. When we turn to a little notebook labelled 'Cash Account for own expenses', 1868–72, internal evidence reveals it to be hers. It is a modest, retiring record, speaking of the Victorian spinster found in so many households. In 1868 Tillie was a struggling single woman living in Chippenham, who had a tiny annuity of £10 a half year, earned as a governess or companion a salary of £10 a quarter, and was thankful for a 'kind present' of £1 towards a new dress or water-proof cape. Her expenditure was mainly on clothes, though she also had to pay for her washing. She bought calico for drawers (12 yds) and nightgowns (16½ yds) which only cost her 14s 5½d, but she managed some flourishes too: ribbon for cap 3s 3d, and parasol 12s 6d. The material for her new silk dress cost £3.10 and the dressmaker's bill was 16s. When she bought a new velvet bonnet for £1.5., she also spent 4s on 'strings and border' for doing up the old one. She had her stays cleaned and repaired for 6s. (How she would have been shocked at their mention: at night she always covered her folded underwear with a cloth lest they be open to public gaze.) Like all the family she was a prolific letter-writer, so paper, envelopes and stamps take a sizeable bite out of her tiny income. She notes everything: barley-sugar drops for cough 1½d, 'corks for Globule bottles' 3d, a beggar 4d, 'pictures for little ones' 4d, 'wrong change given 6d', tract ('He's Overhead') 1d. But even her meticulous memory nods occasionally and we meet such items as 'Forget 8d'. In spite of the minute scale of all this, Matilda gave presents and tips to servants, found 5s for a 21st birthday or 1s for 'toy for the dear little one' and paid visits, especially to Bratton. She even went to Ryde at the cost of rail-fare to Frome 9d, and then to Ryde 13s 7d, and in 1871 to London (rail fare £1.10), where she dashed around in cabs and omnibuses to see the 'International team', the Royal Academy and numerous relations. Curiously, there is no record of subscriptions or donations, but a mysterious item 'Transferred to other Purse' occurs on almost every page, involving quite substantial sums. One guesses that here is a case of generous reticence: let not your right hand know what your left doeth. Not often do accounts leave such a moving picture in the imagination: here is the authentic Aunt Tillie, a dignified little person, managing her own tiny budget with great care, ready to accept presents from her better-off relations in the spirit in which they were given, warm-hearted in her own giving, independent in all her ways. And so she remained until her death in 1939 at the age of 104, remembered by younger generations as a delicate-featured little old lady in a lace cap (20) who loved, so long as she was able, to sit in the kitchen chopping mint or making spills or ironing handkerchiefs with meticulous care.

These ladies' sewing-baskets were very full and all kinds of relics remain. A bundle of scraps have sample embroidery designs on them, while an envelope of Mrs Saffery's holds patch-work patterns. There are directions for making a 'sovereign purse with two coloured silks'. 'Fancy', rather than 'plain', sewing was in vogue and much of this work must have been for bazaars. Bead-work for chair-seats, footstools, cushions, tea-cosies, and even watch-pockets to hang by the bed, must have been popular work, and much in vogue were flower designs stencilled on velvet. One surviving piece of woolwork on canvas was a co-operative effort started for some good cause by a ladies' working party, for it consists of medallions of embroidery, each with a name pinned on it; some are finished, some are not. Knitting, tricot and crochet needles turn up in large quantities, and the netting-tools with which the ladies netted ham frills for the immense hams that appeared on their tables. An envelope marked 'On Her Majesty's Service' actually contains a yellow crochet pattern, while another, addressed to Miss Salter, holds a sample and directions for 'the feather pattern'. An intricate piece of curly knitting was apparently done on needles as fine as hat-pins. Two exercise books with marbled covers (1852) contain Matilda Brinkworth's crochet patterns for a Mary Stuart Collar, a D'Oyley for a round cruet-stand, an Anti-Macassar and so on. A particularly cosy type of antimacassar has a thick wool edge round the embroidery to keep the draught out. The many bookmarks which drop out of Whitaker books show us another type of handwork popular with Victorian ladies.

They are embroidered with texts and neat little patterns on thin card or stiffened canvas and then stuck on ribbon. Other things produced in this work include a little stamp container with this verse worked on it:

In England letters find no grace,
  Unless they bear Victoria's face,
To keep her head from dust and damps,
  Accept this case for Postage Stamps.

One amusing relic of all this stitchery is a complete paper of new pins headed The Royal Jubilee Pin Sheet and produced by William Avery & Son of Redditch. Each row is marked by an event, starting with 'Queen Victoria born May 24th, 1819' and ending 'Queen Victoria proclaimed Empress of India, 1878', topped by Victoria Regina and Britannia. Events selected show the march of progress: Introduction of Penny Post, 1840; Electric Telegraph Introduced, 1843; Great Exhibition, 1851; Abolition of Slavery, 1862. How cheering to survey the glorious reign as you sewed!

At her elbow, no doubt, Polly Whitaker kept the comprehensive guide to domestic affairs: *Enquire Within upon Everything,* now in its 540th edition (1873). A note on the front page announces:

Whether you wish to model a flower in wax; to study the rules of etiquette; to serve a relish for breakfast or supper; to plan a dinner for a large party or a small one; to cure a headache; to make a will; to get married; to bury a relative; whatever you may wish to do, make or enjoy, provided your desire has relation to the necessities of domestic life, I hope you will not fail to 'Enquire Within'.

At the top of each page is a proverb, for example 'A liar should have a good memory'; 'Children and chicken must always be picking'; 'For the light of the day we've nothing to pay'. There are some surprising items: a list of words which made good charades, a story to illustrate when, and when not, to pronounce an *H*, information on a Roman lady's toilet and 'the habits of a man of business'. It is the kind of book to be dipped into endlessly.

Sophia, their first child, had arrived quickly and easily, but John and Polly suffered a tragedy over their second, Joshua, who was born and died in 1872. The next, Edith, came in 1877 and was followed quite quickly by Philip (1878) and Jane Saffery (1881). Because of the gap the three younger ones were closer together on companionship. Their possessions tell us small things about their childhood. A charming little girl's work-box with red roses and blue forget-me-nots wreathing the lid holds cotton reels, tiny wooden ones and old bone ones, with the label 'Victoria Thread' on one of them. Which of them filled a little basket with everything that pleased her by way of quaint pin-cushions and knick-knacks, including a button-hook and a tiny purse? At the bottom, perhaps most precious, is a tiny homemade envelope decorated with a witch riding her broomstick with glee and the appellation ME! And who created the joke doll, comically constructed with scraps of silk and artificial flowers, with pins for eyes and mouth? (5) Beside her in a wicker basket lies a dog's head that puts out a long tape-measure tongue. As a child Polly Brinkworth and her sisters had done the regulation samplers and she brought to Bratton an elaborate one in which Isaac Watts' verse for such an occasion stands in the midst of pillars, lions and flowers:

Jesus permit thy gracious name to stand
As the first efforts of an infant's hand
And as her fingers o'er the canvass move
Engage her tender heart to seek thy love.

But she never set her own daughters to such work. The sampler tradition was dead.

Their books were more varied in style than the small, finely printed and engraved volumes of an earlier age. For one thing, cheap paper editions had come in; these children had the Alice books with the Tenniel illustrations in Macmillan's Sixpenny edition, as also *The Pickwick Papers* and *Black Beauty*. Coloured illustrations were now commoner, eye-catching but often inferior in style to the older striking black-and-white examples. There were, however, some charming productions. These Whitaker children had six of Mrs Ewing's stories with the Caldecott illustrations. One of Edith Whitaker's favourite books was *Kisses*, the story of a seaside monkey, which told you on the title-page:

Kisses was clever
But sly as could be
Poor Kisses was drowned
In the waves of the sea.

The large picture-book for the very young was beginning to appear and in 1886 Philip (aged eight) inscribed his name laboriously in *The Large Picture Primer* which begins with a picture alphabet and goes on to graded stories with good black-and-white pictures. But some very crude productions like Call and Inglis' *Scripture ABC* show how taste in cheap children's books had deteriorated.

There is an atmosphere of cheerful cosiness about Victorian jig-saws which conjures up a vision of the parlour on a winter's evening, fire-warmed and lamp-lit, with puzzles in progress on the big mahogany table. One is Our Daily Bread, picturing round the border scenes of sowing, reaping and so on, and in the middle 'Consuming', in an ample Victorian kitchen where everyone, including the children, the dog, the cat and a grateful, very tidy tramp all rejoice in eating just bread. Another is Red Riding Hood in a very authentic cloak. Her terrible drama could also be constructed in six scenes with highly-coloured cubes. At Christmas, 1884, when she was seven, Edith was given The Fifteen Cube Puzzle which created the story of Bo-Peep in the same way. For Sundays there was The Good Samaritan in Betts' Series of Parable Puzzles. But the jolliest of all the jig-saws was a gay scene of Victorian children at the Zoo, riding the elephant and camel and feeding the bear with a bun on the point of an umbrella, duly attended by Nurse – for fear of finding something worse.

Toys for construction again mirror their period. Stone building-blocks with pillars and arches have an ecclesiastical flavour, while a large box of wooden pieces in various shapes invited you to make models of 'Classical and

Modern Architecture'. Most interesting is a primitive kind of meccano from which 'Crandall's Bridge', patented 11 October 1875, was to be made. This is a pointer to the future, but when we turn to Victorian card-games we are in a traditional world again. Happy Families was played with all the old trades of a country town that knew not super-markets: Mr Bones the Butcher, Mr Bung the Brewer, Mr Dose the Chemist. And their families gather round them in late Victorian costume. Edwardian Snap cards (for the grandchildren, no doubt) included such gems as a morning shave with antique equipment and the caption 'Another gash! Oh my poor chin!' or the snake-charmer with a too lively snake exclaiming 'Oh you little monster!'

The delights of their magic lantern can only be imagined from a set of painted glass slides with bright little scenes of snowballing, Father Christmas, tropical jungles and so forth. Worn and scratched as they are, they still carry the enchantment of pre-cinema days. In the room at the end of the house which was at this period called the schoolroom they would set up the bagatelle board on a table, to play miniature billiards or, on a similar board, The Devil among the Tailors, which you played by spinning the devil (a top wound up with a piece of string) among 12 wooden pegs. Scissors never fail in their attraction, and making cut-outs was as popular as ever. We stumble upon two delicious little fashion-plate ladies, with bustles and wasp-waists, carefully folded inside a piece of paper with a drawing of school laboratory apparatus on the outside. And someone has left a box-full of cut-out horses, all shaded in pencil and attached to wooden stands, but perhaps these are the work of a Brinkworth cousin who was noted for such skill. He has differentiated them beautifully and named them to match: Lady Dash, Young Trotwell, Miss Kitty, Fleetfoot and Old Ambleside.

When it came to schooling, it is clear that the last generation had to be educated less expensively than at places like Mill Hill. Sophia was able to go to school at Winchester under the eye of her Aunt Anna Gotch (the Anna of the Hodge-Podge), but Philip, like his future brother-in-law,

Robert Reeves, went no further afield than Keyford School, Frome, where the headmaster was now Arthur Coombs, who in 1891 married Sophia. Edith and Jane were sent to a school in Wine Street, Frome, kept by the Misses Coombs. Three programmes of Musical Afternoons in 1892 and 1893, given by the pupils of Wine Street House in the Y.M.C.A. Hall, afford us just one glimpse of what they did there. Edith played violin solos, duets and trios, while Jane appears in 1893 playing from Mendelssohn's *Songs Without Words*. The only other echo that reaches us is from a merry little letter written by Edith, 10 May 1892, from Wine Street. At the top she has drawn a bottle of claret, a house and rows of eyes peering over desks. It begins:

My dearest Mamma and Papa (the gloomy old couple), I didn't say anything about the exam because I shall & you will hear rather too much about it soon from Miss Amy and myself.
How be 'ee? As shur I da of'en dink of 'ee, I be zure thee twa mus' be glad *zometimes* all we caddlin' leetle toads be out of the way – fur that's what we've allus a bin.
Well Miss Brown came & it was dreadful, we had to talk French *all* the while, or try to . . . Please forgive the writing but I'm rather crazy tonight I think.
'*Slowboots*' sends her kind regards to J.S. and Mrs. Whitaker Esq. C.C. & C.W.B.G. and she be main happy . . .
I feel inclined to laugh at everything this evening. 'Jeanie's top knot is coming down'. Ethel and Jeanie are very amusing. . . .
    Your very loving child,
        Edith.

When we turn to the Yew Trees bookshelves we are confronted, of course, by all the major poets, often in the opulent bindings of school prizes. But it is the cheap popular literature of the Victorian age that most interests us. In the 'Run and Read Library' we find *I've Been Thinking or The Secret of Success* (1853), a story of enterprise 'making good'. The new philosophy of literature for the million is so eloquently set forth on the front that it must be quoted:

If ever there was a time when the saying received fulfillment, that many shall run to and fro and knowledge shall be increased, it is in the present day, when the Rail, the Road and the River are teeming with intelligent beings; and the unprecedented demand for cheap literature plainly shows that they who run will read ... the great evil is that the worst stands about an equal chance with the best ... It is ... a duty, at certain intervals, to relieve the intellect and feelings from care and effort, and devote ... time to works of mere recreation and amusement; and the most elevating and the most refining of all amusements is the exercise of the imagination ... persons who have the taste, invention, sprightliness, humour and command of diction that qualifies for a successful novelist, may become the greatest of public benefactors by skilfully providing the *healthful aliment* that may be employed in supplanting the pernicious leaven. It is to supply this acknowledged desideratum that the Run and Read Library has been projected.

John Whitaker used *Penny Readings in Prose and Verse* (1865), perhaps as a stand-by at village entertainments. It contained the most marvellous mixture from Milton's 'Hymn on the Nativity' (sic) to 'The First Grey Hair' by T. H. Bayley and 'Eccentric Sermon on the Word Malt'. Chambers' *Miscellany of Useful and Entertaining Tracts* (1847) is in the same class – a mixture of biographies and stories with unexceptionable morals, while advancement through knowledge is the theme of another miscellany, *Excelsior: Helps to Progress in Religion, Science and Literature* (1854) which begins, under the title 'Onward and Upward', with the declaration: 'Since the Fall, indolence has been a besetting sin of our species'. Two interesting oddments of John Whitaker's are *The Battle of the Petticoats* (1874), a satire on elaborate ecclesiastical vestments which would please the Nonconformist, and a local curiosity, *The Wiltshire Centenarian: Her wonderful life and happy death at the age of One Hundred and Two Years*, written by William Jeffery of Westbury and sold by the local printer, W. Michael.

The enormous part played by the Religious Tract Society and other similar tract-distributors in disseminating reading-matter is aptly illustrated by the Whitaker collection. Besides little bound volumes, such as *The Working Boy's Sunday Improved* and *Scripture Mountains*, they accumulated some 300 little tracts, as well as 'Sacred Gems' to slip inside letters. The English Monthly Tract Society provided artless little stories for children and teenagers. Some tracts covered wider ground, such as 'Kind Words to Domestic Servants' and 'How to Improve A Bad Memory'. 'A midnight Ramble in the Streets of London' describes experiences while distributing tracts to 'unfortunate women'. The most interesting group was published by The Ladies Sanitary Association. Here we find advice 'on Dress: Its Fetters, Frivolities and Follies from a Sanitary Point of View'; 'On Washing the Children'; on 'Rubbish, or A few words for rich and poor ... on the use and abuse of ashpits'. Charles Kingsley contributed 'The Two Breaths', on ventilation and good breathing. From the National Health Society came 'How to be Strong and Beautiful. Hints on Dress for Girls', while an amusing poem, 'The Lady's Dilemma', reaches the conclusion 'that we must have machines to sew, now hands can sew no more'. There is, indeed, a progressive note in many of these tracts, yet a leaflet on 'The Rights of Women' would horrify Women's Lib. today:

> The Rights of Women! what are they?
> The Right to labour, love and pray;
> The Right to weep with those who weep;
> The Right to wake while others sleep.
> The Right to show a spirit meek
> When angry words a quarrel seek;
> The Right to wear a modest dress,
> When fashions bold around may press ...
> The Right by scripture and by choice
> To be without a public voice,
> Humbly at home her Bible search
> Meekly keep silence in the church.
> Are these thy Rights? then murmur not
> That woman's mission is thy lot;
> Improve the talents God has given,
> Live to His praise, and rest in heaven.

Some of the periodicals which came into John Whitaker's household show their interest in culture and politics. There was the Saturday journal *Great Thoughts*, which had a literary and philosophical flavour, but also carried sentimental stories. On each front page there was a picture of a 'great man' – Landor, Cowper, Andrew Lang, Canon Barnett and the Maharajah of Jeypore keep curious company – and above them sits the Muses of Poetry and Philosophy. Chambers' *Journal of Popular Literature, Science and Art* represents the same type of interest. Alas – nothing remains of political reading, except some numbers of *Picture Politics, A Penny Popular Monthly*, with cartoons by F. C. Gould. This was a kind of *Punch* with a Liberal slant, anti-Chamberlain and pro-Gladstone – just right for a Non-conformist household who would note that the *Methodist Times* said: 'This wonderful pennyworth ought to find its way into every Liberal household'. The Whitakers – and in the 1900s Reeveses too – did indeed form part of the great Nonconformist Liberal vote. Other relics of a Liberal attachment are an address from Sidney Herbert announcing his resignation as member to the Electors of South Wilts in 1861 and a Liberal Calendar sent to John Whitaker 'with Mr J. M. Fuller's compliments' at Christmas, 1906. A splendid 'find' is a booklet of Liberal and Free Trade Songs for the 1906 election, which include 'Stamp, Stamp, Stamp, upon Protection', 'No more Joe' to the tune of 'Poor Old Joe', 'Oh we ken Bob Peel' and 'Free Trade will triumph yet'. Another is a pamphlet of political cartoons around the Lords crisis of 1910. On the cover is the modern Canute in peer's robes trying to hold back the tide of the People. Someone in the family obviously liked political cartoons, for we come on a bunch of 'cartoons of the week' saved from the *Westminster Budget* for 1903.

Some of the little things that a pious Victorian household gathered are most evocative. There are the little books they loved – bijou anthologies or selections from great poets, such as *Gems of Sacred Poetry* in green watered silk, with a tiny slip-case embroidered with bead flowers, or *Milk and Honey, A Collation of Many Christian Sentences*. There are small text-books like the minute *Diamond Text Book* and *A Threefold Cord, A Precept, Promise and Prayer for every day*. Birthday books were essential in an era when one kept up with cousins and had large extended family celebrations.

'Autograph albums' and scrap-books were their delight. Friends and relations were cajoled into 'putting something' – verse, drawing, quotation, picture, aphorism – into the prized book. The pages speak of so much. Little sketches embellish them with birds, flowers and rural scenes. When literary and artistic inspiration gave out, Christmas and birthday cards, texts and pictures of all sorts filled the gaps, so we get in amusing juxtaposition portraits of Frederick William of Prussia and Napoleon, a poem entitled 'Warm Hearts' and a picture of an enormous white champion cock and hen. Then there was the continuing habit of the Whitakers of making their own anthologies or commonplace books. Here, for instance, is a substantial book into which 'A Whiteley of the West. A Unique Advertisement' has been copied from *The Rambler*, 14 August 1897 – and then there is nothing else. But another has a great range of pieces, including a poem called 'The Burial of Moses' from the *Dublin University Magazine*, of all places. A mid-Victorian anthology includes a piece headed 'Prince Albert's Poetry', while Mrs John Whitaker had a book full of poetry including a quaint piece called 'A Swarm of Bees' which begins:

B patient, B prayerful, B humble, B mild,
B wise as a Solon, B meek as a child.

Nor had they lost their passion for composing verse themselves, both serious and light. There are odd little collections of poems in notebooks and on scraps of paper. 'A Professor' (of the Faith) is thus described:

With sober look and moderate walk
A tongue smooth tip'd with Bible talk,
Religion's track he'll seem to tread
Tho' number'd still among the dead.

A Possessor, A Hearer and A Doer are similarly delineated. A pious little poem is headed 'The following lines were composed by a Young Lad of 12 years of age while sitting by the fireside, many talking round about him'. Another begins: 'We will never give thee up. O thou sadly erring one' – to whom was this written, we wonder? John's second daughter, Edith, gets two poems, one on her ninth birthday, and another 'To my little Cousin with her first Bonnet':

Fairies guard the Baby's bonnet
Set a special watch upon it ...
Neat as neatness – white as snow
See you ever keep it so.

Even 'The Pulpit Cushion, Bratton' gets its own poem in 1860:

...A Pulpit Cushion now,
  My heart elate with pride,
  I judged all eyes below
  Would hence on me abide.

  But soon, too soon, I learned
  When placed upon my shelf,
  Those eyes on me that only turned
  Could learn the least of self.

They would poetize on anything, for someone turned the History of the Kings of England into verse. A poem on Wisdom is written on the back of a recipe for killing weeds in paths. Their serious poetry, one must admit, is pretty lame, but how they (and we) enjoy their capers in light verse, often written for the amusement of those famous aunts. Here is one of 1886 with an obvious point:

Who with kindly heart and eye
The produce of her Farm doth spy
To see what delicacies rare
She to her London friends can spare?
    Aunt Thomas

Who when some amiable pig
With gratitude is growing big.
Doth tell her foreman John to give him
A little more – and then to kill him?
    Aunt Thomas

At a later date a similar gift by John Whitaker to his brother Cecil's family in Birmingham produced a postcard which began:

For your gift of a hare

This postcard will bear
The grateful thanks due
From our house to you.
It arrived just as we
Were assembled at tea
An unlooked for surprize
We gazed on it with eyes
Admiring . . .

(This recalls an entry in Polly Whitaker's diary – 21/12/74: 'Hamper gone off to London with eight nice turkies'). In patriotic mood are 'Grannie's Words composed for the Prince of Wales' Wedding Day', set out in lines to be sung by Soprano, Mezzo-Soprano and Chorus:

Solo.   Our Prince hath won a lady fair
        To be his royal bride
        And Britain's heart uplifts one prayer,
        All blessings them betide!   (repeat)
        All are rejoicing, hasten then
        To sound the joyous lay   (repeat twice)

Chorus.   Up rouse you then, ye loyal British men
          It is the wedding day   (repeat ad lib.)

We even have the music for this ditty – a copy of 'The Celebrated Gipsy Glee in Guy Mannering arranged for three Voices', in which slips with Grannie's words have been pasted over the original text. The event took place in 1863, so Grannie must be Mrs Joshua and the young who chanted it, John Whitaker's family.

Aunt Thomas and Aunt Tillie were each a source of poetic inspiration in their day. There is a poem on Aunt Thomas's little white cat and one on an expedition to the Crystal Palace led by herself. She herself took to verse:

Lines composed by Aunt Thomas when Sophie broke her collar-bone, May, 1878:
Dear little Sophie sat on a wall
Dear little Sophie had a great fall
And broke her collar-bone.
Out rushed the women and out came the men
But Dr. Smith put it together again
And so she got safely home.

When dear little Sophie next gets on a wall

Let dear little Sophie remember her fall
Not always can doctors or women or men
Put poor broken bones together again.

A charming reproof for a rather wayward little girl. One amusement produced for Aunt Tillie was 'A little Petition to the House of Commons for the widening of Tinkers' Lane' (this was the narrow path up which the diminutive Tillie would go to shop in the Village). And one of the children must have produced the rather juvenile effort on her 60th birthday which begins:

Our venerable Aunt we greet
On this auspicious day
And hope that long her little feet
May live to run and play.

It ends:

May Health and Happiness and Hair
Long crown your precious Head
And to this end mind you prepare
To take three pills 'fore bed.

It is the ephemera that have survived by chance – the cards not thrown away, enclosures in letters, doodles on scraps of paper – which most create the feeling of immediacy. The Whitakers did sums on the envelopes they received and allowed the children to draw animals or houses, or even Punch, on a most serious letter. There are clever pen-and-ink sketches of faces, and one of an old lady in a feather boa and feathered bonnet which catches the Victorian matriarch to a tee. We open an envelope to discover a sample of bright rug wools – which the sender had asked to be returned. Another has pressed harebells 'belonging to my dear, very dear Sister Sarah', and a third, a paper cut-out flower with a love poem on its petals. A packet labelled 'Hair' holds bright ringlets from various children. A male note is struck in this pronouncement:

A Description of some of the affected modern fine Ladies, comprised in six words, the initial of each is L:
Literary. Literry (sic). Lazy. Loquacious. Luxurious. Lavish.

If I were fifty years younger than I am, rather than I would be united to one possessing the above characteristics, I would be Transported to Botany Bay or the wilds of Africa.

Riddles delighted grown-ups as well as children. Here are two:

A point of the Compass and a Clergyman's Office is the name of a Town well-known in Wiltshire.

Many cannot live without my first
By day and night 'tis used;
My second is by all accursed,
By day and night abused.
My whole is never seen by day,
And never felt by night,
'Tis dear to friends when far away
And hateful when in sight.

Perhaps there are too many coloured texts and not enough Christmas cards among the survivors, but three little cut-out girls of the 1890s are very gay, though one has lost her head. The Christmas card sent by Willie Brinkworth in 1889, in the form of a railway season ticket on the Health and Prosperity Line, issued to Mr J. S. W. Whitaker, Wife and Family, has a moral:

Here's a Season Ticket that unto you I send,
It was issued by the Company of Love, my Friend,
And if you'll only show it, wherever you may go,
It will carry you quite safely on your journeyings, I trow.

Never part with it or lose it, and then you need not fear
Collisions at the junction, for the line is always clear,
For Love's the only ticket in this world of din and strife
That can ever bring you safely to the Terminus of Life.

Another curiosity is a New Year's card in the form of a clock with a dial which turns round, exhorting you to Lay Aside Guile on Monday, Hypocrisies on Tuesday, Envies on Wednesday, and so on.

The whole family sang, while Polly Whitaker played her Victorian piano (complete with candlesticks and pleated silk front) with plump, nimble fingers. Her daughters, Sophie and Edith, played violins. Sophie, her mother and Phil may have sung the glees for three voices which come to light.

There is 'The Horn of the Chase' from an opera *The Persian Hunters*, performed at the Theatre Royal. Others include 'Tell Her, Oh Tell Her,' with words of Thomas Moore's, and 'The Bark before the Gale', a setting of words from Scott's *The Lord of the Isles*. Two bound volumes of songs tell us what Polly and her daugher Sophie were singing in the 1880s and 90s. They evoke a whole world of gentle sentiment: 'Love's Old Sweet Song', 'Fiddle and I', 'Hidden Angels', 'The Queen of the May' and 'The Brook' from Tennyson, 'Oh that we two were maying' from Kingsley – one could quote these titles *ad lib*. 'Robin Redbreast' has a haunting little tune, remembered by Polly Whitaker's grandchildren, and there is a melting song which begins: 'Darling, I am growing old, Silver Threads Among the Gold'.

Topical songs give an amusing slant. Here is a rashly prophetic one of 1885:

I've heard people say that the world they'd surprise,
But they can't do it, you know.
With ships like balloons they would soar to the skies,
But they can't do it, you know.
While some other fellows who haven't a cent,
Are on some most wonderful patent intent,
And perpetual motion they'd like to invent,
But they can't do it, you know.

By the turn of the century Phil, the youngest, was singing humorous pieces such as 'We Sing for the Fun of it', from a light opera, 'Cigarette', by J. Haydn Parry, and 'The Polka and the Choir Boy', from a musical sketch called 'My Aunt's in Town'. The most amusing find is a song published in Trowbridge, 'The Fly be on the Turmuts, newly arranged ... from the Authenticated Melody of the March of the Wiltshire Regiment by H. Millington, Late b.m., 1st Wilts R.V. and Western Countie Brigade', with a picture of the Turmut-hoer on the cover. The Millingtons were a great musical family in Trowbridge: they tuned pianos far and wide, gave music lessons and performed as a family quartet at concerts. Here is the first verse of the song:

I be a turmut Hoer, from Glostershire I came,

My Parents be hard working folks, Giles Whapstraw is my name,
Twas on a summers morning and at the break of day,
When I took my hoe and off did go, Some fifty miles away.

There's some delights in haymaking, And some be fond of mowing,
But of all the jobs as suits I best, Give I the turmut hoeing.
The Fly, the Fly, the Fly be on the turmuts,
For its all my eye and no use to try,
To keep 'em off the turmuts.

On some occasion this must have been sung at a concert by a group of lads whose names are scribbled at the top: W. Flower, C. Whatley, T. Cox, J. Smith, W. Smith, W. Aubertin – well-known names, all.

Beecham's must have done a real service for amateur music-makers when they published their *Portfolios*, handy little volumes of songs and piano pieces. Tattered remains of numbers up to 19 are found among the piles of Whitaker music. The mixture is marvellous: 'The Death of Cock Robin', 'There's a beautiful land on high', 'Tell me, Mary, how to woo you' and 'The Little Old Log Cabin' all come in quick succession. But there is other matter too. 'Love was once a little boy' ends with two 'Heigh-hos' and below we read:

It is a question whether more Heigh-hos are sighed from the heart or the liver: if the former, the contents of this book may be of assistance to the weary one, but for any Heigh-hos which express that tired feeling emanating from 'that horrid liver' ... there is nothing so beneficial as Beecham's Pills.

A nice thought – are other advertisements scattered through the pages intended to be apt? Were 'The Children of Jerusalem' to use Beecham's Tooth Paste, or 'The Highland Queen' Beecham's Cough Drops for Hoarseness? Certainly there seems a connection between a nostalgic song, 'In this old chair my father sat' and the comment below:

Sleepy? If a man is drowsy in the day time after a good night's sleep, there's indigestion and stomach disorder. Beecham's Pills – Worth a Guinea a Box.

Finally we turn up a manuscript music-book in which some-one has collected items in startling incongruity. Starting with 'They say I'm but a waggoner', it goes on to 'None other Lamb', to the tune All Hallows, and then rescues from oblivion an engaging little ditty, much loved by several generations in the nursery which begins:

There were three little Owls sat a-singing in the barn,
    Dingy, dingy, do, dum, day.

'Oh merry goes the tune when the heart is young' seems rather appropriately juxtaposed to 'The fool hath said in his heart'. At the end is a popular chorus item which featured at Bratton concerts, the Old Trombone:

There was an old man played on a trombone, Pow! Wow! Wow!
The dismallest tune that ever was known, Pow! Wow! Wow!
He was very very old and very very lame,
But it wasn't for that he was most to blame,
But the tune that he played was always the same, Pow! Wow! Wow!

We can imagine how the audience yelled the chorus.

To be at home with the Whitakers on Sunday would not, I think, have been a dismal experience. Sunday School and chapel services took a good chunk of time, but there were plenty of special things to do at home. Instead of the Sunday crossword, both grown-ups and children went in for text-hunting to fill in their Scripture Almanacs which gave a text for each day to which you had to find the Biblical reference. In 1891 Philip, aged 12, was working through the Baptist Visitor's Almanac: every month was completed, and the book was marked 'Perfect'. Another game was making a Scripture Clock. You drew a clock face and divided it into segments for each hour. You chose a key word, like Love, Repentance, or Wisdom and then hunted for texts which contained this word and had the right number of words for each hour. Then the texts were triumphantly inscribed in the appropriate segments.

The Sunday At Home was part of the staple reading at the Yew Trees. It carried a nice mixture of stories, articles on religious leaders and national events and items such as 'Golden Gleanings for Young Folk', 'Bible Competitions' and 'Far and Near' on world religious news. It was a real family magazine. *The Church*, a monthly Baptist magazine, started in 1874 and only costing a penny, was a more low-brow affair, with more stories and less solid reading. Serials, such as 'With Cords of Love', were a great feature, and the constant theme in the stories is the Family: struggling in poverty, stricken in sickness, conquering evil and triumphing through goodness. The drama is heightened by eloquent pictures and captions, such as 'Every tendril of her bright hair seeming to express indignation' – at not being allowed to dance.

On Sunday evenings there was singing round the harmonium in the 'long room'. Several manuscript music books contain favourite hymn tunes, beautifully copied in four parts. One belonged to Philip Whitaker in 1841, another to John, his grandson, in 1853, when he was 13. (Again, rather incongruously, one of these books begins with a three-part setting of ' 'tis the voice of the sluggard'). 'Sankey's Sacred Songs and Solos' provided other items and 'The Sunlight of Song, A Collection of Sacred and Moral Poems' was a great favourite. It had a wonderful frontispiece of the Victorian family at song. Sophie and her mother used to sing soprano/alto duets, as for instance, 'He shall feed His flock' and 'Come unto Me' from *The Messiah*; 'I waited for the Lord' and 'O Rest in the Lord', from Mendelssohn, were also in their repertoire. Mrs Whitaker had songs in Topliff's 'Sabbath Melodies' series, as for instance, 'The Infant's Prayer', sung by Mme Clara Novello, with a moving picture of The Infant on the cover. Her sister Tillie gave her 'Is there no balm in Gilead?', composed by R. Reynolds from the Bristol Blind Asylum and published by A. Demoline of Bristol. Somebody in the family sang the ever-popular 'Rosary' ('The hours I spent with you, dear heart, Are as a string of pearls to me'). Having turned this up, one looks for that other favourite, 'The Lost Chord' – and there it is.

Finally we realize that we can actually view this family

who have left us such vivid relics of their lives. Consider what the invention of photography did for middle-class families who did not so lightly commission portraits of themselves. It seems that with one accord they all went to be photographed. Four imposing albums and boxes of loose photographs present us with the last Whitakers and their tribal ramifications. The leather-bound, brass-clasped albums, with their stiff frames into which the photos slipped, symbolize the seriousness with which family ties were maintained. Here we review rows of patriarchal, bewhiskered gentlemen, younger ones in morning dress with top hats beside them, ladies in crinolines, and later bustles – nearly all seated or standing beside a piece of furniture which seems to be essential to the photographer's art. There are babies in long robes and children who look surprised or coy. Most are now unidentifiable, but we can find our own Whitakers: Joshua sits by a table, with large tomes behind him, looking like a poet rather than a farmer; Mrs Joshua we have already observed, also reading. Old Aunt Thomas was photographed at an age perhaps past merriment, but her face is still shrewd and full of character. John looks at us with bright, deep-set eyes and square figure, while his purposeful wife, Polly, has smooth hair parted in the middle and a wonderfully calm face; delicate-featured little Aunt Tillie ponders on the past. From the next generation we may pick out Jane, a bright-eyed, alert little girl who lived to save all these albums for us.

Groups mark the passage of time. There is an early one of John and Polly, with a rather pathetic little Sophie and the powerful addition of Aunt Thomas who dominates the young people. We move to a charming picture posed by their new tennis-court, with John and Polly in middle life, Sophie as a pretty young woman and Edith, Phil and Jane as teenagers. Here retiring little Aunt Tillie has taken Aunt Thomas's place. And so on to another garden group, with John and Polly as grandparents and Sophie with her brood of three. There are many groups of relations and friends drinking tea under the yew trees or on the brick court, and several groups of John and young members of the family setting out to ride on the hills. Sophie, riding side-saddle in voluminous habit, sits her horse most elegantly, while Phil bestrides a little nag. John Whitaker himself seems part of his mare, as indeed he might, for he spent so much of his life riding. So we should close this picture gallery with a final photograph of John, still in riding-kit with bowler and riding-crop, but now seated on a garden seat, quietly reflecting, towards the end of his life.

9 Chapel Folk

It is difficult to put one's finger on the moment when the eighteenth-century word 'meeting-house' died and people began to talk about 'church' and 'chapel'. By the end of the nineteenth century they commonly said: 'They're church' or 'They're chapel', and the distinction was quite a sharp one – strangely, it seems, sharper than in the previous century. Perhaps this was because from a devoted little band the Baptist community had grown to be, for a time, the dominant religious group in the village. In 1777 there had been about 20 members. In 1800 there were probably about 50. In 1807 the chapel was enlarged by the addition of the gallery and in 1810, 56 members joined to invite Mr Edminson to become their minister. By 1812 there were 79 members and by 1822 the number had risen to 117. The membership was about 150 in the 'thirties and over 160 in the 'sixties. A series of evangelistic meetings caused it to jump to 206, and though it fell back again, right up to 1914 it remained between 160 and 200. In terms of families this meant many more, since children did not become members by baptism until they had attained years of discretion. The advent of National and British Schools in the mid-nineteenth century meant a deepening of the rift between Church and Chapel, since the children were segregated. This was a village with two clear religious foci, and a change of loyalties, such as when a 'chapel' family turned over to 'church', could be a socially disturbing event.

The century started with two leading figures in Baptist affairs: Joseph Goodenough Blatch and Philip Whitaker. They were solemnly elected as deacons in 1800 and until a succession of regular ministers began again in 1805 they virtually conducted the chapel business. Even after 1805 the deacons were more in evidence in the records than ministers. In 1813 two more deacons, Thomas Williams and John Newman, were elected. In the continuous record which was kept after this we find elected to the diaconate Joshua Whitaker (1833), Robert Reeves (1847), John Whitaker (1880), Henry Reeves (1886), Robert John Reeves (1907). But the list also includes a number of names to be found among the servants and employees of the two families: John Newman, James Newman, Lewis Snelgrove, Reuben Ashley, Benjamin Coleman and so on. This highlights the distinctive mixture of hierarchy and democracy that characterized the Nonconformist community.

Whitakers and later Reeveses kept the accounts and minutes and wrote the letters but within the Church they were 'brethren' with the rest. This can be illustrated almost visually from the first Trustees Account Book. In 1806 a new Trust Deed, listing all the property and funds, was read at a Church Meeting and signed by all the members present. For some years after this the accounts were kept in Philip Whitaker's elegant hand, but each year they were audited by two or three other members who signed them. Many were farm-workers whom we can recognize: their clumsy signatures reveal the painfulness of their schooling, while one 'James Coulrick' appears uncertain of his own name. The oldest Church Minute Book shows a closely-knit society, deciding in 1801 to hold a Monthly Church Meeting to promote 'Godly discipline and Christian love'. Everyone was subject to its rulings and everyone had an equal vote. Letters inviting new ministers were signed by all the members. The workings of this village democracy are recorded all through the nineteenth century in the solemn, dignified language proper to a Church Minute Book. Yet physical arrangements in the chapel show clearly how the social hierarchy was ordered. Among the Whitaker papers is an exercise book which starts with a neat plan of all the pews in the chapel, upstairs, in the gallery, and downstairs. It then lists all the families and individuals who paid for the various sittings, starting with the gallery pews: No. 1, Mrs J. Whitaker's servants and Miss Salter's; No. 2, Mrs T. Whitaker's servants and Mrs Whitaker's. Most of the rest of the gallery is occupied by people whose names are recognizable from the 'servants' ledgers'. Downstairs there is a quite democratic mixture, but Mrs T. Whitaker reigns over a whole pew, and Mr J. Whitaker over another, while John Carr, Reuben Ashley, Philip Drewitt crowd into one. There is a discriminating use of the appellation 'Mr'. Mr R. Reeves needs two pews (he had a considerable family), while Mr T. Reeves and Mr J. Reeves have one apiece. One pew of seven seats at the back is graciously labelled 'Free sittings for old people'. The members of the Church were beyond doubt sincerely 'Brothers in Christ', but they recognized necessary social proprieties.

Religious experience, however, gave an authority which transcended social demarcations, and sometimes a natural eloquence to people who did not easily handle a pen. It was entirely accepted that the children of 'the master' were taught in Sunday School by their father's employees. The deacons who took their places at 'the Lord's Table', when the Ordinance of the Lord's Supper was celebrated month by month, prayed with a fervour born of long practice in the faith. Indeed, the memory still lingers of the last of those saintly old preachers and pray-ers who rambled on with marvellous eloquence but little sense of form. The fraternal handshake outside the chapel, which took much longer than the usual perfunctory affair, was performed with mutual dignity. The letter from Lewis Snelgrove to John Whitaker, quoted in chapter five, well illustrates the mixture of deference and equality before God, of dignified language and illiteracy, which seems to me to characterize the common culture of the chapel. In the presence of death all were united. Another letter, written by T. Havel of Newport to 'Mr Widdicar' in 1851, reveals the typical attitude:

Having received a Letter bearing the news of the death of my dear Father, and the kind manner you acted in seeing him so respectably returned to his mother earth, I consider it to be my duty to return you my most sincere thanks for your kindness. It must indeed have afforded you some comfort as well as my dear

199

Mother and Friends, to know that whilst you were committing his body, earth to earth, and ashes to ashes, it was with a sure and certain hope that it would rise again to a life of Glory and happiness. The knowledge you had of him for so many years, his conduct through life, and his last moments, his triumph over death, his confidence in the merits of his redeemer enabled you to say without a doubt, that his soul had taken its flight to the mansions of eternal bliss. Death was for him no trouble . . .

Happy indeed should I have been could I have had the pleasure of hearing your discourse on the death of my father. I am certain you done justice and my sincere and hearty prayer is that some poor sinner was awakened to his lost condition while you were speaking . . . You, Sir, and my death (sic) Father enjoyed sweet fellowship together on earth, may it be your happy portions to be united in eternal fellowship before the throne of mercy . . .

There were three main points at which the activities of this Baptist community were concentrated: foreign missions, the Sunday School and education generally, and the needs of the surrounding villages. The first brought a new dimension into village life which sprang initially from a Whitaker incentive and went back to Philip's marriage with Anne Andrews of Salisbury. This, as we have seen, brought him in touch with the dynamic John Saffery, minister of Brown Street Baptist Church in Salisbury. Saffery's imagination took him outward in concentric circles from his own church: first to the villages of Salisbury Plain, then to evangelizing campaigns in neighbouring counties, then to tours in Cornwall, Ireland, Scotland. But especially he was fired by William Carey's setting forth for India and the foundation of the Baptist Missionary Society in 1792. He immediately formed a Wiltshire Auxiliary in 1793 and started collecting money. Saffery was remarkable for three things: his white-hot zeal for the B.M.S., his untiring energy in touring the country by coach, gig and horseback, and his extraordinary capacity for raising subscriptions from all kinds of persons, including the Bishop of Salisbury and clergy of the Establishment. We have an example of his eloquence in an appeal from which I quote a few sentences:

The poor Idolater has listened and renounced his gods, and even Brahmins, the zealous devotees of a cruel and debasing superstition, have embraced the Gospel ... the genius of that compassion which instructs the children of poverty in Great Britain is employed in rescuing from vice and degradation the childhood of an immense population ... But the most stupendous effort of the Mission is the Translation of the Scriptures into the numerous languages and dialects of the East ... These exertions, designed to promote, not the interests of a party, but those of Christianity in general, are conceived to possess a forcible claim on all by whom that Christianity is valued ...[1]

Saffery's chief memorial lies in four neat little collecting-books which demonstrate his powers of persuasion, and in the multitude of letters which flowed in to him from all parts, and especially from India and Jamaica. He died in 1825 after falling from a gig during a tour in Dorset. Some time afterwards Mrs Saffery gathered together all his papers and brought them to Bratton. A second link with the Whitakers was formed when Joshua married his cousin, Jane Saffery. Old Mrs Saffery lived near her daughter in Bratton until her death in 1858.

John Saffery's portrait looks like a man of action rather than of meditation and one wonders what his impact was on the introspective Philip Whitaker. The first spur seems to have been given to evangelism in the villages. We have a fragment of an account book for 1797 which looks like Philip's. It records subscriptions from a wide area around which were obviously used for preaching, while the balance was 'transferred to the Money for Horse Hire in Village Preaching'. At this time Saffery was forming the Imber Church, amongst others, and this became the special responsibility of the Bratton Baptists. As for the missionary spur, the ground for a wider vision had already been prepared by Western Association Letters which in 1782 had recorded with thankfulness the spread of religious toleration in Europe and in 1788 had pledged itself to the abolition of the slave trade. Baptists were to be no longer an inbred sect but, as the Association Letter of 1793 put it, 'members of a community at large, parts of a vast body of mankind,

[1] See p. 66 for cut-outs made by or for Philip Whitaker's children from a B.M.S. Appeal.

citizens of the world'. John Saffery brought this claim to life. The first recorded collections for the 'Baptist representatives in India' in Bratton were made in 1811 and 1812. In 1814 the Bratton Church's Letter to the Association notes the establishment of a penny-a-week society to support the B.M.S. By 1820 John Saffery's collecting-book records a long list of subscribers in Bratton, including a row of Whitakers.

So Bratton became a missionary church and the missionary vision gave a new colour to the outlook of Bratton people. The *Missionary Herald* and *Juvenile Herald* brought strange new pictures and stories; 'missionary deputations' preached a new sort of sermon and brought exotic objects and costumes to exhibit. Perhaps the box of Saffery papers itself became a stimulus to the imagination, for it is something one would not have expected to find in a remote village. Saffery's Indian correspondent was Joshua Rowe, a Wiltshireman who went out to Serampore in India in 1804. His first long letter was written aboard the ship *Samson* and gives a vivid account of experiences on the voyage. Thereafter he wrote regularly from India until 1822 – 16 letters in all. There they are: sheets of notepaper folded longwise, sealed on themselves and franked with strange marks. Their sheer physical presence evokes the picture of sailing-ships crossing the Indian Ocean or battling round the Cape, all the more so since Saffery methodically noted on each the date when received. They could take up to 200 days to come. Perhaps these and other letters Saffery had received from Jamaica were read in the Whitaker family, but in any case the stimulus of strange, far-off happenings came from other sources too. From 1800 to *c.*1825 Whitakers and Blatches took the *Evangelical Magazine*, and later the *Baptist Magazine*. This carried much missionary material. In the 1800 bound copy one meets straightaway an engraving of 'Temoteitei of the Marquesas, or as he has been called after the ship which brought him to England, Jn. Butterworth'. He is described as a 'young heathen Islander who has been for several months under the care of the Missionary Society', and the tone of the article about him brings out vividly how far removed we are from the racial attitudes of those early devoted evangelizers. A regular feature in this journal was 'Religious Intelligence' which brought together a fascinating medley of information. To read, for instance, 'Extracts from Dr Vanderkemp's Journal of a Journey from the Cape to Roodezand' (1799), or a letter from Parramalta, New South Wales, or an account of disturbances in Tongataboo must have been an absorbing geography lesson. On the Whitaker bookshelves we also find the *Journal of Mr Anthony N. Groves, Missionary during a journey from London to Bagdad, through Russia, Georgia and Persia* ... which Alfred Whitaker bought when it came out in 1831. An appeal by the Patagonians, *Jamaica: Enslaved or Free* and M. L. Whateley's *Ragged Life in Egypt* also represent the widening outlook of the household. In 1845 Joshua Whitaker bought two 'missionary maps' from W. Michael, Westbury.

We do not always realize how powerful the engraving was as a medium of education, often so much more dramatic than the modern flat photograph. What strikes the eye among Whitaker books and pamphlets is the large number of these exciting windows on new worlds, as, for instance, from a book on India, 'Indian jugglers', 'the Mango-tree trick', 'Festival of Juggernaut', 'the Monkey Temple', or again, a moving picture of a fair English girl clasping hands with a hopeful young African. Title pages were exciting too: for instance, a book showing specimens of Sacred Scripture in eastern languages put out by the Serampore Mission has a lovely design to illustrate 'The People that walked in darkness have seen a great light'. This was also true of the *Missionary Herald* which, as we know from their cash accounts, the Whitakers were taking regularly. A copy of 1839 has on its cover a half globe, partly in light, partly in darkness, with representative heathen crouching round and gazing upward where the clouds are rolling back and, in a dramatic shaft of light, the angel with the Everlasting Gospel is flying earthward – so much more stirring than later covers. Besides the *Herald*, the adults took the Annual Report of the B.M.S. which gave the list of subscribers.

When the *Juvenile Herald* appeared in 1845, the

Whitakers were on to the first bound number. It is a neat little volume with eye-catching engravings of far-off places, stories and exhortations. There are geography lessons on coffee, sugar-cane and the like, and poems, such as 'The Little Negro's Joy' from which I quote:

Little negro, why so gay?
Hast thou gained a holiday?
Where's thy driver? prythee say.
Little negro, why so gay . . .
[Reply]:
Me thankful too for every gift
My kindest friends do give;
For nice clean clothes, and holy book,
Which teaches me to live;
But all these things, and nothing mo'
Would leave my heart quite full o' woe.

Yet me *is* glad; I tell you why
My little heart so full o' joy;
The holy Bible which me read,
Say, *Jesus make me free indeed.*

There is a picture and a poem on the sending forth of the missionary ship *The Dove,* and this is accompanied by an exhortation to support her:

The missionaries much wish to visit all the poor heathen on the coast and up the rivers . . . The Dove will help them . . . going backwards and forwards carrying the tidings of Jesus and of eternal life to the wicked and cruel heathen . . . I hope it will go quickly and safely across the sea. Will you pray to God, dear children, that he may graciously preserve the Dove . . . But you must remember it when it is there. It is hoped that the children of England will collect money enough to pay what this ship will cost each year. Take care, dear little reader, that you do your share.

The little reader could then sing 'God speed *The Dove!*' to music provided.

The Jubilee of the B.M.S. in 1842 spurred the churches on to fresh efforts. We still have the poster advertising celebrations in Westbury and district. Lurking among packets of letters there came to light a Bratton list of subscribers to the Jubilee Fund and some collecting cards. Here again nice social distinctions are observed, for the list is headed by Whitakers, Blatches, etc., who subscribe sums varying from the Whitaker 2s 6d per week to the Reeves 6d per week, while the collecting-cards mainly deal with contributions of $1\frac{1}{2}$d to 3d a week from labouring people. These cards are interesting partly because of the working folks' signatures on them and partly for their design. The card is headed by Carey's famous motto – 'Expect great things from God, attempt great things for God' – accompanied by a picture of an altar with an open Bible on it, flanked by two rejoicing natives, with a missionary proclaiming the Gospel and angels trumpeting in the sky. Around the picture are dates and statistics showing the progress of the work. To this effort the Sunday School contributed 17s $10\frac{1}{2}$d, while a chapel collection produced £5.12.7 and 'A.J.W.' gave a gold coin worth £1.19. It was a general effort of high and low in the church and the final result must have been about £80 for the Jubilee Fund.

After this the missionary effort seems to have been continuous. The Sunday School had collecting boxes through which the pennies dropped with a satisfying rattle. Once a year a fascinating operation was performed with a penknife in the bottom of the box by which a concealed aperture was opened up, the box emptied and the opening pasted over again: all immensely absorbing to a child. Bazaars and Sales of Work became fashionable, with ladies' working parties and children's handwork efforts. A ticket of admission to one of Mrs Thomas Whitaker's Juvenile Missionary Bazaars survives. It has this little verse on the back:

Like little rivulets that creep
To find the fountains of the deep,
Let Mercy flow to lands afar,
Through streamlets of a Child's Bazaar.

Under Mrs John Whitaker the women's effort was focused on the Zenana Mission to the women of India. We have a series of letters from Dacca and elsewhere in India thanking for parcels and describing the work. Each year a box of garments and other requested things was dispatched and lists of what was sent between 1899 and 1914 have come to light: jackets are the chief item, but almost every year dolls were dressed and sent, along with marbles, beads, scrapbooks, penholders, writing slates, balls, skipping ropes, puzzles, etc. Pictures, almanacs, old cards, pencils, sewing materials – all sorts of things went, but the chief glory was the display of dolls, exhibited in a show before dispatch and still remembered by Mrs Whitaker's granddaughter.

Serious missionary study for adults centred on a chosen study-book and we still have a Whitaker notebook on one of these, *The Desire of India*. For children *Wonderlands* succeeded the *Juvenile Herald*, changing its style of picture and story with the times. In the last period before 1914 John Whitaker's daughter, Jane, ran a Junior Missionary Circle in which for 'expression work' they painted pictures, coloured texts and mottos and cut out cardboard figures – quite advanced handwork for those days. Year by year the missionary 'deputation' introduced a village congregation to strange scenes and curious objects. It is impossible to estimate the impact of all this on the imagination in pre-television days, but it was certainly a major educational force in this period. Perhaps the greatest impact on successive generations of children was made by the story of William Carey, the Northamptonshire cobbler who looked at a world map as he cobbled and saw the narrow range of his life opening out into a global vision. Many times must Bratton children have heard this story and many times must his famous motto have been coloured and cut out in cardboard. Even Baptists have their saints' relics and among a collection of missionary material at the Yew Trees was a folded piece of paper containing a piece of wood from William Carey's chair.

Sunday School at the beginning of the nineteenth century meant basic skills as well as Bible stories. Reading and writing were essential for bringing up children in the faith. Probably the first enthusiasm for education was fired by Jeffery Whitaker's legacy for the education of poor children. From the Trustees' Account Books we see that year by year this was faithfully expended on the education of specified children, both boys and girls. Here again we meet the names of Newman, Smith, Bristow, Cook and Callaway, once Reeves. From £1 to £2 is expended for one to two years' education. These are clearly weekday scholars, but one of the teachers named, Miss Gibson, was also connected with the Sunday School. Here our main source is a most illuminating Sunday School Account Book, found among the Whitaker papers, which runs from 1804 to 1874. In 1804 it was financed by collections and subscribers, amongst whom the first are a Dr Ludlow, Mrs Whitaker, Mr P. W. Whitaker and Mr Seagram. Miss Gibson was paid a salary, and the earliest purchases on record were '1 doz. Dr Watts Psalms and Hymns, 2 doz. sets of both the First and Second School Catechisms, 2 doz. spelling books, *Sunday School Hymns* and 20 Wicks and Candles.' A little later six *Devizes Spelling Books* were bought and in 1810 four Bibles, 26 Testaments and 80 Spelling Books (1st and 2nd parts) were ordered from the Sunday School Society. The children must eventually have reached the formidable lists of words in Part III, for one copy of this bleak book in brown paper covers has survived. Orders go on in much the same way. We may note in 1811 the purchase of *Lessons for young people in humble life*, the *Child's Memorial, Daniel Cusan* (?) and Small's *Sermons*. Handkerchiefs were bought to be given as rewards and in 1813 we meet the entry: 'Handkerchiefs distributed to those who did not go to Bratton Revel'.

Until Miss Gibson's death in 1817 the schoolchildren sat on wooden forms in a room hired from a Mrs Humphries, probably in the Duke William Inn of which she and her husband were landlords. In 1818, however, the schoolrooms were built on the west side of the chapel and the school started a new phase, though still sitting on white scrubbed forms, probably those still there today. There must have been voluntary teachers from early days, for we still have Anna Jane Whitaker's Fourth Class Attendance Book from 1812 to 1817, but after Miss Gibson the teaching appears to have been entirely voluntary. Anna Jane had around ten in her class of girls, once again with all the familiar surnames. Incidentally, the fact that in 1810 she presented a book to the 'Bratton Meeting Library' tells us that the chapel lending library was already in existence. Our first real guide to numbers in the school comes from the Church's Letter to the Association for 1832, when there were 110 scholars. The Letter of 1837 records 120 scholars and 18 teachers. For the period 1843–53 we have the Superintendent's register for the girls which shows c. 80 girls at the beginning, dropping to c. 50 by the end. This tallies quite well with a *total* number of 96 reported to the Association in 1853. The Sunday School remained roughly of this size through the rest of our period.

It was an orderly Sunday School in which proper records were kept of the scholars, with their ages when admitted and how 'dismissed' in the end. Whitakers and Reeveses figure largely in its affairs. From his bills with Michaels, the Westbury printers and stationers, we see Joshua Whitaker buying, for example, a dozen *Sunday School Companions*, 25 *Pious Child's Delight*, 14 *Infant Pilgrims* and ½ hund. *First Spelling books*. Bibles, hymnbooks, catechisms and tracts were regularly bought for it and sold, as both the Sunday School Accounts and Joshua Whitaker's Cash Accounts show. Mrs Thomas Whitaker gave the *Juvenile Herald*. In the 1850s Robert Reeves was involved in this provision of materials, buying *Heralds* and 'reward books'. Later John Whitaker was Superintendent, then Henry Reeves and finally Robert Reeves (jun.).

We do not have much evidence, apart from these purchases, of what was taught in the mid-nineteenth century, except for one Whitaker book entitled *The Teacher Taught; or The Sunday School Instructor furnished with materials for his work in a series of Questions upon Scripture History to which answers and appropriate texts are appended*, published in 1844. This volume was on Leviticus and was planned to last one month. Here we find the class struggling with such questions as 'What do you mean by "within the veil" ?' and 'What does the Jewish day of atonement set forth?' It may be only a matter of chance that two other surviving relics are a set of teaching cards on the Jewish sacred year, with pictures on one side and information on the other, and a pamphlet issued by the Sunday School Union in

1859 entitled *Pictorial Description of the Tabernacle in the Wilderness*. There is also a large-scale model of Jerusalem. One has the impression that much teaching was concentrated on the Jewish background of the Old Testament.

Some Sunday School equipment survives among the Whitaker books. There is a neat little *Collection of Hymns for the use of Sunday Schools*, published in 1816. Its preface, addressed to the Children and Youths belonging to the Sunday Schools, states that those hymns have been

selected as appeared most suited to your capacities, notwithstanding which there may be several expressions that you do not understand and some subjects which you cannot at present comprehend. In such cases you will do well to apply to your Teachers, who will be pleased to perceive that you are anxious for information and will readily give you all needful instruction according to the wisdom God has given them.

There are some engaging hints on how to praise God in singing which include the following:

3. Avoid a drawling tone, sing with animation, but not too loud; the sweetest singing is the best, and so modulate your voice that you may sing the highest as well as the lowest note without straining it and making a disagreeable noise, and at the close of every verse, let your voice diminish like the sound of a bell.

Did the Bratton children pay any heed? Later, this book was perhaps superseded by *The Sunday Scholars' Hymn Book* published by the Sunday School Union, of which John Whitaker had a copy in 1867. *The Child's Own Hymn-Book*, edited by John Curwen in 1865, was designed 'to aid the pious child in giving full expression to his religious feelings and to invite all children to thoughts of piety by the beauty of the hymn and the charm of the tune'. After this it is a little damping to find that the very first verse reads:

Our evil actions spring
From small and hidden seeds;
At first we think some wicked thing,
Then practise wicked deeds.

But also in this collecton are two charming little paper editions of Isaac Watts' *Divine and Moral Songs for Children*, issued by the Religious Tract Society, and adorned with telling little pictures. We may presume that the Sunday School Lending Library ran continuously, but the only surviving catalogue dates from 1906. There were 283 scholars' books and 13 for teachers. The library was a grand mix of Bible and missionary stories, biography, geography and children's tales. Acquisitions were simply added to the list. Thus the last three items read: 'In touch with nature', 'Bits from Blinkbonny', and 'Oowikapan'.

In the early twentieth century the Sunday School was meeting both before morning service and in the afternoon. At some point – rather ahead of its time in its ideas – it was reorganized into Infants (upstairs), the main school (downstairs) and the Bible Class (in the minister's vestry). At first the Infants sat crowded up together on wooden benches built in tiers, one above another, with the eldest at the top and the youngest at the bottom. Descent by falling or being pushed off was only too easy. Jane Saffery Whitaker took charge in 1900 and during her long regime, the Infants became the Primary Department, the benches were transformed into little seats and tables, and the children sat in small groups. A rather rickety piano led the wandering singing while the children marched round singing 'Hear the pennies dropping'. The bravura with which Jane Whitaker would strike up one of their favourite ditties is something still remembered. The main school was a more dignified affair with a succession of rather weighty superintendents in the persons of John Whitaker, Henry and Robert Reeves. After opening exercises the scholars were taught in small groups. Preparation classes were held for the teachers and the local Sunday School Union often held a monthly prayer-meeting and a quarterly Tea, Business and Prayer-meeting. These were dedicated men and women, intent on 'bringing the lambs into the fold'. History does not disclose what the Bible class did.

There were several highlights in the Sunday School Year. No doubt in the scholar's memories the two first-ranking ones were the Treat and the Christmas Party. The Treat went back at least to the mid-nineteenth century, for in 1847

Robert Reeves was collecting money for it. We do not know what form it took in earlier days, but later it is remembered as beginning with a motley procession 'up the Castle', headed by the waggons with the 'swing boats' and other vehicles with provisions, tea-urns and trestle tables, followed by the ladies to 'cut up', and finally everyone else. It was a festival of sliding down the earth-works, pulling yourself up on the swing-boats until you could see the blue country spread far below the White Horse, of singing games, and – finally – of playing 'thread-the-needle' helter-skelter all down 'the Castle' again. The Christmas treat was more conventional and probably of more recent origin, but one suspects that the summer treat may have begun as an alternative to that mysterious and wicked Bratton Revel. For the teachers, the Sunday School Anniversary in early summer was the most important occasion. The whole school turned out in its best pinafores to sing and recite to a chapel filled with its parents. Special hymns were practised beforehand, there was a special preacher and a special collection for the school. We still have copies of the Services of Sacred Song they performed and early printed programmes of these occasions. Latterly, one of the attractions was the sight of all the primary children (aged 3 to 7) sitting packed together on the rostrum under the pulpit and capable of a 'demonstration' on their own at any minute.

Linked with the Sunday School was the Band of Hope, the league to guard the young against alcoholism. This was a Victorian development. The Whitakers, for one, had always in the past drunk beer and cider, as their account and recipe books testify. But somewhere in the 1880s John Whitaker became a 'tea-totaller' – a word invented in the drive against the social evils of alcohol. His move created a minor stir among his farming friends at market and one is reported to have said: 'I would give a lot to make John Whitaker drunk'. Perhaps the temperance movement in Bratton was partly sparked off by horror stories of the great cities, for in the period 1865–76 a Miss Whitaker was collecting for the London City Mission. At any rate, the Band of Hope became a flourishing social institution. It issued brightly decorated membership cards, with a pious girl and boy kneeling in opposite corners and the legends: 'Lead us not into temptation' and 'I promise to Abstain from all Intoxicating Drinks'. The example in front of me belonged to Jane Whitaker, dated 1888, and across the smug little girl's face someone has written 'Jeanie'. The only surviving Programme Book starts in 1903, from which we see that the session began with an opening meeting and address in the autumn, followed by periodic lectures, on, for instance 'The Best Teatotaler' or a Magic Lantern show, like one entitled 'Brave Benny'. The chief focus of attention was, however, on the socials and entertainments. The socials follow a regular pattern of which the following is a sample:

Temperance Social. Nov. 4th 1903.
1. Hymn 14
2. Prayer
3. Hymn 91
4. Roll Call ....Mr. N. G. Reeves
5. Chairman's Remarks..............Mr. H. Reeves
6. Recit........'Eddie's Pledge'......Percy Aubertin
7. Hymn 124
8. Recit........'The House that Jack Mr. N. Staynes, Miss
                built'   M. Staynes
9. Recit........'The Pride of Battery Emily Flower
                B'
10. Song........'Little Rosa' ....Mr. P. J. Whitaker
11. Dialogue ....'Evidence of Sam   Willie Barnes
                Weller in the trial   Jack Smith
                of Bardell v.   Willie Smith
                Pickwick'
12. Refreshments
13. Hymn
14. Benediction

The entertainments became major village events and as such deserve a place in my last chapter. There is little about actual teaching on the evils of alcoholism in the surviving material, except in the *Hymns and Songs for Bands of Hope* which featured at the meetings. Here the heart-rending appeals and calls to battle are so eloquent that it is hard to select:

212

Hark! The Temperance trumpet calling,
See around you sights appalling,
See the wretched drunkards falling,
RALLY, TEMPERANCE MEN.
Drink is spreading desolation,
Hail the dawning reformation,
One and all, throughout the nation,
RALLY, TEMPERANCE MEN.   (Sung to 'Men of Harlech'.)

The concern for education which characterized the Baptist community is clearly seen in its efforts for elementary education in the village as a whole. The grants from Jeffery Whitaker's bequest for the education of poor children go on until 1843, the last payment being to Jemima Callaway 'till her giving up school'. The next year and thereafter 'Mr Whitaker's charity for educating poor children' goes to the treasurer of the newly erected British School. The appearance in Bratton of the National School in 1820 and the British School in 1844 reflected the controversy throughout the country on non-sectarian v. sectarian education. The Baptists were, of course, passionate supporters of the latter and both Whitakers and Reeveses threw themselves into the support and management of the British School. We have already referred to the Account of Subscriptions for Building the British School which was the responsibility of Joshua Whitaker. Two more of the innumerable little notebooks which fetched up with the Whitakers concern the British School. One is an account of subscriptions to the 'British Girls' School' from 1855 to 1865. All the leading Baptist ladies gave regularly and there are frequent Whitakers and Reeveses in the lists. Folded inside is a revealing collection of accounts paid, mostly for sewing materials. William Couzens, Linen & Woollen Draper, Silk Mercer, etc., of Westbury supplied yards and yards of calico. The other book gives an account of the garments made and sold: shirts at 2s and chemises at 1s 3d brought in very small profits, but the girls were obviously expected to earn something towards their education. Among the Whitaker papers is also a letter from the Committee of Council on Education in Whitehall, written to the minister of the Baptist Church (Rev. G. W.

213

Fishbourne), dated 28 March 1846. It acknowledges receipt of a copy of the Deed of Conveyance of the British School, sent by Mr Whitaker, and authorises payment of the Government Grant towards the erection of the school. It is signed by no less a person than J. K. Shuttleworth. In this same period Joshua Whitaker also records subscriptions to 'the British School at Imber', but – so far as I am aware – nothing more is known about this school. Later the Nonconformist belief in non-sectarian education found strong expression at a public meeting held in Bratton on 14 June, 1902, at which John Whitaker took the chair and Henry Reeves proposed the motion of protest against the Education Bill before Parliament which would, they believed, 'strengthen the whole system of sectarian education.'

Quite apart from the British School, apparently, Mrs Joshua Whitaker for some years ran an Infant School in a building which can be seen near the chapel in an old picture. We know little about this: a fragment of accounts has survived and the attendance register for 1854–60 has been rescued. It begins with ten on the register but climbs to 45 in 1857 and 63 in 1858, remaining stationary at 50–60. The same basic Bratton working families appear, with some new ones. Caroline, Mary and Martha Reeves all attended, but no Whitakers. The school must have faded out at some point, for the next we hear of it is in 1887 when the Baptist Trustees met to 'consider a proposal for making the building formerly used as an Infant Schoolroom a Public Room for the benefit of the village'. They agreed to this on condition that the building was removed to a central site in the village. The Trustees were to be residents in the village, five churchmen and six nonconformists. Mr Whitaker (John), as acting trustee, was to communicate with the principal residents of the village with a view to calling a public meeting. The project was duly carried through and the result was the original Jubilee Hall. It is said that the floor of the Infant School was hauled up intact.

Both Whitakers and Reeveses were also closely involved in running the Evening Continuation School held at the British School. For this we have the Log Books of the years

1893–1906. The session ran from October to February, and in 1893 25 boys and 12 girls enrolled for a curriculum which consisted mainly of the three Rs, relieved by 'vocal singing' which Beatrice Reeves taught. John Whitaker was a manager and Henry Reeves was correspondent. Both visited regularly, signing the log book and sometimes taking classes. Later the curriculum was widened to include geography, the 'science of common things', map-drawing, etc. There were lectures on Chalk, Coal, Bones and so on. Henry Reeves characteristically gave a lecture on 'The Pump' with diagrams, and later, on 'Water'. From 1895 to 1898 Edith Whitaker was one of a group of teachers, after which Mr and Mrs King, well-known teachers in the British School, took over the evening classes. This was a serious effort on the part of both pupils and teachers, and the inspectors who came (since a grant was involved) usually praised the ordderliness, effort and progress made. In 1900 efforts were extended to a twice-weekly Reading Room Session during the winter. Over 400 young men came, with Robert and Nelson Reeves of the younger generation in charge of 'good order'.

In the third place Bratton Baptists developed a strong sense of responsibility towards the surrounding villages. The zeal for village preaching which had been sparked off by John Saffery had not waned and the Church became committed to an energetic plan of founding and serving its own village 'stations'. Help for a Sunday School at Coulston is evident from those earliest Sunday School accounts, while the Baptist group at Imber formed part of the Bratton Church until it became a separate church in 1839, with continued support from Bratton. The chapel papers include a lease of Tinhead Malthouse to P. Whitaker and others in 1801 for the holding of services. Soon involvement in such causes led to the building of chapels. Once more the Whitakers played a major part and some of the documentation turns up among their papers. We have fragments of a notebook beginning with Donations to 'Coulstone' Chapel and accounts of rent and repairs in 1831, running to 1844. This is, I think, the only evidence of a chapel there at that date. Later we find among donations to Coulston the following:

215

R. Reeves £5, John Whitaker £3, Henry Reeves £2, Mrs J. Whitaker £2, J. Reeves £1. The work in Steeple Ashton began with a week-evening meeting in 1861, held in a shop, which was attended by 80 to 100 people by the time a Sunday evening meeting was started in 1862. A house was found which could be converted into a 'neat and commodious chapel' and the Whitakers, particularly the young John and Cecil, threw themselves into the project. The first bills came to their father Joshua and when he died in 1864 his brother-in-law, P. J. Saffery, collected 'a personal tribute to the memory of one "whose deep and prayerful interest in Evangelistic efforts made at Steeple Ashton contributed so largely to their success" '. In all about £260 was collected for Steeple Ashton chapel and they broke even. Finally, the Cheverell story must be briefly mentioned. There was already a building in use there as a chapel when it was adopted by Bratton in 1877 as a village station. John Whitaker wrote an appeal for renovations costing £40 and collected this sum, not only in the pounds of leading families, but in the shillings and sixpences of poorer members. Unfortunately this rented building was auctioned and bought by the Vicar at Cheverell in order to keep the Baptists out. The Nonconformist reaction was strong. A Bratton deacon, Alfred Pocock, bought another piece of land, contributions flowed in to J. S. Whitaker, Henry Reeves acted as architect and in 1907 the new chapel was opened in great triumph. Two photographs recall this moment of 'battles long ago'. One could be called the Four Patriarchs, that is, the bearded and venerable figures of Alfred Pocock, Henry Reeves, John Whitaker and Charles Hobbs (the minister) outside the door of the new chapel (17). Into the other all the excited congregation at the Opening crowd, a tribute to those shillings and sixpences and a symbol of Nonconformist democracy.

But evangelism in the villages meant not only raising money for buildings. It meant lay preachers and Sunday School teachers who had to get there, and this meant walking, riding, driving in a horse-vehicle or – latterly – cycling. There is a story of three Baptist worthies driving back from a Sunday evening service at Imber in a pony trap. On the steep downward road one says to the others: 'Whose is that wheel running down the hill in front? Why, it's ours!' Bratton leaders were indefatigable in this work. Two 'Preachers' Plans' survive for 1897 and 1898 which show them going regularly to Ashton, Cheverell and Coulston on Sundays. At Coulston there was a week-night meeting as well. John Whitaker and his son, Henry Reeves and his son, appear several times in these plans. But only for John Whitaker does any record over a long period survive. Characteristically he ferreted out an old school notebook to re-use. On the cover we read '34. John Saffery Whitaker. Aug. 11th 1856' and the first and back pages have pieces of translation from Herodotus and Terence. Clearly it was a relic of his Mill Hill days (perhaps unused because of illness) in which he now wrote on his starting page: 'My first Sunday Service was at Tinhead on the evening of 18th October, 1868'. In this book he recorded methodically all the places at which he preached and all his texts between 9 May 1869 and 20 June 1915 – about four months before he died; it is an astonishing record. The places were mainly Tinhead, Steeple Ashton, Coulston, Shrewton, Cheverell, Littleton, Imber and Bratton itself. Occasionally he preached at Westbury or Melksham. Often he took both afternoon and evening services. At the end of each page he totted up the number of services taken and he maintained a running total. In the first year he preached 22 sermons; by January 1875 he had reached 200 and in this year he preached 54 times. Thereafter he gives both the total for each year and the running total. The number in each year is usually between 40 and 50. Once he took a service at Grants Farm. In 1885 there is a break and down to 1889 the yearly total is below 30, but in 1890 he is back to 41 services and after that sometimes rises above 50. He reaches the grand total of 1,000 in 1896. In 1901 he took 57 services on 32 Sundays and he maintained this level of activity until 1905 when the number begins to drop back to the thirties and then the twenties. In 1911 he could still take 27 services on 18 Sundays, but thereafter he only managed one or two until the last two at Cheverell (13.6.15) and Coulston (20.6.15), only months before he died. He still totalled the last full page triumphantly as 1,582 sermons preached so far. The record speaks for itself. Others were certainly as faithful but no one else quite so methodical.

The chapel community was one in which people of many different types, varying education and recognized differences of social standing found a common ground in religious experience and activity. It was a warm community which provided for most social needs. Characteristically, the Bratton Friendly Society was started in 1843 out of the concern of Baptist leaders. The 'Sabbath' (more favoured term than 'Sunday') centred on the two – sometimes three – main services in which the regular pattern was a sandwich of hymns, prayers and Bible readings, with a Long Prayer and Sermon towards the end. Hymns were important and had to be sung to the right tune. There still survive manuscript tune-books containing favourites not to be found elsewhere. People were connoisseurs of tunes and metres in days when hymns were started by a deacon, with or without a tuning fork, or perhaps led by a violin. There are various reminiscences of starters who sent the congregation quavering up into the skies or tried to fit a long metre hymn to a common metre tune. Probably sometime before 1866 a harmonium was introduced and in 1884 a new American organ was installed in the gallery: successive generations of Whitakers and Reeveses played it with the choir grouped around. In 1895 John Griffiths left £100, the income on which was to be used 'towards improving and supporting the choir'. The fund was handled by Henry and then Robert Reeves. Amongst members of the choir named at that time were P. J. Whitaker (bass), R. J. Reeves (tenor), O. J. Reeves (tenor). Favourite hymns were ones with repeats or choruses and when people got tired of the staid *Psalms and Hymns* they turned to the rollicking selection of Sankey's *Sacred Songs and Solos*. A number of people enjoyed singing a part, often from tonic sol-fa. Basses and tenors in particular seemed to have their special passages for self-expression. One old bass is still remembered for his performance of the runs in a repeating tune to 'Crown Him with many crowns' which

218

allowed him to come down the scale on 'Cr-wow-wow-wow-wow ...' We have an indication of the general interest in tunes in John Whitaker's record of tunes played between 1866 and 1876 which he kept at the back of his preaching notebook.

There is no record of the first Harvest Festival but it became a major event, with a decorating team on Saturday afternoon, who, amongst other things, put red apples all round the gallery ledge, the chapel packed with extra congregation on Sunday, thundering out 'Come ye thankful people come!', and a public meeting in the week. This event became linked with concern for the poor in great cities, and in latter years the produce was afterwards sent to the West Ham Central Mission. To a Bratton child 'West Ham' spelt a poignant contrast. Here was the chapel, filled to the brim with abundance: sheaves of wheat and a large harvest loaf, potatoes and apples tumbling about, yellow marrows like half-moons, immaculately scrubbed carrots, beetroot, parsnips ... all in profusion. And there, in the imagination, were those pale little children creeping along pavements with not a blade of grass in sight, who never had enough to eat. So the packing of the boxes for West Ham was the climax of Harvest Home. There is other evidence of concern for poverty in a wider context than just local need. For instance, at the time of the Lancashire cotton famine in 1862, the Baptist congregation in Bratton contributed £24 and that at Tinhead £1 'for the relief of Lancashire distress'.

Among special occasions were various types of revivalist meeting or 'tent mission' held in the neighbourhood, at which people would gather in great numbers. When the main Great Western Railway Line was being built just north of Bratton c.1898–1900, a great evangelistic opportunity presented itself in terms of the Irish navvies at work there. Mr Seagram organized a mission at Bratton House which was run by Baptists, one of whom later recalled playing the harmonium for the Irishmen. Many chapel occasions were marked by 'tea-meetings' in the schoolroom, with a public meeting in the chapel afterwards. Here the ladies took control, ordering lardy cakes, buns, etc., 'cutting up' beforehand

219

with their own favourite knives which they brought and took away again, and presiding behind the tea-urns at the ends of the long trestle tables in a strict order of precedence. Tea-table 'greetings' and speeches were in vogue and there was much exchange of fraternal good wishes, with a certain amount of sedate joking and story-telling. It was a warm, cosy kind of occasion. In 1863, and roughly at ten-year intervals after this, the Wilts and East Somerset Baptist Association met in Bratton, requiring to be provided with lunch and tea (15). These larger numbers must have strained resources somewhat, but the ladies' tea committee always seems to have coped. There are still extant some of the precious little notebooks in which they wrote down quantities to order for different sorts of occasion.

It is difficult now to recover the flavour of village Nonconformity in its hey-day, when the chapel gallery was full of families, as well as the downstairs pews. It represented a way of life with its own language and vocabulary, its high earnest purposes and mild enjoyments, its variety of self-expression and its sometimes very funny happenings. There was, no doubt, plenty of hardship and tragedy, back-biting and quarrelling, but one is left with the impression that the really committed members were established in a solid loyalty which transcended the very evident social hierarchy.

10 Occasions

Families in the past created their own occasions. They visited each other with enthusiasm, even in the winter, and in the summer 'the Bratton season' summoned them to rural pleasures. In the later part of the nineteenth century – when railways made it easy – families seemed to pour in by tens and dozens, but even before this, letters, diaries and the village magazines show them arriving regularly in horse-drawn vehicles, if not on horse-back. There were the Greens from Holcombe, Attwaters of Bodenham, Safferys of Salisbury and London, Wassells of Bradford-on-Avon. John's wife, Polly, brought in a large tribe of Brinkworths from Chippenham. John's eldest sister, Anna, married W. H. Gotch and in due course brought five boys and a daughter to holiday in Bratton. John's brother, Cecil, married Polly Brinkworth's sister and after he had settled in Birmingham as a Baptist minister, the Yew Trees opened its doors to the 'Birmingham Whitakers', with their five children. There were also fringe relatives, such as Tuckers and Woollacotts. At the end of the century, after John's daughter, Sophia, had married Arthur Coombs, three small children of the next generation began to look forward to summer holidays in Bratton. Luckily the Yew Trees would accommodate a lot of small fry on its top floor and Polly Whitaker might well have quoted Christina Rossetti: 'Yea, beds for all who come'. A large family net-work provided a great deal of social life in an all-age group of almost clan-like proportions.

Village magazines were still a summer amusement, and so we come across a tattered number of the *Bratton Gazette* for 24 July 1875. It announces Fashionable Arrivals, notably of

Lady Chapman de Maizey and Grafin von Pulverthurminger, and informs us that Mrs Cross at the Post Office had a postcard, left there yesterday evening, written in a language hitherto unknown in this locality. It carries a leading article on the White Horse (once again an object of fascination) which puts forward the theory that it was established by Julius Caesar to mark the place where he first landed in Britain ('we have seen several shells there which seem to show that the sea once came up to this spot'). The highlight of this number, however, is a poem to be sung to the tune of Old Hundredth:

Oh Bratton on the banks of Brat!
Where Muses oft have sung and sat
Thou art the place to grow so fat
Oh Bratton on the banks of Brat!

Thy natives turn with souls so flat
From natural beauties to gaze at
Miss Minnie Wassell's grand new hat
Oh Bratton on the banks of Brat!

So the erroneous idea that the village was named after the stream was already circulating.

'Expeditions' were the great thing. They drove out in waggonettes or brakes, with large hampers of food for the picnic – no one had yet thought of eating-houses on the road. We have already heard about expeditions to Stoke (Erlestoke); the park was still apparently stocked with deer and enjoyable to visit. Once a year Lord Bath allowed his tenants the use of the boathouse and boats at Shearwater on the Longleat estate, so there was usually an all-day excursion, with much boating and a large picnic. A faded photograph shows a boatload, with John Whitaker, an impressive figure in a tall hat, Aunt Tillie in a bonnet and younger women in full-blown hats. One of the Whitaker silver spoons is allegedly still at the bottom of Shearwater. Stonehenge was another objective. Mrs Saffery wrote a sonnet to young Alfred Whitaker, 'On the Plain at Stonehenge, August 1831', which evokes the spirit of a summer expedition:

. . . how many a lofty thought must climb
From thee, ere long – from thee whose laughing eye
Surveys it now with looks so gaily sweet
And wildly sportive as the summer fly,
Companion of the harebell at thy feet.

Later photographs bring back the days when there was no
fence or guard and you could group yourselves as you
wished on the stones. Here we see Polly Whitaker and her
sister-in-law, Anna Gotch, well fortified in cloaks and
bonnets, surrounded by a tribe of young Whitakers and
Gotches. Perhaps 'The Ballad of Wild Whitakers and Stonehenge' belongs to this era:

The Whitakers sat in the Yew Trees hall
Planning to cross the Plain;
'Good Uncle, lend us a brake to take
Us there and back again'.

To see Stonehenge, to see Stonehenge,
To Stonehenge over the Plain,
'But who will choose us a day', they said,
'When there shall be no rain?'

Then waited they full many a day
But ever, alas, rain fell,
And so it chanced in a storm that they
Set out, as I shall tell.

So manfully the horse did plod
And manfully plodded he,
While the wind did howl, and the rain did fall
Till the land was like the sea.

At length they reached the ancient stones
And three times round drove they,
From east and west, from south and north
Gazed thrice and drove away.

Home, home again across the Plain
While all the world did drip
And squelched and oozed each rider's shoes
Ere he did end that trip.

But nothing could dampen the passion for excursions. When
bicycles came in, younger members of the clan made their
own expeditions. Another photograph shows a bicycling
party at Stonehenge (18) and this brings back a reminiscence
of Edith Whitaker's – that she had to bicycle up every hill

on the road to Stonehenge not to be beaten by the Gotch boys. The Whitakers had some of the first bicycles in the village and, while the men went in for special cycling knicker-bockers, the women had to have dress-guards to keep their long skirts out of the wheels. One famous expedition of the younger Whitakers with Arthur Coombs to Longleat was celebrated by the latter in a parody of Cowper's well-known hymn which begins: 'What various hindrances we meet/when coming to the Mercy-Seat'. Arthur's version ran:

What various hindrances we meet
When coming home from sweet Longleat!
Yet who that knows a picnic's fun
But wishes it were oftener done?

Restraining oil, our lamps go out;
Which makes us stop and stay about,
And Sophie trembles when she sees
Her lamplight flicker in the breeze.

Were half the breath on cycles spent
To wagonette and carriage lent
Some panting lungs would often feel
'Give me a horse and not a wheel'.

Nearer home there were always large picnics at Grant's Farm over the top. The children had rides on the sack trolleys, slid down the grass slopes and played in the big barn on its 38 staddle-stones; everyone was weighed on the big corn-scales. And of course there was a big tea in the shooting lodge. Several photographs outside the big barn at various dates bring back vividly the reality of the large family gathering. Here is the patriarch, John Whitaker, venerable but still upright, and the matriarchal ladies in bonnets and capes (with little Aunt Tillie bobbing in at one side), their children in the costume of c. 1900 and a succession of grandchildren now appearing. In a final Grant's Farm photograph of c. 1909 (19) John Whitaker holds his youngest grandchild (Edith Joan Reeves, born 1907). The on-going family life seems so secure, but behind John stands a schoolboy, his eldest grandchild Henry Whitaker Coombs, too soon to be killed in the First World War, that great disrupter of the society they knew and believed in.

A photograph of a wagon full of children recalls halcyon days when the sun shone on the hay and the children romped in it. In the early 1900s a picnic was arranged for the younger ones when the hay in the last field was ready to be carried. The ride down in the empty waggon had a special spice of excitement, for this particular field lay on the other side of the new railway-line, crossed by a farm track. So there was careful negotiation with the station-master at Edington as to the habits of express trains, but there was always a faint shiver of apprehension lest a wayward train would break the laws. Haycocks are made for endless games and when the last one had been lifted, the ride home on top of the loaded waggon brought hay harvest to a blissful conclusion in infant minds at least. Of the autumn harvest supper only one record remains – a poem addressed to Aunt Thomas in 1857:

Draw, Draw, Draw
Beer in the morning like rain,
Draw, Draw, Draw,
Beer in the evening again.
Boil, Boil, Boil,
Pratees and Bacon and Beef,
Roast, Roast, Roast,
The eatin's beyond belief.

One summer occasion for the village was the Whit Monday procession and dinner of the Bratton Friendly Society, recalled for us in an old photograph.

An odd assortment of handbills and tickets bears witness to a variety of occasions of quite a different sort. We should so much like to know who went to Signor Bertolotto's 'Extraordinary Exhibition of the Industrious Fleas' in Bath. The handbill advertising this was wrapped round a bundle of letters (21). It tells us that there will be a Ball Room scene in which two Fleas dressed as Ladies and two as Gentlemen dance a waltz, while twelve fleas, as an orchestra, play instruments of proportionable size: 'the Music is audible'. There is a Mail Coach drawn by four fleas who are belaboured by the Flea Coachman in royal livery, while the Guard blows the horn. The Marquis of W— will appear in a pea-green coat and white trousers, driving a tandem and other spirited flea-performers are the Great Mogul, 'The Three Heroes of Waterloo – Wellington, Napoleon and Blucher – riding on fleas with gold saddles, and 'Two Fleas deciding an Affair of Honour'. The period of this flea-show would have been just about right for Joshua and his brothers and we hope the young men enjoyed it. Another handbill announces that on 5 October 1852 the Westbury Athenaeum would be opened, when J. Sheppard of Frome would lecture on 'The Life and Times of Alfred the Great'. The bill informs us that, as the new building is now completed, with every attention to comfort and at a considerable expense, the committee relies with confidence upon the cordial co-operation of the Gentry and Tradesmen of the Town and Neighbourhood. There were to be lectures every fortnight and alternate lectures would form a popular course on Experimental Chemistry given by Dr Gibbs. This would have been much more in Mrs Joshua Whitaker's line than flea shows.

We have a programme for concerts in the Town Hall at Warminster in 1855, when the Mistress Dolby and Mr Dolby would sing in 'Mr. P. Dyer's Grand Evening and Morning Concerts (reserved seats 4/–)'. Some Whitakers probably went to one of these concerts, for against certain items the word 'ordered' is written and on the back details of three more numbers are written: two from 'Rigoletto' and a quartet 'Brighter than the stars above'. In Bratton itself, Willie Brinkworth, Polly's brother, came from Chippenham to give concerts. He had a good voice and brought the house down with his comic songs. Once he raised £3.1.2. for the Bratton Cricket Club. Local Flower Shows were already established in the mid-nineteenth century, for a Members' Ticket to the Keevil District Floral and Horticultural Society's Show on 29 August 1866 has survived. For a later date there is a handbill of 1903 announcing the Cheese and Butter competitions in the annual Chippenham Agricultural Show – did Jane Whitaker enter for the butter section? One amusing survival shows one of the visiting families putting on an entertainment for Bratton consumption. The programme of the 'Alfredo

Opera Company' announces that it will perform a comic operetta, 'My Uncle the Ghost' and selections from 'Gilbert and Cellier's' comic opera *The Mountebanks*. The General Manager was Signor Edgarello and the Musical Conductor A. P. Whitaker, so these were clearly Cecil's sons indulging in the literary capers beloved of their father while on a summer visit to Bratton.

No doubt there was always village cricket, but records do not appear until we come across the account book of the Bratton Cricket Club from 1896 to 1904. Whitakers always seemed to be keeping accounts and in this case the treasurer was John's son, Philip. The Captain was then Benjamin Emm, Vice-Captain, Fred Burgess, and the Committee, Ernest Smith, John Scull, George Walter, W. H. Smith and 'Alfie John' Smith. They collected subscriptions from honorary members, such as W. H. Laverton, W. H. Seagram and some of the Reeves family. The vicar and minister subscribed and, at one point, Sir John Fuller, the M.P. Members paid 1s. each and out of the funds they bought equipment, paid for a pitch in 'Great Ground' (a field on the east of the Trowbridge road), hired the Jubilee Hall at 6d for their A.G.M. and even sometimes expended 6d on 'fetching tea'. In 1897 the club had to hire a water-barrel, presumably because of the dry season and in this year provisions for the 'Royal Artillery Match' appear to have cost 3d. Alas – an account book can give little inkling of triumphs and defeats, of the memorable innings and the long evenings of pleasure, but occasionally it lifts the curtain on disaster: 'Doctor's Bill for sewing up Harvey Smith's chin cut open at Cricket Match at Heytesbury, 4s'. In 1903 the members' subscription went up from 1s. to 1s. 6d. – ominous sign.

From the early 1890s onwards tennis was the great summer game among the upper ten in the village. Whitakers and Reeveses together organized the large parties that played on each other's courts through long summer evenings. There is no record of when the tennis court was cut out of the orchard at the bottom of the Yew Trees garden, but an early photograph shows a foursome of young Whitakers playing against a background of leafy apple trees. In 1894

Philip began – true to type – to record his tennis wins and losses, in a notebook once dedicated to German at Winchester High School. Almost the only person who could beat him in singles was his sister Edith who was well-known for her over-arm service at a time when many ladies still did underhand lobs. Those parties, when they played as long as the light lasted, must have been very agreeable occasions and the photographs, with ladies in long white skirts and blouses, take us straight back to the days of leisurely amateur sport. At the Yew Trees the way to the tennis court lay through an enormous box hedge in which the children happily played 'houses' to the sound of hitting racquets. Henry Reeves made a similar orchard court at The Butts, Oswald Reeves squeezed one in on his front lawn at The Beeches and – just before 1914 – Robert Reeves made a new tennis court in the garden of The Elms. Among the quaint bits to survive is the record of a Tennis Tournament held on the Butts/Beeches courts some time before 1914. It shows the social circle of the tennis players nicely: all the younger Whitakers and Reeveses, together with the Dermers (the family into which Gracie had married), George Brent from Luccombe, Miss Bird (the doctor's daughter) and some visiting friends. It is amusing to see that Edith Whitaker, by this time Mrs R. J. Reeves, won the Ladies' Singles, her brother Phil the Men's Singles and Oswald Reeves, with his cousin-in-law, Mrs R. J., the Mixed Doubles, beating Mr R. J. and Mrs Nelson Reeves.

Still turning over the sports material we come on *The Book of Croquet* by Arthur Lillie, Champion, Grand National Croquet Club, 1872, with a quotation from *The Tempest* on the front: 'Why hath thy queen summoned me hither to this short-grassed green?' This is a real period piece, with its pictures of Victorian ladies and gentlemen in earnest combat and its advertisements for croquet equipment. The introduction remarks on the simultaneous appearance in the world of 'tight croquet' and of short petticoats with fascinating borders which showed pretty ankles and gives as one reason for the phenomenal success of croquet as a national pastime 'the fact that it is the only game that brings gentlemen and ladies together in the open air'. It arouses in the breasts of its players strong rival feelings, excitements ferocious and excitements tender, so that whether for flirtation or downright hard play it holds the palm. Front lawns were the place for croquet and several in Bratton were dedicated to the game, though at the Yew Trees, it had to be played on the sloping lawn at the back, under the yew trees and with considerable hazards. The croquet played in Bratton must have been very like 'Garden-Party Croquet' as described by Mr Lillie:

Some play Croquet for the game; some play it for idleness, or an excuse for a gathering on a fine summer's afternoon ... The great beauty of Croquet is its elasticity; it amuses children of five, and I have seen a fine old gentleman of ninety take delight in it ... We all remember the difficulty of running the cage on the side where the grass was worn away. We can all call to mind the amicable wrangle about two hands and one; the hunt after Two-blue who would persist in imagining that her partner was playing in that distant set under the laburnums; the almost tragic excitement of One-red when they were putting out his rover

and – I would add – the unmitigated tragedy of the youngest player when croqueted into the shrubbery.

When the summer visitors had disappeared and the tennis nets had been stored away, Bratton settled down to amuse itself through the winter. In November, 1886, the Bratton Mutual Improvement Society was inaugurated – surely symbolic of the Victorian spirit. Its object was the intellectual improvement of its members, but it was specially ruled that 'nothing at any meeting shall be introduced which (either in Religion or Politics) is of a party or denominational character'. Members were elected and paid a subscription of 1s. Women were at first excluded, but in the Minute Book which we have this rule has been crossed out and they were, in fact, admitted by 1888. The committee which drew up the constitution consisted of the Vicar and Baptist Minister, J. S. Whitaker, H. Reeves and G. Cleverley (a well-known farmer), but at the opening meeting on 5 December, the 40 odd members who joined represented a real cross-section of village society, with Smiths, Newmans, Meads, Hobbses in plenty and many other familiar names. One rule, which elaborately limits speaking time in discussions and imposes a severe discipline on offenders, makes one wonder if they were providing for the rambling old boy who was notorious for lengthening Baptist Prayer Meetings.

They opened with a concert on 9 December, given to a packed house in the National School. Non-members paid 3d. and oddly they took 29/10d at the door. Songs and duets were 'ably rendered by the members kindly assisted by their lady friends', as the newspaper report puts it. The post-master, Mr Cross, and his son played in a violin trio, the vicar's daughter played piano pieces, John Whitaker read from Cowper's 'Conversation', and lots of people sang, ending with a glee, 'Silvery Moon' by Alfred and Isaac Pocock and others. This effort must have been highly successful, for new members continued to crowd in until the season closed in March. There were lectures, debates and readings, as well as the ever-popular concerts. We notice that when they had a reading and recitation meeting, a small approval committee was appointed to vet the items beforehand. The Society soon settled into a programme of lectures, debates and impromptu speeches which reveals clearly the local and national concerns of its members. For instance, on 14 October 1887 impromptu speeches were made on: Should Museums be opened on Sundays?; Small Holdings; Local Option (on public houses); Will England fall into decay like the nations of antiquity?; Use of Tobacco. Animated discussions are recorded as when Mr W. Reeves read a paper on 'Ought not a man to be paid according to his personal worth?' and the meeting concluded 'in Theory it was right but in Practice impossible'. The concerts went on enthusiastically. There was one on 15 December 1887 at which Mr, Mrs and Miss Whitaker sang a glee, 'The Barque before the Gale', which we find among the Whitaker music, and then, on 29 December of the same year, the committee had to arrange tea for 120 and a concert in which last-minute performers press in with much goodwill. Magic-lantern shows and even charades varied the programme. In 1888 a farming pupil of John Whitaker's, Hector Waylen, became secretary. He was regarded as a rather eccentric young man – it was rumoured that he bathed in the dew-ponds and danced naked on the hills – and he certainly gave a new slant, lecturing on Vegetarianism and 'Delusio Vacci-nationis', and writing up vigorous minutes. Typically, the vicar lectured on the Crusades and Henry Reeves on the Steam Engine, with models. It is, however, the subjects for debate and short papers that are most revealing, as these selections show:

1st November, 1888. Impromptu Speaking. Subjects of Debate.
   Should not compulsory education be a free one?
   Have men as much brains as women?
   Do animals think?
   Is tightlacing injurious?
   Who does game rightly belong to?
   Which is best, three acres and a cow, or one acre and three cows?
   Does it pay at the present time to convert arable land into pasture?
   Is it well to make jokes in the pulpit?
   Is there any objection to comic songs in Public?
   Do you believe in ghosts? If not, why not?

24 January, 1889. Short Papers.
   (Mr. Applegate) Our present army and navy, are they neces-sary?
   Conclusion after discussion: Yes, certainly.
   (Mr. Cleverley) Signs of the Times.
   Mr. Cleverley drew attention to the marvellous advances that were being made in every department of art and science. He closed by asking the question Are we going too fast?, which on being debated was answered in the negative.
   H. Waylen then read a paper on Hygienic Clothing, pointing out that it should be of wool throughout and should fit closely to the body in every part. Tight lacing came under severe condemnation. From the nature of the subject no vote could be made upon it.

Was Bratton conservative or forward-looking in outlook? How difficult to tell, when the Society gave an unfavourable reception to a scheme for a local Cooperative yet already, getting on for 100 years ago, voted for a Channel Tunnel by a majority of six.

Teas and entertainments now took place in the Jubilee

Hall. No doubt jollifications for 120 to 140 people put a strain on the tiny hall. John Whitaker, we remember, complained of the fearful row at one of the concerts. The ventilation was inadequate and in 1890 £1 was voted by the Society to improve it. And there were other difficulties. We come across a minute such as this: 'Complaints were raised as to the disorderly conduct of members at the last meeting and it was resolved that should it continue, severe and immediate steps should be taken to secure harmony and that the objects of the Society might be attained'. At the January concert in 1891 it was noted that the new ventilation had done something, but 'the piano gave most uncertain sounds during the latter part of the programme and the air was thick as pea soup'. In spite of these conditions, enthusiasm for the Christmas concert mounted, each being accounted the best ever. Here is the programme of the concert on 1 January 1891:

Pianoforte Duett (sic)		Misses Jacob & Reeves
Song	'Queen of the Earth'	Mr. J. J. Newman
Song	'The Star of Bethlehem'	Miss Bird
Song	'Captain of the Lifeboat'	Mr. Robertson
Song	'My old friend John'	Mr. I. Pocock
Song	'Never lose a friend'	Miss Jacob
Song	'My Lady's Bower'	Miss Whitaker
Song	'The Railway Porter'	Mr. C. Stiles
Song	'Hark, hark, the Dogs do bark'	Miss Ashby
Song	'The Last of the Boys'	Mr. Pepler
Quartette	'John Bull & his three brothers'	Mr. Robertson & Messrs Newman
Pianoforte Solo		Master R. Reeves
Song	'We swept the seas before us, boys'	Mr. C. Stiles
Song	'The song that reached my heart'	Miss Drew
Song	'Killaloe'	Mr. W. Newman
Song	'He, She, It'	Miss Bird
Song	'The Skipper of St. Ives'	Miss Jacob
Song	'The Postman'	Mr. G. Bailey
Song	'The workaday world'	Miss Ashby
Song	'Auld lang Syne'	Mr. I. Pocock
Dialogue	'The Sick Man's Dream'	

232

Soon after this the minute book begins to peter out, and we do not know how long the Society lasted. Although the upper ten were always the most vocal and managing, the record shows that this was a genuine village effort in which working people spoke, debated, read papers and took part in concerts. In the early 1900s something like this society was revived in 'literary evenings', when people recited or read works of a chosen author. Tennyson and Longfellow 'Evenings' are recalled. There was even a 'cafe chantant' in 1902. But these were less genuinely village occasions. Some were initiated by the Baptist minister Charles Hobbs, and his artistic wife, and were probably too 'precious' to take on. Looking back, they do not rouse memories of roaring evenings in the Black Hole of the Jubilee Hall.

In the early 1900s it seems to have been the Band of Hope annual concerts that supplied the occasion for a display of village talent. The concert would begin with the smallest children in 'action songs', accompanied on the piano with great verve by Jane Whitaker. Wonders could be done with coloured crepe paper, and they would be dressed as Bluebells, or Japanese ladies or Spanish dancers and trained to wave, rattle or shake the appropriate prop – somewhat waywardly, it must be admitted. The programme went on to recitations, dialogues, songs of all sorts, moral, sentimental or comic – no inhibitions about the latter by this time. There would probably be a temperance item (such as a part-song, 'No more strong drink', in the 1904 programme), but mostly the concert was for the fun of seeing the performers on the little platform. The hall would be packed with parents and friends and the whole audience would turn out into the street for air at the interval. Part Two contained the older talent and worked up to a climax in the dramatic piece at the end, usually a dialogue or a cantata. In 1901 this item took the form of a take-off on celebrities, entitled Mrs Jarley's Waxworks. In 1909 the cantata 'Little Snow White' made a dint on collective memory through the remarkable performance of the seven dwarfs. In 1910 there was a daring innovation in a cantata called 'Coons at Play', of which we still have some of the music. This involved blacking faces, an exercise no one would agree to until the 'upper ten' led the way. In the next concert they went back to sobriety in a Temperance Drama entitled 'Fast Life'. Whitakers and Reeveses figure in all the programmes. Humour was supplied by Philip Whitaker, in such songs as 'The Old Trombone', and his brother-in-law, Robert Reeves, who was noted for his musical monologues, such as 'When Father laid the carpet on the stairs'. When he forgot his words he would improvise wildly, leaving his accompanist-wife quite bewildered. Reading this Band of Hope minute-book into which all the programmes have been so carefully pasted brings back a whole world of Bratton families in the pre-1914 years. Here is the 1910 programme:

Part I

1. Duet	'Happy Days of Childhood'	Misses K. & A. Mead
2. Recitation	'The Three Dolls'	Hilda Pike, Nellie White, Edith Newman
3. Action Song	'My Precious Teddy Bear'	Children
4. Recitation		Kathleen & Madgie Reeves
5. Screen Song	action with screens	Twelve girls
6. Recitation		Mr. W. Hobbs
7. Musical Monologue	'The Man with the Single Hair'	Mr. R. J. Reeves
8. Charades		Children
9. Duet	'Mary & Eliza'	Misses E. Whatley & A. Walter
10. Recitation		Hilda Pike
11.	'The Vanishing Orchestra'	Conductor: Mr. R. J. Reeves
12. Recitation	'What would you think'	George King
13. Dialogue	'Alfred the Great'	Miss A. Walter, Messrs. Bert Merritt, Frank Mundy, Willie Newman

Part II

1. Song	'The Suffragettes'	Misses K. & A. Mead, J. Smith, E. Newman, E. Prior, D. Powell, E. Pike, A. Cruse

2.	Recitation	'Nothing to Wear'	Mr. W. Hobbs
3.	Song	'Four Jolly Sailormen'	Mr. P. J. Whitaker
4.	Recitation	'Memory'	Misses Laxton
5.	Dialogue	'The Fancy Fair Bazaar'	Five Girls
6.	Recitation		Miss Greta Hobbs
7.	Cantata	'Coons at Play'	Misses A. Boone, A. Stokes, E. Whatley, Mrs. R. J. Reeves, Messrs. W. Smith, R. J. Reeves, P. J. Whitaker and Chorus

Although I have not included them all, the name of every performer is carefully written into the record. Another small notebook gives a vivid sense of involvement in village occasions. There are lists of provisions needed, cutters-up and tea-makers to summon, and sports to be arranged for the Whit Monday jollification. There are mysterious rehearsals noted: 'Parrots 4 p.m.; Dr. Quack 7 p.m.; Hen Convention 8 p.m.' There are programme notes ('Ask Rob to sing'; 'Cheer, boys, cheer, if wanted') and memos of props to provide, such as 'Mouse's tail and forepaws'. Life was busy and entertaining.

Seaside holidays were coming in. Collections of shells, bathing-costumes fit for the hippopotamuses, old picture-postcards and souvenir presents mark the trail. For the earlier nineteenth century we only have one tantalizingly enigmatic entry in a pocket-book of 1824, owner unknown:

Beggars 2d. Ostler 1½. Letters 2d. Lobster 1/-. Fisherman 6d. Bathing 1/-. Guide to Church 1/-. Boat 6d. Woman at Lighthouse 1/-. Shrimps 6d.

The anonymous traveller also copied out a verse seen 'at Brockenhurst Inn'.

Strangers and friends alike here find
Accomadation (sic) to their mind
Fatigue finds rest
Dejection cheer
In well-aired beds
And Home-brewed beer.

A tea-pot stand with a view of Osborne House and later picture postcards indicate the popularity of the Isle of Wight for holidays. John Whitaker took his bride, Polly, there for their honeymoon. And now we come on real treasure trove in the shape of 'A Journal of our visit with Aunt Thomas to the Isle of Wight'. The writer is unknown. Aunt Thomas was 69 at the time – the age of an old woman in those days. Selections from the journal will speak for themselves:

Wednesday, August 17th, 1859. Left our hospitable Cousins Charles and Ellen [Roach] at Devizes at 7.30 a.m. met Aunt Thomas all ready for anything at Westbury Station at 8.20 – came on to Salisbury and thence to Southampton – stayed at Southampton two hours – Aunt Thomas bought a very nice and I am glad to say neat (not gaudy) checked shawl . . . Left Southampton at 2 p.m. in the 'Gem' . . . at Cowes saw the 'Fairy' and 'Elfin', and off Osborne the 'Victoria and Albert' – all dressed in colours, there being a fete at Osborne that evening – saw the Channel Fleet at Spithead and a Russian squadron . . . [they disembarked at Ryde and lost their luggage for a while] . . . came on to Shanklin in a Caravan Omnibus, the carriages being too small for the luggage – it was a queer conveyance to look at but proved a very good one to go and very comfortable – went at a terrific pace *down* the hills – got to Shanklin about ten . . . just one set of rooms to be had in our dear Everton House where we hastened and got comfortably settled.

Friday, August 19th. The weather very fine – no great undertaking in the way of walking – Aunt T. and all of us much amused in the Afternoon with a Monkey and an amiable Italian boy.

Saturday, August 20th. Took a carriage to Ventnor – saw Banchurch on the way – whilst looking in a very serious mood at the gravestones the Monkey suddenly appeared peeping over the Churchyard wall . . .

Sunday, August 21st. Fine – Church and Chapel – very flowery preachers at both.

Monday, August 22nd. After much consideration resolved to go to Carisbrooke and the Needles and back in the day. Started at ½ past 8 in a Carriage for Carisbrooke . . . (sightseeing on the way) . . . Went on to Newport and ordered another carriage to meet us at Carisbrooke – went to Carisbrooke Castle – much to my horror Aunt T. walked all round the top of the walls – I remained below in great fear for the result of this presumptuous conduct . . . went to the Red Lion at C. where we had a good lunch and some extremely good porter (N.B. Aunt

T. and Mary will vouch for this *last* fact) – Went on in a fresh carriage to the Needles Hotel ... walked from thence down to Alum Bay – stayed there about 2 hours ... back to the Needles Hotel – a very good tea dinner – returned to Newport, a very beautiful ride – saw Tennyson's place near Freshwater – stopped at Newport where Aunt T. and Mary *much refreshed* themselves with —— and came on in our Shanklin carriage home – Aunt T. and Mary *very* talkative – on the way the drag broke but no damage ensued – got home about 10.

Tuesday, 23rd. Rather disposed to be quiet today – the weather very hot I worked at law papers till dinner time – Aunt T. and Mary *more quiet* than when coming from Newport – got better when they had had some dinner only gentle strolls today.

Wednesday, 24th. Calcutta heat – went down very lazily to the beach not intending to do *anything* – tide out – strolled on and on till we got to Luccombe Chine – nothing then would do but Aunt must go up the Cliff – went to work and at last got up – sun baking hot – no beer to be had anywhere for love or money – Aunt T. and Mary lost themselves in a wood – thought we should all have had brain fever – but at last cooled ourselves on the top and walked home ...

Thursday, 25th. Calcutta Hole Heat – but no keeping Aunt in or still – so off along the Cliff to Sandown – reached there about noon in a deluge of heat – rested a little while and am sorry to say their Newport fit came upon Aunt T. and Mary again and that they could not be induced to leave Sandown without some refreshment of the liquid sort – walked them home briskly by the beach and got them into tolerably decent trim by the time we reached home ...

Friday, 26th. (Charles and Ellen Roach arrived)
Aunt T. bought a Crab of the iniquitous rascal Tolan the Lapidary – for a wonder good and cheap – had a capital supper – all very merry ...

Saturday, 27th. a beautiful day – started for Blackgang at 9 with Daish's best carriage and a capital horse – *very hot* – broke the drag at Luccombe Hill – mended and broke again at Banchurch Hill – ladies alarmed but the Driver a very good fellow who managed all nicely – stopped at Banchurch and had the drag repaired ... (at Blackgang) went off to the Fisherman's Cottage – Aunt T. very brave in the descent – sent the Fisherman's crazy daughter and her little sister with a Pitcher and jar up to the Hotel for Newport ale – laid out our dinner consisting of a couple of fine Wiltshire Fowls and a tongue – after a long time the crazy child and her sister returned with the liquid – things looking better – got well refreshed – went down the remaining portion of the Chine – Aunt T. assisted (with his usual gallantry) by Charles got down capitally – walked sometime on the beach – Aunt T., Mary and Charles then climbed up what they thought a shorter path ... Cousin Ellen and I returned by the regular route ... (they all met for tea and started home)... horse going in grand style – all well save a *little* troubled by C.R.s' *peculiar* and somewhat *suspiciouus* attention to dear Mary – made a note to note that heard M. say 'speak to me only with thine eyes' – she *might* have been merely talking about the song of that name but still it sounded strange felt inclined by way of reproof to poor Mary to play off the same game with Cousin E. myself – tried it a little – Aunt T. greatly pleased with this very delightful day's excursion ...

Sunday, 28th ... to Church – heard the ugliest and most extraordinarily stupid man preach I ever saw ... (went in the evening hoping for another preacher) ... but alas Caliban got into the pulpit again and preached the most atrocious nonsense about Ahab and Jezebel, matrimonial connections and chemical experiments till it was dark and every one tired ... catching C.R's eye once just as Ellen had been *nudging* him, I *burst* but I hope and believe concealed it by a cough and sneeze was sorry Aunt T. did not go with me as we had proposed to the Bible Christians Meeting House instead – *Note* I always have remarked that when one takes a dissenting friend or relative to Church some most undesirable person generally happens to preach.

Monday, 29th. very beautiful sea – the roughest since we came – I, Walter and Charles bathed – Charles very frisky in the water ... C. and M. much alone when opportunity served and very singular and evidently well-understood signals passing between them ... must talk seriously to poor M, but feel sure it is only a temporary delusion to which alas we are *all* subject at times.

Tuesday, 30th. ... caught Aunt T. and Mrs. Roach *in the Bar*!! – retired till they had left – then returned with Charles and had a long chat and parting glass with Mr. Daish (the hotel-keeper).

Wednesday 31st. Up at ½ past 6. Walter, Charles and myself went down and bathed – water very cold ... took an affectionate leave of the Bathing Machine man and head of the Bible Christians – a very good fellow indeed and a man one envies ... a most amusing ride to Ryde in the Caravan Bus ... much amused with the Driver who had been at the Bombardment of Sebastopol and afterwards at Canton ... to Portsmouth – strong wind and heavy sea – poor M. very ill directly we got on board – Aunt T. not the least upset and greatly pleased. C. not at all attentive to M. in her distress – so it is always with these heartless flirtations – so different from true love ... landed and went to the Fountain where we had lunch – Aunt T. much enjoyed some *good porter again* – left poor M.

on the sofa and went off with Aunt T., C, E and Walter in a small boat all up the Harbour to the Queen's Yacht – *very rough* . . . after a long pull against the wind and tide got to the Victoria and Albert went all over the Queen's apartments which were left just as when she used them last – very beautiful sight . . . returned to our boat – hard pressed for time but put up a sail and ran back very quickly to the Victory – went on board and all over – Aunt T. very active in running up the ladders and most delighted with the many sights – back to shore up to the Hotel – *more porter* as Aunt T. *could not get on without* – up to the station and to Salisbury by train – when we got there the Great Western *last* train gone – . . . Aunt T. very vexed and perplexed for a few minutes but at length all settled that the whole party should go to Britford (home of Attwater relations) for the night. So off in four wheeler and fly – a very merry evening at Britford . . .

And now ends my journal for our good little Aunt T., C. and E. got up at 6 next day and off home – and I am ashamed to say without my seeing her. I hope she will be amused with this poor rigmarole of mine – and I will conclude by telling her that we were most delighted to have her cheerful company this pleasant fortnight and that we may all live to meet again next Autumn and go together to some other pretty seaside place— We shall also hope to see C. and E. too and I can only add that I trust by that time C. will have become steadier and wiser and will not cause me so much pain as he did at Shanklin this year.

Since the identity of the writer is not certain, there is nice scope for deduction from internal evidence: male, young, law student, indolent, fancies himself as his sister's guardian? Aunt Thomas, at any rate, goes home with flying colours perhaps carrying two glass paper-weights with views of Shanklin.

By the early years of this century postcards are proliferating and seaside holidays are the regular thing. The Isle of Wight is still popular and 'the Front' at Sandown in 1907 brings back the old days of seaside boarding-houses and the sedate promenade. And here, on a card dispatched on the same holiday, are the bathing-machines at Boscombe, all ready with their horses to drag them into the sea for the convenience of ladies. From a Swanage holiday come large pictures of Edwardian ladies and gentlemen exploring the Tilly Whim Caves and examining the Great Globe, while a visit to Eastbourne has preserved for us the perfect picture of holidaying on the beach: rows and rows of prosperous Edwardians reclining in deck chairs, ladies in stupendous hats and gentlemen in boaters.

Finally, there were national occasions to be suitably celebrated in Bratton. The glorious reign of Victoria provided several of these, but we have no surviving relics earlier than the medals commemorating the 1887 Jubilee. On this occasion the chief celebration in the village was the opening of the Jubilee Hall, planned in March and opened in June, 1887, at a final cost of £173.9.4. Under a committee whose chairman was Robert Reeves, Vice-Chairman, John Whitaker and Secretary, Thomas Reeves, 150 people sat down to dinner that day in the new hall, at a cost of 1s 6d per head. The medals were presented to Baptist Sunday School children by Aunt Thomas (aged 97) and showed the Queen's head, with, on the reverse, Victoria being acclaimed by Sunday School Scholars, and the motto 'The Throne is established by righteousness'. For the Diamond Jubilee of 1897 we have the programme of the Athletic Sports. There were 11 events, of a conventional kind except for the Steeple Chase and Pair Race. Some are ear-marked for *boys* under a certain age; the rest are for 'Any Age' – query: Any Sex? One suspects that the women and girls did not get a look in. Prizes to the value of £4 were given, with a slightly grudging note that 'These Sports are open to the Inhabitants of the Village of Bratton only'.

For the Coronation Festivities of 9 August 1902, we have three commemorative medals and a complete programme, with pictures of Edward VII and Queen Alexandra at the top, flanked by two swallows. Ceremonies began with the assembly of the Band outside Messrs Reeves' Office and they paraded round the village before establishing themselves in 'Mr Pickard's Field where the day's rejoicings will be held'. At 2.30 p.m. came the Sports. J. S. Whitaker was one of the judges; R. J. Reeves the referee; Nelson Reeves and P. J. Whitaker were secretaries for the whole proceedings. The Sports were now more novel, including a Bicycle Race, a Sack Race, a Potato Race, an Egg-and-Spoon Race and a Bucket Race. *Girls* were specifically allowed in some items but the ambiguous 'Any Age' remains. At 5 p.m. there was a free tea for all and afterwards Band-playing and the rest of the Sports until at 9 p.m. fireworks brought the celebrations to a climax.[1] Swinging Boats, Coconut Shys and other sideshows were provided free, and 'All visitors staying in the Village are respectfully invited'. This suggests a more open attitude than in 1897 and would have suited the Whitakers very well.

For the Coronation Festivities of 22 June 1911, again our only documentation is the notebook recording the sports – and the winners. But this time living memory can fill out some of the detail. First there was a carnival procession round the village, led by the band. A motley collection of conveyances was entered in the competition for 'the best-dressed vehicle', but the only one which was 'memorable' to one small girl was a highly colourful and dramatic representation of a red-bearded Alfred burning the cakes, staged on a dray. This, according to the notebook, won first prize. Also in the procession was John Whitaker's little pony trap, with fat Tommy between the shafts and led by Tom Cox, an undersized but remarkable little man, a humourist with a shrill voice and a great reputation in the village. In the trap were three little girls representing the United Kingdom: England had a beautiful wreath of roses and behaved with decorum; Wales had a cardboard harp which she broke by leaning too heavily on it; Scotland's only memory is of the prickles surrounding her basket of thistles. But they won a special prize of 2s 6d. According to the book, one of the competing vehicles was the Bratton Fire Engine; another prize-winner was a waggon full of Haymakers, while 'The Three Old Maids of Lea' were also there. Behind the vehicles came competitors for 'The Best Costumed Pedestrian'. In this prizes were won by Ethel Whatley, C. Smith

[1] In fact, two programmes are extant: for June 26th (the original Coronation date) and August 9th. The first ends with a torch-light procession and bonfire on the White Horse Hill, but Edward VII's illness cancelled this. After anxious debate, it was decided that the bonfire would not keep, so on July 5th, a 'very successful' procession and bonfire took place, while on August 9th the fun ended with fireworks.

241

and Bert Annitts, but – alas – we do not know what they wore.

The Sports took the usual form: to read down the list of competitors in the flat races, the hurdles, the jumps and so on brings a certain sadness, for so many of the boys and young men were too soon to be killed in the War. First prizes in the walking-race for over fifties went appropriately to the two shepherds, Frank and Robert Whatley. What exactly, one wonders, was the 'Menagerie Race' in which Harry Humphrey was 'Ducky', Frank Whatley 'Ferret', Charlie Smith and Oliver Maslin 'Goats', George King, 'Cockerel', W. Mead, 'Bat' and a member of the Walter family, 'Pig'? They were generous with first, second and even third prizes (such things as knives, pepper-pot, button-hook, hair brushes, box of paints, all carefully priced), but the total account for the sports was only just over £6 and they ended with 5s 10d in hand. There must have been a free tea for all, run by one of the Bratton Ladies' Tea Committees. But the little notebook in which they were wont to record quantities and prices of buns, lardies, 'fancies', etc., does not survive for this occasion. Finally, of course, the day had to end with bonfire and fireworks, this time on the top of the White Horse, where corresponding conflagrations could be seen all round. It was a halcyon day, well-concluded, celebrating a reign begun in confidence. But the end of the fireworks was not very far away from the end of an era.

11 End of an Age

On 28 August 1900 Edith Whitaker married Robert Reeves. Although the two families had been associated in Bratton affairs for three generations this was the first time they had intermarried. Some of the Whitakers thought that Edith was marrying beneath her. Her Aunt, Anna Gotch, protested to her father: 'But John, his grandfather used to lay our carpets!' But it was a real village affair. Although they were married in the Baptist chapel, the bell-ringers, who were mostly Works men, insisted on ringing the parish-church bells. The wedding procession walked up through the leafy lanes and back to the reception under the yew trees. Relatives and friends flocked in. The wedding photographs (22), taken on the brick court at the Yew Trees, seem to encapsulate the society of 1900. There is the bride in a cream brocade gown, with a skirt that almost stands by itself and a minute waist; there are the bridegroom and best man, very correct in morning dress; there are the bridesmaids, Jane Whitaker and Ethel Reeves, in quantities of striped silk, with high, boned necks, and hat-creations piled with tulle and flowers, while three little Coombses, a page and two little girls, look engagingly out of their muslin and frills. In the general photograph matriarchal presences in bonnets and venerable bearded heads of houses proclaim an unshakeable belief in the stability of families. Roundabout gather relatives and friends of all ages, the younger women in those wonderful hats which were to be the glory of the Edwardian age – a concourse of faces affirming their confidence in the propriety and morality of their society.

Everything seemed so permanent. Yet in less than two decades the age had passed. Whitaker farming fortunes were already on the decline, though the old regime went on. In spite of all his efforts, John Whitaker continued to lose money, until finally Grants Farm was given up and its contents sold in 1913. John and his wife both died within months of each other in 1915. Their son, Philip, had been developing a threshing business of his own and was already beginning to pull the farm together when he died, as the result of a fall from an apple tree, in 1917. Jane Whitaker was left alone in the Yew Trees and the name of Whitaker was eventually to disappear from Bratton.

The Iron Works was still prospering then, but with hindsight we can see that one cause of ultimate decline was already present. As large-scale agricultural machinery developed, Reeves's became agents for tractors, combine-harvesters and so on. Their elevators still sold well and even after the First World War a new, all-steel version was successfully marketed. But the coming of the baler killed the elevator trade almost at a stroke and, though the business was kept alive for some time by good craftsmanship and ingenuity, an inexorable decline set in which ended in the destruction of what had been a humming centre of village activity for 150 years and more.

In 1909 an article on Bratton, published in the *Oxford Times*, began: 'Two sounds break day by day the stillness of the village, the low tinkling of sheep-bells and the rhythmic beat of a steam-hammer and between these two lies the history of Bratton.' It was still possible then for a summer visitor to feel the impact of a traditional pattern of life. But economic opportunities were not expanding and just before the First World War a restless mood produced a wave of emigration in the village. Kings, Smiths, Whatleys and others departed for Canada and wrote back describing a new and exciting life. Movement and change became a possibility, yet the old order appeared unshaken. In August, 1914, there were 69 employees at the Iron Works, grouped in the following categories, which include apprentices and labourers: Office (2), Smiths (13), Fitters (11), Foundry (15), Boiler Shop (3), Carpenters (10), Paint and Erecting Shops (8), Tinman's Shop (2), Saw Mill (2), Carters (3). The names still read like a roll-call of old Bratton families, with some newcomers. Most of the men had been in 'The Foundry' all their working lives and their fathers before them – a number of them for over 30 years and a few for over 50. So we come to the outbreak of the First World War. There was much enthusiasm. Many rushed to enlist and when the men of the village set out in a body to take the King's shilling at Devizes, they had a great send-off. So we end with a photograph taken in August, 1914, outside the Duke Hotel, with the Works behind (23). The cavalcade of old cars is filled with village men, with O. J. Reeves driving the first car; wives and children crowd into a corner of the picture; Mrs Scull is still taking a loving leave while Nelson Reeves steps forward to remove her from the picture; Union Jacks wave. It is the end of an age.

Index

ker's servant, 32, 39, 40
Hepplewhite, George, 73
Herodotus, 169, 217
Heytesbury, cricket match at, 227
Hill, P. L., ironmonger, Trowbridge, 155
Hilperton, 17
Hobbs family, 112, 229; W., 234; Rev. Charles, Baptist minister, 216, 233; Greta, 235
Holcombe, verses on, 146-7; relations at, 150, 153, 221
Holloway family, 39, 112
Honeybridge charity, 102, 108, 109
Houlton family, Seagry, 62; John, 48
Humphrey, Harry, 242
Humphries, Mrs, Duke William Inn, Bratton, 207

Ilchester, Richard Gay imprisoned at, 49
Imber, Baptist Church at, 201, 214-15, 216-17; British School at, 214, 215
India, letters from, 200, 201-3, 205
Ireland, workmen from, 124, 219; J. Saffery's tour in, 200
Isle of Wight, holidays in, 174, 236-9

Jacob, Rev. S., vicar of Bratton, 229, 231; Miss, 232
Jamaica, letters from, 201, 202
James, Fox & Co., drapers, Devizes, 156
Jeffery, William, author of The Wiltshire Centenarian, 183
Jerusalem, model of, 209
Johnson, Dr Samuel, 141

Keevil, Flower Show at, 226
Keevil, Mr and Mrs, 109, 110
Keyford Academy, Frome, 168, 169, 182
King, Mr, 41; Mr and Mrs George, school teachers, 215, 234, 242, 244
Kingsley, Charles, pamphlet, The Two Breaths by, 184

Lancashire, Bratton aid for cotton famine in, 219
Lang, Andrew, 184
Langham, North Bradley, fulling mill in, 20

Laverton, W. H., 227
Lawes, John, 41
Lille, Messrs Reeves exhibit at, 122
Lillie, Arthur, author of The Book of Croquet, 228, 229
Littleton, Baptist cause at, 217
Lloyd, T. W., 'professor of music and dancing', 152
Lloyd, Mrs, W. R., author of The Flower of Christian Charity, 163
Locke, John, 55, 100
London, Fly Waggons from Frome to, 155; trips of Whitakers to, 38, 153-4, 176, 188; Alfred and Edward Whitaker in, 143; Ward, bookseller in, 33, 38; London City and West Ham Missions, 211, 219
Longleat, estate of Thynnes, 22, 26, 62; expeditions to, 222, 224
Ludlow, Dr, 207

McCormick, Messrs, agricultural engineers, 128
Macmillan's sixpenny books, 179
Maidenhead, 38
Marlborough, 38
Marsh (Dilton), 118; Fair at, 32, 35
Marsh, Edward, clockmaker, Salisbury, 74
Maslin, Oliver, 242
Mavor, William, writer of children's books, 139
Mead family, 112, 229; Misses K. and A., 234; W., 242
Melksham, 32; Baptist cause at, 217
Mendelssohn-Bartholdy, F., 182, 194
Merritt family, 115; Francis, 76; Bert, 234
Michael, W., printer, Westbury, 125, 183, 203, 208
Millard, T., 110; Ann, 115
Mill Hill School, Hendon, Whitakers at, 168-72, 181, 217
Millington family, musicians, Trowbridge, 191
Milman, H. M., books by, 101, 153
Milton, John, 88, 100, 183
Moir, I. J., author of Wiltshire C.C. Handbook on Practical Dairying, 107
Mompesson family, J. Whitaker acquires lands from, 20

251

Reeves, Messrs, (contd.)
logues of, 122–3; employees of, 124–7; promoters of gas, telegraph, telephone in the village, 128–9; buyers of first motor car in Bratton, 131; decline of, 244

Riley's *Chart of English History*, 58–9

Roach, Charles, draper, Devizes, 156–7; his wife ,Ellen, 167; holidaying with Whitakers in Isle of Wight, 236, 237–9

Rode, Revel at, 34

Roger le Hoppe, fourteenth-century landowner in Bratton, 62

Rollin, M., author of *Ancient History* etc. (1788), 162

Rowe, Joshua, missionary to India, 202

Russell, John, author of *A Tour in Germany* etc., 151

Ryde, Isle of Wight, 176, 236, 238

Ryland, Dr John, 60

Saffery, Jane, later Mrs Joshua Whitaker, 141, 147–54, 156–62, 164–7, 169–74, 188, 195, 198–9, 201, 216; Infant School run by, 214, 226

Saffery, Rev. John, Baptist minister, Salisbury, 67, 148, 200–202, 215

Saffery, Mrs John, see Andrews, Maria Grace

Saffery, Philip, 150, 174, 216

Sage, Rev. Carey, Baptist minister, 128

Salisbury (Sarum), 32, 122, 153, 236, 239; Bishop of, 200; Baptist Church in, 43, 67, 68, 148, 200; Mrs Saffery's school in, 138

Salisbury Plain, 15, 17, 18, 122, 127; described by Cobbett, 121; villages of, 200

Salisbury and Winchester Journal, 47

Salmon's Mercury (1781), published in Bath, 89

Salter, Miss, 150, 177, 199

Sandown, Isle of Wight, 237, 239

Sankey, author of Sacred Songs and Solos, 218

Saunders, J. K., clock-maker, Warminster, 155

Scammell, carrier, 100

Scotland, 123, 200

Scott, Sir Walter, 85, 191

Scott, Mr, of Gawcott, school master, 138

Scull family, 112; John, 227; Mrs, 245

Seagram family, 23, 128, 157, 207; Dr, 152; W. H., 219, 227

Seagry, 48

Sebastopol, bombardment of, 238

Serampore, India, 202, 203

Shanklin, Isle of Wight, 236, 239

Sharp, Thomas, Westbury, 104

Shepherd, J., chemist, 176 Fleet Street, London, 60

Sheppard, J., Frome, lecturer at Westbury, 226

Sheraton, Thomas, 73

Sherwood, M. M., schoolmaster, 138

Shorland, E. P., family doctor, 107

Shrewton, Baptist cause at, 217; Philip Ellis, schoolmaster of, 30

Shuttleworth, J. K., 214

Smith family, 112, 207, 229, 244; George, 112, 115; George James, 112; Henry (milkman), 112; Henry (thresher), 112; Jane, 166; Lydia, 115; Philip, 111, 115; T. C., butcher, 154; J., 192; W., 192; Jack, 212; Willie, 212; Ernest, 227; W. H., 227, 235; 'Alfie John', 227; Harvey, 227; Charlie, 242

Snelgrove family, 112; George, 113, 116; Lewis, 113, 115, 116–17, 198, 199; R., baker, 154; N., cobbler, 155; Mrs William, 166

Sobersides, Solomon, author of children's books, 52

Southampton, 174, 236

Southey, Robert, 101, 144

Spain, war with, 31

Spithead, 236

Staynes, Mr N., 212; Miss M., 212

Steele, Anne (Theodosia), 49–51, 57; 'Sylvia' (Anne's niece), 50, 51

Steeple Ashton, Whitaker property in, 19, 20; Baptist cause at, 110, 111, 124, 216, 217

Stevens, Robert, tailor, 154–5

Stiles, Joe, 131; C., 232

Stokes, Miss A., 235

Stonehenge, expeditions to, 222–4

Stradbrook, Bratton, 18